Healthcare Financial Accounting

A Guide for Leaders

Healthcare Financial Accounting

A Guide for Leaders

First Edition

Cristian H. Lieneck
Texas State University

cognella®
SAN DIEGO

Bassim Hamadeh, CEO and Publisher

John Remington, Executive Editor

Gem Rabanera, Senior Project Editor

David Rajec, Associate Editor

Alia Bales, Production Editor

Emely Villavicencio, Senior Graphic Designer

Kylie Bartolome, Licensing Associate

Natalie Piccotti, Director of Marketing

Kassie Graves, Senior Vice President of Editorial

Jamie Giganti, Director of Academic Publishing

This book is designed to provide educational information to our readers, and is not be interpreted as direct financial advice. Healthcare leaders should consult their organization's CPA for specific, organizational-related questions. It is sold with the understanding that the purpose of the book is to educate readers on the principles of healthcare financial accounting. The content of each chapter or reading is the sole expression and opinion of its author, and not necessarily that of the publisher. No warranties or guarantees are expressed or implied by the publisher's choice to include any of the content in this volume. Neither the publisher nor the individual author(s) shall be liable for any physical, psychological, emotional, financial, or commercial damages, including, but not limited to, special, incidental, consequential or other damages. Our views and rights are the same: You are responsible for your own choices, actions, and results and for seeking relevant topical advice from trained professionals.

Cover image copyright © 2020 iStockphoto LP/sasirin pamai.

ISBN: 978-1-7935-6282-1

3970 Sorrento Valley Blvd., Ste. 500, San Diego, CA 92121

Brief Contents

---

*   Available via Cognella Active Learning, see Introduction on page xxiii for details.

Detailed Contents

---

* Available via Cognella Active Learning, see Introduction on page xxiii for details.

Cognella Active Learning

ACTIVE LEARNING

This book has interactive activities available to complement your reading.

Your instructor may have customized the selection of activities available for your unique course. Please check with your professor to verify whether your class will access this content through the Cognella Active Learning portal (http://active.cognella. com) or through your home learning management system.

Foreword

As a business term, the word "accounting" comes from the word "accountable." It should not be lost on us that financial accounting belies the importance of the seismic industry shift that is underway to deliver care that is more accountable for outcomes. The economics of American healthcare is systemically broken in every way possible, with spending in 2019 that topped $3.8 trillion dollars—nearly 18% of the gross domestic product. Prior to the COVID-19 pandemic, the Centers for Medicare & Medicaid Services (CMS) Office of the Actuary projected health spending would continue to grow at a rate of 5.3% a year, reaching nearly $6.2 trillion by 2028. If those increases were to continue over the next 20 years, health spending could reach a staggering $11.8 trillion by 2040 (Gebreyes et. al, 2021). That spending trajectory presents a bleak scenario if unabated, as we would see a collapse in various facets of our society due to the opportunity costs associated with our massive medical-industrial complex. Simply stated, there is much responsibility on the next generation of healthcare financial management professionals to ensure that we meet the economic and moral imperatives to hold the industry more accountable.

I am not an "accounting guy." I am deeply passionate about healthcare as both a professional and a citizen, and I have experienced a level of success in the industry; however, I have always struggled with accounting. In my many years as a healthcare executive, I have longed for an entry-level healthcare financial accounting textbook that could illustrate complex accounting topics more simplistically. In knowing that simplicity is the ultimate form of sophistication, Dr. Lieneck has stepped up in a big way to meet an unmet need. In writing this book to assist MHA/MBA students prior to enrollment in a graduate-level healthcare financial management course, as well as undergraduate healthcare administration students taking either accounting and/or finance courses, he has built a bridge to understanding. He has empowered students to have a healthier relationship with financial accounting which can then propel them throughout their career. By better understanding the development process and formatting and of valid and reliable financial statements for healthcare organizations (hospital and non-hospital entities), the next generation of healthcare executives will be better equipped to lead in the new paradigm of value-based purchasing.

I can think of no one more qualified to write this text. As a teacher, scholar, and experienced medical practice executive, Dr. Lieneck has taught numerous courses and published multiple papers on healthcare accounting and finance topics. He is a recognized servant leader in our industry who understands the unique challenges in learning and applying financial accountability. Through his experience in the industry, he understands that healthcare executives must be well-versed in financial accounting principles to ensure appropriate financial management decisions for the organization. Such actions support patients receiving the proper care in the most cost-effective way. This manuscript is artful in the way complex financial concepts are presented. His decade of physician practice administration experience, coupled with a practical approach to teaching complex healthcare accounting practices allows for a welcomed view of financial accounting from a nonfinancial manager's perspective. This textbook fills a much-needed gap in healthcare administration literature and related curriculum.

It is undeniable that there will be an increased need for accounting in health care that is more accountable for both patient and cost outcomes. This book follows a rich tradition of providing important instructional resources to both students and practitioners, but it also contributes a new approach to advancing industry capability. It is my hope that as the healthcare industry continues to evolve towards value-based payment this book will serve as a continued resource to ensure accountability in healthcare financial accounting.

Eric Weaver, DHA, FACHE, FACMPE, FHIMSS
Executive Director, Institute for Advancing Health Value
March 2021

Reference

Gebreyes, K., Davis, A., Davis, S. Shukla, M., & Rush, B. (2021). Breaking the cost curve: Deloitte predicts health spending as a percentage of GDP will decelerate over the next 20 years. Retrieved online on 3/01/2021 from: https://www2.deloitte.com/us/en/insights/industry/health-care/future-health-care-spending.html

Preface

A T EVERY LEVEL of my healthcare administration career, I was expected to possess a high level of competency in financial accounting. Specifically, an expectation regarding the accumulation and interpretation of the basic financial statements was an inherent requirement at all my physician practice management positions. While physician leaders (who are often the organization's owners) were able to identify and interpret major financial statement values at board meetings, it was my ability to look deeper into the statements and associate underlying operational practices and protocols to the account values that fashioned these reports. Regardless of what segment of the healthcare industry one chooses to specialize in, it will be those who take the initiative to truly understand the intricacies and relationship of healthcare financial accounting and the follow-on subject of healthcare financial management who will make an impact on operational successes. Financial accounting knowledge will cut through all healthcare administrator job duties and related competencies—and rightfully inform and affect organizational processes and protocols. In my experience, this thorough knowledge of the organization's financial statements resulted in the delivery of higher quality patient care.

This textbook is not designed to impress, but rather to teach. It is specifically written to address daily healthcare management operational questions and therefore does not focus on any single specific type of healthcare organization or industry segment. This book is not a hospital financial accounting text, yet it does incorporate many hospital accounting concepts, scenarios, and example financial statements. The last chapter is available in a 100% online format via the publisher's Active Learning online platform, so ongoing Financial Accounting Standards Board (FASB) Accounting Standards Updates and other industry changes are kept up-to-date, maintaining textbook relevancy for andragogy purposes.

I have written this textbook and corresponding online materials to assist two primary groups of students in higher education:

- undergraduates enrolled in a healthcare administration or related degree program who require a financial accounting course and solid understanding of healthcare organizational financial statements prior to enrollment in a healthcare financial management course; and

- MHA, MBA, or other graduate-level management degree program students who require an initial introduction to healthcare financial accounting or possibly an immediate refresher prior to enrollment in a healthcare financial management course.

Healthcare financial accounting is the *required predecessor* to any healthcare financial management course. Based on my experience in healthcare administration, it is imperative that a *healthcare financial accounting course* be required and successfully completed prior to enrollment in any *healthcare financial management course*. One must learn the language of business and finance before attempting to make decisions on behalf of the organization's stakeholders. Attempting to learn healthcare financial management without healthcare financial accounting knowledge does not offer the learner an ability to interpret financial statements at a level that is required of today's healthcare leaders. Further, most business school financial accounting courses are not healthcare-specific and are limited to a broad overview of basic financial accounting procedures—often lacking implications organic to the healthcare industry.

I have taken all my learnings, acquired industry best practices, and physician practice administration application examples and incorporated them into this textbook. Additional, extensive online resources are also available to assist students, faculty, and even current healthcare leaders in their professional development to support lifelong learning initiatives. As a prior healthcare administrator with over a decade of physician practice administration experience and over a decade of teaching and researching the development of future healthcare leaders in higher education, I wish them all success in current and future healthcare leadership positions.

I encourage any instructors of healthcare administration (or related degree program) to contact me at any time regarding this textbook and/or accompanying online resources. The presentation of financial accounting topics throughout the textbook, number of chapters, and online resources have been designed for a variety of teaching venues (fully online, hybrid, and/or traditional, in-residence course offerings). This initiative to assimilate the textbook and related materials to a variety of course delivery formats and various semester lengths was initially to support the development of future healthcare leaders and associated industry stakeholders enrolled at various healthcare administration programs. The COVID-19 global pandemic has influenced the delivery of course material in higher education and further highlights the accessibility and flexibility of this textbook and related online content. Please reach out if there are questions—as it is the collaboration and ongoing teaching and research initiatives that make this profession most enjoyable for me.

Dr. Cristian Lieneck is an associate professor of healthcare administration at Texas State University in San Marcos, Texas, and can be contacted at clieneck@txstate.edu.

Texas State University faculty profile: https://faculty.txstate.edu/profile/1921808

LinkedIn profile: https://www.linkedin.com/in/cristianlieneck/

Introduction

How the Book is Organized

Strategically organized, this textbook supports a learner's pathway towards the competent creation of valid and reliable financial statements for healthcare organizations. In this effort, chapters and their related content are organized in a manner to support an individual's cognitive processes according to Bloom's Taxonomy. The application of the healthcare accounting cycle and chapter sequencing transitions in a general manner from knowledge to comprehension (Chapters 1–3), application to analysis (Chapters 4-7), and concludes with synthesis and evaluation (Chapters 8–12). Putting all parts (chapters) together as a whole, the ultimate objective is for the reader to understand the intricacies of the development and formulation of the healthcare organization's three main financial statements. Naturally, a deeper understanding of organizational workflow processes and related activities associated with the provision of care—and how they affect the financial statements—is an inherent learning outcome that will truly support healthcare leaders in their everyday financial management decisions.

* Chapter 13, Adherence to Healthcare Financial Accounting Standards and Updates

Accounting standards, protocols, and practices change over time. The healthcare industry continues to adapt to how healthcare activities are represented on the financial statements regularly. Chapter 13, "Adherence to Healthcare Financial Accounting Standards and Updates" is the final chapter of this textbook and is only available online via the Cognella Active Learning website. This enables a continuous explanation of FASB (Financial Accounting Standards Board) updates to support changes/updates related to Generally Accepted Accounting Principles (GAAP) protocols, as well other healthcare industry application of related standards. Our industry is quite unique – and therefore requires constant reflection and alteration regarding how such intricate patient care and related processes are to be presented on the organization's financial statements.

A solid foundation in healthcare financial accounting and ongoing awareness of industry updates supports the leader in their generation of valid and reliable financial statements and follow-on financial management decisions. It the healthcare leader's fiduciary duty to thoroughly understand healthcare financial accounting (and ongoing updates) prior to engaging in financial management decision making, which ultimately affect the multitude of stakeholders associated with the healthcare organization.

Acknowledgments

T his textbook is dedicated to one of my most honorable graduate school faculty mentors: Dr. Michael Nowicki, EdD, FACHE, FHFMA, professor of healthcare administration at Texas State University. It was what he taught me in graduate school that provided the backbone for successes I experienced while working in the field as a physician practice administrator. I am very grateful for his teachings, compassion, and servant leadership as my prior healthcare finance instructor, professional colleague in higher education, and good friend. Over a decade ago he assigned me to teach an undergraduate healthcare financial accounting course, and I have continued to enjoy this teaching assignment even today, every semester (including summer semesters, all scheduled at 8:00 a.m., twice a week).

A significant amount of his 2006 textbook, *HFMA's Introduction to Hospital Accounting*, fifth edition, published by Health Administration Press, was the basis for my healthcare financial accounting pedagogy framework utilized in the classroom, beginning over a decade ago. This book remains a seminal reference in the field of healthcare administration, even today. Dr. Nowicki's collegiality and ongoing collaboration on multiple healthcare financial accounting and financial management teaching methods and techniques demonstrate his immense knowledge in the field and his influential motivation to develop competent healthcare leaders.

Peer Review Contributors

The following individuals contributed valuable time and effort by participating in an additional informal review of this textbook manuscript. Each reviewer offered their own personal perspectives and important andragogical notes to make this manuscript successful.

Dr. Sandra Collins, PhD
Professor and Program Director of Health Care Management, Distinguished Faculty
Southern Illinois University Carbondale

Dr. Warren McDonald, PhD
Professor and Chair of the Department of Health Administration (retired)
Methodist University

Dr. Michelle McGowan, PhD, CPA
Professor and Program Director of Health Administration
King's College

Dr. Eileen Morrison, EdD
Professor of Health Care Administration (retired)
Texas State University

Dr. Eric Weaver, DHA, FACHE, FACMPE, FHMISS
Executive Director, Institute for Advancing Health Value
Western Governors University

Ms. Brook Herzog
MHA Student, Graduate Instructional Assistant
Texas State University

Ms. Katharine Heinemann
MHA Student, Graduate Instructional Assistant
Texas State University

Important Textbook Navigation Notes

THE FOLLOWING INFORMATION is provided to ensure an optimal learning experience while reading/reviewing this textbook.

- Simple interest (rate × principal) is utilized in all calculations. Compounding and other interest calculations are purposely omitted from this textbook to assist with the ease of learning healthcare financial accounting fundamentals. Time value of money is most often addressed in the follow-on healthcare financial management curriculum.

- To avoid obsolescence due to financial accounting questions/problems with example calendar date(s), the decade (tens) digit in all years has been substituted with an X. Readers are to utilize any single decade year in place of this X placeholder value for any one problem, being sure not to change decades (always assume the same decade).

- Any rates (%) utilized in this textbook are assumed to represent a 1-year interest rate (interest rates are annualized). From there, monthly rates can be calculated. The number of single days and/or number of days in any single month are not considered. The monthly time frame is the shortest time period utilized in this textbook's accrual calculations.

- Many calculations throughout this textbook utilize rounding at various points, and therefore final answers may be slightly different. Problems in this textbook and accompanying online resources were not generated to ensure answers landed on an even dollar amount (with zero cents). Keep this in mind when rounding during any calculations and when reviewing any textbook accounting problems. If rounding occurs earlier in the calculations, a greater answer variance will most likely result, but still be correct.

- To further assist with the understanding and fluid comprehension of healthcare financial accounting, this textbook offers a significant online learning platform to assist healthcare administration students in their learning progress. Readers are highly encouraged to access these additional teaching and learning resources on the textbook's accompanying Cognella Active Learning website during and after reading each chapter.

Financial Accounting and the Healthcare Financial Environment

Introduction

A healthcare leader's ability to apply the principles of financial accounting properly within the healthcare organization is a management skill that differentiates *good* healthcare administrators from *great* healthcare administrators. The United States has the only private healthcare system in the world, driven by the necessity of proper structure, process, and outcome initiatives in coordination with dynamic, ever-changing external environmental conditions (Donabedian, 1980). These initiatives are all supported and implemented by healthcare leaders using a multitude of management concepts and problem-solving tools. The healthcare organization's financial statements are a vital instrument in this detailed process, and they are readily available in the healthcare administrator's decision-making toolbox. How they are generated and interpreted will determine the healthcare organization's success in the delivery of care.

As with most healthcare administration programs (both undergraduate and graduate), each course's content and related (mapped) competencies should overlap across the curriculum. This same practice should also occur with healthcare financial accounting.

For example, healthcare financial accounting knowledge will further assist the leader by doing the following:

- Providing a solid basis to understand the organization's financial statements. This is vital in the development of healthcare leaders prior to enrollment in any follow-on healthcare financial management course (where operational decision making occurs).
- Emphasizing the use of healthcare strategic planning and process control/ improvement initiatives to support organizational objectives.

- Supporting the moral and ethical obligations associated with the fiduciary duties of healthcare leaders and their respective organizational stakeholders.

The healthcare leader will take one of the greatest steps in developing their career by learning how to develop ***valid and reliable financial statements***. Applying these statements and analyzing financial trends over time assist with the delivery of consistent and effective healthcare operations. This skill set makes the healthcare administrator a valuable asset to the organization and all of its stakeholders. With regard to professional degrees, there is no management program in higher education with the word "administration" or "management" in its degree name (for example, MHA, MBA, BHA, BBA, etc.) that does not involve mathematical concepts and calculations to some extent. The same applies to the field of healthcare administration and the requirement to be fully competent in the subject of financial management—which must be preceded by the study of financial accounting (this textbook). To go from a *good* healthcare leader to a *great* healthcare leader, one needs to learn the basics behind the numbers on the financial statements in order to then move on to making decisions for the organization based on the information drawn from these statements.

Discussed in the Preface, an investment in the study of financial accounting (this textbook) assists with a better understanding and learning experience in a follow-on healthcare financial management course. Therefore, investing time now in learning financial accounting will assist the student in subsequent enrollment in a healthcare financial management course. To begin this journey, Chapter 1 will introduce the subject of healthcare financial accounting, emphasize the importance of generating ***valid and reliable financial statements***, review the current healthcare financial environment, and address how basic healthcare services are financed.

Learning Objectives

By the end of this chapter, the student should be able to:

- Define financial accounting.
- Discuss the relationship between healthcare financial accounting and healthcare financial management, including how knowledge of one must be obtained prior to attempting to learn/implement the other.
- List the four financial statements to be thoroughly investigated throughout this textbook and applied to healthcare operations.
- Describe how healthcare is financed in the U.S. healthcare system.

- Discuss the current healthcare financial environment in the United States, including an ongoing challenge as related to government payer reimbursement for services and commercial (private) health insurance reimbursement cost-shifting.

Key Terms

1. Healthcare financial accounting
2. Healthcare financial management
3. Gross vs. net revenue
4. Cost-sharing methods: premium, deductible, coinsurance, and copayment
5. Charge master
6. Cost-shifting
7. Patient Protection and Affordable Care Act (PPACA) of 2010
8. Medicare Access and CHIP Reauthorization Act (MACRA) of 2015
9. Indigent patients

Introduction to Financial Accounting

The disciplines of accounting and finance are both extensive in nature, yet also highly related. As previously discussed, one cannot be totally competent in healthcare financial management and related operational decisions without a strong understanding of healthcare financial accounting. Otherwise, this would be like attempting to take the second semester of a foreign language course prior to successfully mastering the first semester's content. To make matters a little more complicated, the names of these two disciplines involve similar words that can lead to additional confusion.

- Healthcare **financial accounting** entails the accumulation and communication of the organization's history (represented using the dollar sign) *to develop valid and reliable financial statements.*
- Healthcare **financial management** involves taking properly developed financial statements and *making informed financial decisions regarding the organization's future.*

Table 1.1 demonstrates a more detailed comparison of healthcare financial accounting and healthcare financial management concepts. These differences will be frequently referred to in future textbook chapters and further established as the principles of financial accounting are introduced.

TABLE 1.1 Distinction between healthcare financial accounting and healthcare financial management

Distinguishing characteristic	Healthcare financial accounting	Healthcare financial management
Timing/time period	Provides historical information up to current day (retrospective, looks backward).	Provides decision-making information from current day into the future (prospective, looks forward).
Decision making occurs?	No	Yes
Utilizes Generally Accepted Accounting Principles?	Yes	Yes
If errors present?	Financial statements with accounting errors will affect future management decisions made if based on the incorrect accounting data.	Financial management decisions made will affect the future revenue/expenses of the organization, which will then result in future accounting data being recorded based on such decision-making efforts.
Statement analysis of organization position and performance	Provides the bookkeeping data (account values) for use in financial management analyses.	Utilizes established ratios and other financial management formulas to pull information out of the financial statements for use in decision making for the organization's future.

As a result, the purpose of the study of healthcare financial accounting and of this textbook is *to develop valid and reliable financial statements*. There are three primary financial statements to be addressed:

- balance sheet
- statement of operations (also known as the statement of revenue over expenses, income statement, and/or the profit/loss statement)
- statement of net assets (and the statement of changes in net assets)

In addition, the statement of cash flows will also be addressed for those healthcare organizations operating under the accrual method of accounting. These financial statements are available for review in their most basic form in Appendix A. Additional information regarding their format and other basic characteristics will be addressed and thoroughly expanded on throughout this textbook. As a result, the final, more detailed financial statement formats will be discussed and solidified in forthcoming chapters. Readers are highly encouraged to review the Financial Accounting Standards Board (FASB) Accounting Standards Updates (ASUs) and other healthcare financial statement format changes in Chapter 13 (an online, continuously updated chapter located on the accompanying Cognella Active Learning website).

These financial statements are not mutually exclusive to only the healthcare industry and related healthcare service organizations. They are used by both for- and not-for-profit organizations, healthcare and non-healthcare organizations, as well as private and public organizational types. Financial accounting concepts addressed in this textbook expand beyond the field of healthcare administration and will assist learners in management of non-healthcare organizations as well. As an added benefit, the study of financial accounting will also assist with a stronger comprehension of personal financial status and future personal financial goals. Directly transferrable to other industries, the leader knowledgeable in healthcare financial accounting may easily apply these textbook financial accounting concepts to many other types of organizations beyond those in the healthcare industry.

Paying for Healthcare in the United States

As previously mentioned, the United States is the only privatized healthcare system in the world. It consists of multiple types of business entities (such as for-profit and not-for-profit systems, private and government). However, all healthcare organizations have one underlying, inherent initiative in common: they all must earn a profit. This is required in order to continue to care for patients and thrive successfully as an organization in the future. Regardless of organizational type and/or classification, the ability to generate a profit while still providing high-quality patient care is a primary responsibility for healthcare administrators. These professionals are entrusted with the overall management of the organization and possess a fiduciary duty to ensure its ongoing, future existence to support all stakeholders involved.

One reason why the U.S. healthcare system remains a competitive environment is the private industry approach, which is still dependent on the volume of care provided to its various stakeholders. The more healthcare services that are provided by a healthcare organization, the more revenue it will generate to help offset its operational expenses. When an organization's revenues exceed total expenses in any given time frame, a profit is earned. When operational expenses exceed revenues generated (or received), a loss

Helpful tip: The terms "healthcare leader" and "healthcare administrator" are utilized interchangeably throughout this textbook. While a clear distinction can be made for any specific leadership position held by a healthcare professional, they are considered synonymous for purposes of this textbook. The financial accounting discipline cuts across all healthcare leadership responsibilities and therefore applies to those in organizational leadership positions (to especially include clinician leaders), as well as professionals with formal training in healthcare administration.

is incurred for the organization. This current reimbursement method is termed fee-for-service (FFS) and encourages the maximum provision (or volume) of services to patients. The more services provided by a healthcare organization, the more revenue is generated and presumably received by payers. Often, patients finance their healthcare using a third-party payer (for example, healthcare insurance) or other third-party financing source (for example, Medicare or Medicaid). If no third-party payer exists, patients are expected to pay for their care completely out of pocket.

How Third-Party Health Insurance Works

Many people are able to access third-party healthcare insurance coverage through their employer as an employee benefit. Others can access the HealthCare.gov website to otherwise purchase private insurance coverage for themselves and their family members. This online health insurance marketplace initiative was established by the Patient Protection and Affordable Care Act (PPACA) of 2010. Other individuals may be eligible for Medicare based on their age (offered to those 65 years or older and/or those with specific, high-cost diagnoses) or a state-administered Medicaid plans (offered to those with personal or family income falling within a specific percentage below a preestablished federal poverty level). Regardless of the third-party payer type, healthcare organizations can bill any charge they would like for any specific service (termed "gross," or full-billed charge). However, based on the allowed reimbursable amount written into the payer–provider contracts with these third-party payers, the healthcare organization's actual reimbursement amount is usually much lower than the gross, full-billed charge (see Figure 1.1).

Order of events:

1. Chest x-ray provided to a patient.

2. Patient is then charged for the service.

3. A contract exists between the provider and the third-party payer so a 'discount' is provided.

4. After applying the *contractual discount*, the remainder of the charge is now due from the insurance carrier and/or also the patient (net).

$105	*gross revenue* (full-billed charge)
– 25	contractual adjustment
80	*net revenue* (owed for the service by either the patient and/or third-party payer)

FIGURE 1.1   How health insurance works with the third-party payer.

Here, the third-party payer has some leverage against the healthcare organization and its associated medical providers. Specifically, the third-party payer possesses a large number of potential patients in its already established health insurance network (group of covered lives). As a result, the healthcare organization is willing to offer a "discount" to the third-party payer, termed a contractual adjustment. This discount lowers the gross revenue (full-billed, gross charge) down to the net revenue (contracted, allowed reimbursement for the specific service provided). Because these contracts and related contractual adjustments (per procedure) are put in place prior to the delivery of care between the third-party payer and the healthcare organization, the system is termed a prospective payment system (PPS).

In return, the healthcare organization and its associated providers are considered "in network" with the third-party payer. This in-network status then allows for additional patient volume, since the organization is now contracted with the third-party payer and future patients will be directed to the organization for care. By increasing the healthcare organization's access to a third-party payer's covered lives, the number of patients the healthcare organization is able to care for increases, therefore increasing the overall volume of services provided. Increasing volume in an FFS reimbursement environment increases total gross revenue billed and therefore total net revenue received by the healthcare organization.

Assessment of Leverage With Third-Party Insurance Negotiations for Reimbursement

Various amounts of provider and/or health insurance company leverage exists when determining the extent of a contractual adjustment. This discount is the amount deducted from the full-billed (gross) charge and depends on a variety of variables, including (but certainly not limited to) the following:

- quality of the medical providers associated with the healthcare organization and their patient outcomes
- availability of other similar providers/specialties in the given area or locale
- number of covered lives available for treatment under the health insurance company

Based on the calculation in Figure 1.1, the service will cost the health insurance company and/or the patient $80 after the gross charge was

Helpful tip: Most healthcare organizations (regardless of type or specialty) will overinflate the gross (total) billed charge for any healthcare good and/or service. The total billed charge for a healthcare service should technically be delineated based on (a) the organization's total expenses associated with the provision of the good/service, and (b) allowing for an acceptable, prescribed profit margin to be achieved. However, most healthcare organizations' *charge master* document (the list of all goods/service provided by the organization and their total, or gross, billed charges) entails gross charges that are extravagantly beyond such guidelines.

contractually reduced. This is due to contractual adjustment arrangements between the healthcare organization and the health insurance company ($25 discount per contractual arrangements and a prospective allowed amount of $80). Of the remaining $80 due, it is not immediately guaranteed that the insurance company will remit this payment in full. Patient cost-sharing is then applied based on the specific type of health insurance plan in which the patient has chosen to enroll. Patient cost-sharing, in addition to the monthly *premium* paid by the patient to simply maintain health insurance coverage, also includes the following.

- *Annual deductible:* a dollar amount (usually in the thousands) that must be paid out-of-pocket by the patient (or family) each year before any health insurance company payments are made to the healthcare organization on behalf of the enrolled member (patient) and/or family members.
  - The annual deductible resets to $0 on a single calendar date each year (often January 1 of every year, or other stipulated annual date).
  - The contractual adjustment (from Figure 1.1) is still applied (discounted) from the healthcare organization's gross-billed charge, even if the patient has not reached their annual deductible amount. This is because the patient is an enrolled member and pays monthly premiums for coverage to protect them from having to pay noncontracted, full-billed (gross) charges.
- *Coinsurance:* represented by a percentage (examples include 90/10, 80/20, or 60/40) to describe the percentage of the amount due that will be paid by the health insurance company once the annual deductible has been met. The remaining (smaller) percentage of the net charge is to be paid by the patient. This ratio is applied after the contractual adjustment has been deducted from the full-billed charge.
- *Copayment:* an amount (flat fee) paid each time the covered patient visits a medical provider, regardless of whether the annual deductible has been met or not. In other words, this amount is paid to the medical provider per encounter.

It is important to note that only the monthly premium is paid to the healthcare insurance company each month to remain a covered beneficiary for that specific health insurance plan. The remaining cost-sharing methods above require the healthcare organization to collect these amounts from the patient and/or third-party payer directly. The patient is to be billed for a service previously provided and processed as an amount due based on it being (a) applied to the patient's annual deductible, (b) the patient's coinsurance amount due, and/or (c) a simple copayment (which the healthcare organization often collects at the time of service). Therefore, it is the healthcare organization's responsibility to properly record and collect the amount due by the patient after the insurance company processes the patient's healthcare claim. For these reasons, the use of proper financial accounting practices is mandatory to ensure health insurance (third-party) contracts are upheld correctly so the healthcare organization receives the correct, allowed contracted reimbursement for the services it provides. This demonstrates why strong financial accounting skills are vital for the healthcare administrator to possess. Such examples are described throughout this textbook using similar cost-sharing examples.

A Shift of Financial Risk With Payment for Quality Initiatives

While the majority of the U.S. healthcare system remains on an FFS reimbursement method for most of the care provided, a continuous initiative to transition toward a pay-for-performance (P4P) reimbursement methodology has evolved. This program is further supported by the Medicare Access and CHIP Reauthorization Act (MACRA) of 2015. Beyond the scope of this textbook, it should be noted that MACRA (2015) provides modifications to previously enacted P4P initiatives set forth by the original PPACA (2010) healthcare reform policy, including the following:

- new (updated) Medicare identification cards/numbers (to replace the use of the beneficiary's Social Security number)
- repeal of the Sustainable Growth Rate (SGR), therefore abolishing the ongoing and medical provider reimbursement cuts and other associated policy adjustments to physician providers
- establishment of the Quality Payment Program (QPP) through the implementation of the Merit-Based Incentive Payment System, or MIPS (outpatient/ambulatory care)
- establishment of Alternative Payment Models (APMs), which are quality reporting programs in lieu of MIPS participation for eligible healthcare organizations (outpatient/ambulatory care)
- establishment and application of the Total Performance Score (TPS), linking patient outcomes and satisfaction scores with reimbursable amounts to the organization per procedure (hospital care).

The MIPS and APM programs are considered P4P programs within the Medicare QPP initiative for outpatient/ambulatory care organizations. Hospitals are also starting to be reimbursed for P4P quality outcome evaluations using the TPS as calculated by the Centers for Medicare and Medicaid Services (CMS). These P4P initiatives shift payment/reimbursement risk from the health insurance carrier back to the healthcare organization delivering

Helpful tip: Health insurance companies are private companies (similar to car insurance companies). They are in the business of controlling risk. Their mission is to ensure that they are able to stay in business and have funds to pay for future medical claims on behalf of their enrolled members (covered lives). Commercial health insurance companies utilize all of these patient cost-sharing methods by manipulating coverage options in ongoing attempts to help control their financial risk for each patient population enrolled.

the care. P4P programs will provide levels of payment to the healthcare organization only if specific quality outcome goals and/or criteria are reached for each patient encounter and/or otherwise required patient quality reporting requirements are met. Additionally, it should be mentioned that APM programs are budget neutral, meaning that those healthcare organizations receiving additional (or "bonus") payments for reporting and/or receiving high-quality care outcome scores will be funded from payment deductions taken from APM-participating healthcare organizations that failed to meet quality benchmarks. These P4P reimbursement methodologies, while still mostly associated with the CMS, apply only to Medicare patients. P4P initiatives are continuing to be implemented at the outpatient level of care (to include accountable care organizations, or ACOs) and other advanced outcome-related payment models.

Private-Pay Patients and Charity Care

Those without third-party payer coverage who access the healthcare system are often termed private-pay patients. These are individuals who do not have health insurance coverage offered through their employer as an employee benefit and/or have chosen not to participate (purchase) third-party health insurance coverage through the HealthCare.gov website as offered by the PPACA of 2010. Private-pay patients are responsible for 100% of the full-billed charge (gross charges), without any contractual discount offered. This is one of the primary benefits of possessing third-party health insurance coverage—to prevent having to pay the healthcare organization's full-billed charges.

Further distinguishing the U.S. healthcare industry from many other non-healthcare, private businesses is the provision of charity care for *indigent patients. Indigent care is provided to* those individuals who do not possess the financial resources to pay for their own healthcare. Charity care will be thoroughly addressed in future chapters with regard to revenue deductions and the charity care adjustment account. Many FASB changes related to this topic are continuing to develop in the healthcare finance industry, and learners are encouraged to review the updated charity care reporting requirements in Chapter 13 (Cognella Active Learning website). The healthcare administrator should take great care to ensure that a charity care policy exists within their organization, as percentages of gross charges are often awarded to various indigent patients. Such charity care adjustments are often based on their individual financial situation and related financial assessment conducted by the healthcare organization. The healthcare organization providing charity care to medically indigent patients is required to establish a charity care policy and enforce it equitably among all patients who potentially qualify.

The Healthcare Financial Environment

Now that a general idea as to how healthcare services are usually provided, billed, and reimbursed has been introduced, a review of the U.S. healthcare industry's financial environment is warranted. The complicated and ever-changing healthcare financial environment only further highlights the importance of competency in healthcare financial accounting for healthcare administrators. Granted, this is the only private healthcare system in the world, but it does offer both opportunities and challenges to the population it serves—all dependent on what stakeholders' perspective is taken. The ability to properly accumulate and communicate the detailed economic data for the healthcare organization will assist healthcare leaders with challenging operational decisions and help ensure high-quality patient care. These actions are required to help ensure the ongoing, future existence of the healthcare organization.

The United States spends more money on healthcare services per capita (per person) than any other country in the world. The National Center for Health Statistics reports that each person (on average) spends over $10,000 per year on healthcare services (Centers for Disease Control and Prevention [CDC], 2020). This value has increased over 120% since 2000 (CDC, 2020). In other words, all the patient cost-sharing methods previously described in this chapter will sum to an estimated $10,000 per year, per person (on average). This amount is paid 100% out of pocket and is a challenging budget item for a typical American family. There is no price discrimination in healthcare, as all patients receiving care will be initially charged the same amount based on the specific procedure(s) they receive. However, not everyone will pay the same amount for their care. Some will pay more while others will pay less. One thing is for sure—if the system continues to remain unchanged, values will eventually become unattainable for families (with or without third-party health insurance).

As individuals grow older, it is common for their dependency on the healthcare system to increase. This dependency is due to both comorbidities that occur with age and other personal lifestyle choices. Therefore, increased access to the healthcare system in an FFS environment translates to more copayments being paid, more bills applied to the patient's annual deductible, and—once

Helpful tip: While many private-pay patients are those unable to access third-party health insurance for a variety of reasons (or those who choose not to pay for it), keep in mind that there are private-pay patients who simply prefer to pay cash for their healthcare services on a case-by-case basis. While not common, some wealthy patients would rather pay out of pocket for their care in lieu of ongoing third-party health insurance coverage. This action does not permit the use of a contractual adjustment from the organization's full-billed charge for any given service. Private-pay patients without third-party insurance will be required to pay gross charges. However, private-pay patients may be able to negotiate with the healthcare organization for an up-front, cash payment (usually required to be made in full at or before the time of service) for a percent discount from the gross charge. The healthcare organization is required to possess a policy related to private-pay patients if an up-front, cash payment discount is offered.

the deductible has been met—more amounts applied to the patient's coinsurance. This increasing cost of healthcare services, combined with an increased access to the system over time, further supports a strong claim for an individual to maintain a healthy lifestyle. The goal of a healthy lifestyle (an individual responsibility) is to attempt to limit access to the system and prevent future expensive, chronic health conditions that may eventually require the provision of expensive, acute care services. While a little effort now goes a long way in the end, most Americans are challenged by other initiatives with instant gratification, and the healthy lifestyle payoff is continuously challenged by daily behaviors and lifestyle choices.

Healthcare as a Percentage of GDP

The U.S. gross domestic product (GDP) provides an assessment of how productive a country has been by reviewing and monetizing all goods and services produced within a prior year. It is important to recognize the size and scope of the U.S. healthcare industry when comparing to other similar countries. In 2017 healthcare in the United States as a percentage of the country's GDP was 17.9% (CDC, 2020). Hovering close to one fifth (or 20%) of the total annual GDP, this figure has been somewhat stagnant for the past several years (2015: 17.6%; 2016: 18.0%; CDC, 2020). In perspective, the U.S. healthcare system as a percentage of GDP is growing more each year as a significant amount of goods and services is produced in the United States in order to meet the demand for healthcare services in the population.

The goods and services produced by the U.S. healthcare system that make up the greatest percentage of GDP are hospital care, professional (medical provider) services, prescription drugs, and health insurance. These are the industry segments where the most money is spent for healthcare (CDC, 2020). It is a U.S. population with increasing healthcare comorbidities due to ongoing, chronic conditions that supports the increased amount of spending for these specific industry segments. As a result, the healthcare industry is often considered a "recession-proof" industry, offering a significant amount of job security for healthcare professionals. However, no organization (healthcare included) is totally immune from environmental conditions and other global, external factors. The COVID-19 global pandemic easily demonstrated this as routine/outpatient healthcare services declined due to physical distancing and other precautionary protocols enforced by the healthcare system.

Something Will Have to Give, Eventually

Healthcare spending in the United States has reached unattainable amounts for the typical American family. As a result, this trend will continue to stress the system and often limit access for many requiring care. This applies to patients accessing the system for treatment due to chronic conditions as previously discussed or even failing to seek care when significant, acute health conditions require medical treatment. Either situation will eventually compound to a future, increased emergent care intervention. This delay in treatment over time often involves a higher level of care to alleviate the patient's increased health issues. As a result, the costs are higher.

PPACA (2010) Medicaid Eligibility Expansion

Efforts to alleviate such industry concerns have been made in the past, including the PPACA (2010) and MACRA (2015). With an overall initiative to increase access to the healthcare system, the PPACA policy offered an expansion of state Medicaid eligibility. This initiative offered matching funds with additional federal funding to assist with the intended increase in Medicaid beneficiaries now eligible under expanded poverty-level eligibility guidelines. Not every state chose to participate in this part of the PPACA policy and therefore chose to forgo the associated federal funding for state Medicaid expansion initiatives. However, for some states that did expand their Medicaid eligibility criteria, a significant number of people with private health insurance chose to drop their private insurance plans and transition their care to the state-expanded Medicaid policy. Whereas an individual or family potentially did not qualify for their state Medicaid plan prior to the PPACA of 2010, a state expansion of eligibility (expanded percent coverage above a federal poverty level) then enabled Medicaid eligibility. This observation relates back to increased cost sharing for patients with third-party health insurance coverage as a challenge to the monthly family budget and an effort to save money by avoiding insurance cost-sharing methods. This is because there is no monthly premium or other patient cost-sharing associated with Medicaid plans (less individual/family out-of-pocket expenses for required medical care).

Baby Boomer Transition to Medicare

Additionally, there are generational issues in play as well. Members of the baby boom generation—those born from 1945 to 1964—have been entering into their retirement years at unsurmountable numbers. As they reach age 65, they are eligible for Medicare, and they too are choosing to forgo a private healthcare insurance option—primarily to avoid the high out-of-pocket monthly premiums. While Medicare does have a monthly premium associated with it (even after people retire and stop receiving an income), this monthly amount is often much lower than most private/commercial insurance premiums. It is also able to be automatically deducted from the beneficiary's monthly Social Security benefit, therefore avoiding all private health insurance cost-sharing initiatives altogether.

As a result of Medicaid expansion initiatives and the rapid retirement rates of the baby boom generation, the healthcare industry continues to be stressed at levels that will render the program completely insolvent. This issue is also due to Medicare and especially Medicaid reimbursing well below what it costs to treat patients for any given healthcare encounter (on average). In other words, the healthcare organization runs the risk of losing money (incurring a loss) each time a Medicare and/or Medicaid patient is treated if it is unable to get costs associated with any specific treatment below Medicare/Medicaid allowed (PPS) reimbursement amounts. The healthcare leader is charged with controlling such cost and reimbursement issues, and a strong knowledge in healthcare financial accounting is required.

Methods to address government payer (Medicare and Medicaid) reimbursement challenges include the following.

1. All costs involved in treating the Medicare and/or Medicaid patient should be closely evaluated, and work should be done to lower associated treatment costs below the allowed amounts for respective healthcare services. This must be done in a manner that also continues to ensure healthcare quality is not reduced as a result of costs being cut. Medical provider (clinician) input and advice is crucial in this assessment and development of organizational protocols.

2. While the Medicare and Medicaid reimbursement will continue to challenge the healthcare leader's efforts from initiative 1 above, additional *cost-shifting* to private health insurance payers (commercial health insurance, third-party payers) continues to help recover any losses incurred from the lower Medicare and Medicaid allowed reimbursement amounts. The private health insurance companies often reimburse at higher rates than Medicare and Medicaid—as long as the healthcare organization continues to possess an acceptable amount of leverage (as previously discussed in the "How Third-Party Health Insurance Works" section of this chapter). Therefore, it can continue to negotiate higher allowed amounts (or lower contractual adjustment amounts) from commercial insurance companies in an attempt to make up expected (calculated) losses from Medicaid/Medicare payer allowed (PPS) amounts.

In Summary

The journey into healthcare financial accounting has begun, and Chapter 1 demonstrates many reasons why healthcare leaders are required not only to understand financial accounting practices but also to implement them into their everyday healthcare operations. Due to the nature and complicated characteristics of the U.S. healthcare system, an ongoing assessment of the history and status of the healthcare organization needs to be conducted—using valid and reliable financial statements as one tool to get this done. Becoming competent in healthcare financial accounting will assist the healthcare administrator in operational decision making and becoming trusted among medical providers and other leaders on the team. This knowledge will translate into a well-run healthcare organization and, most importantly, the provision of quality care for patients.

Chapter Questions

1. Access your institution's healthcare administration (or related) curriculum. A listing of required courses should exist and be available for review. Does a healthcare financial accounting course (or at least the requirement for it as a program prerequisite) exist? If so, establish whether it is required to be taken *prior* to the healthcare financial management course in the course sequence/schedule. If answers to either of these questions do not align with recommendations of this textbook chapter, ask your program leaders why you are expected to take "Spanish II prior to Spanish I."

2. Identify any third-party health insurance benefits—either your own, your family's, a friend's, or simply using the HealthCare.gov website. Interpret the plan's patient cost-sharing methods and discuss/explain them in your own words if you or a family member were to access the healthcare system using this specific health insurance.

3. Discuss how health insurance companies utilize the various patient cost-sharing methods to balance the risk of financial responsibility as the guarantor for their beneficiaries' healthcare costs.

4. Using your institution's library database, search for peer-reviewed journal articles that address the Medicare QPP: MIPS and APMs. Next, search for articles that address the Total Performance Score (TPS) for hospitals. Identify at least two challenges uncovered by your research that have been encountered by healthcare organizations implementing these P4P initiatives.

5. Conduct your own research to identify at least five distinguishing characteristics (initiatives) for each of the following (related) healthcare policies:
   a. Patient Protection and Affordable Care Act (2010)
   b. Medicare Access and CHIP Reauthorization Act (2015)

   Note: As a healthcare leader, you should be able to recite these policy initiatives at any time.

6. Describe the healthcare financial environment regarding spending per capita, healthcare as a percentage of GDP, and the unsustainable yet ongoing cost-shifting to private (commercial) health insurers.

Chapter References

Centers for Disease Control and Prevention. (2020). *Gross domestic product, national health expenditures, per capita amounts, percent distribution, and average annual percent change: United States, selected years 1960–2017 (Table 42)*. https://www.cdc.gov/nchs/data/hus/2018/042.pdf

Donabedian, A. (1980). *The definition of quality and approaches to its assessment*. Health Administration Press.

2

Mind the GAAP

Accounting Concepts to Guide Processes and Procedures

Introduction

This chapter introduces the accounting concepts that are vitally important to assist the healthcare administrator in successfully leading an organization. The material is cumulative, enabling each chapter after this one to continue to build on the GAAP concepts and protocols introduced here. A solid understanding of these concepts will help ensure the primary focus of this textbook: to create *valid and reliable financial statements* for the healthcare organization.

Learning Objectives

By the end of this chapter, the student should be able to:

- Define what Generally Accepted Accounting Principles (GAAP) are and how they are utilized in healthcare financial accounting practices/processes.
- List and discuss the various types of business entities and how their formation and existence support different types of healthcare organizations.
- List and define all 10 GAAP concepts utilized to develop valid and reliable financial statements for healthcare organizations.
- Demonstrate the difference in recording revenues and expenses using the matching principle versus the conservatism method.
- List and provide examples of all the financial statement notes that provide additional transparency to the financial statements.

Key Terms

1. Generally Accepted Accounting Principles (GAAP)
2. Business entity
3. Consistency
4. Going concern
5. Historical cost
6. Market value
7. Materiality
8. Solvency
9. Matching principle
10. Conservatism
11. Transparency
12. Financial period
13. Financial statement notes

GAAP (Generally Accepted Accounting Principles)

GAAP stands for "Generally Accepted Accounting Principles." Established by the Financial Accounting Standards Board (FASB), these principles serve as general guidelines across all business entities, so a comprehensive and standardized documentation of any organization's financial history is properly recorded. The recording of business activities is done using monetary values with dollar signs ($) for specific, predefined accounts, processes, and related financial statements. This accounting (bookkeeping) standard for the United States requires the use of GAAP methods and procedures so an "apples-to-apples" comparison is enabled for analysis within and between healthcare organizations and their respective financial statements. In other words, GAAP standards help in informing businesses (within the healthcare industry and beyond) to know

- what a balance sheet, statement of net assets, and all other financial statements should look like (formatting and specific account names);
- what specific subaccount(s) should be utilized during any business transaction occurring within the organization; and also
- what ongoing practices and procedures should remain in effect to ensure ongoing compliance with GAAP processes.

GAAP standards in the United States are in place to ensure that all businesses are playing by the rules and reporting the financial history of their organization in a similar manner.

While every business is different (even businesses within the healthcare industry), these generally accepted guidelines establish conformity and procedures to assist in the creation of *valid and reliable financial statements*. It should also be noted that some GAAP concepts to be reviewed later in this chapter may not be able to be fully executed by the organization at any one time and/or may even be in competition with each other as conflicting GAAP protocols. This occurrence does prevent full exploitation of selected GAAP concepts to their fullest extent at times. Accounting professionals will often challenge any particular use of a specific accounting principle over another when interpreting an organization's financial statements. This demonstrates the importance of the healthcare administrator possessing a thorough understanding of financial accounting and GAAP policies to help ensure the future financial success of the organization. Competency in this area will also assist with the establishment of organizational processes and procedures to ensure GAAP protocols are continuously followed.

The Business Entity

Hospitals and other healthcare organizations that provide care to patients in need are all established as incorporated business entities to provide the organization several levels of financial and legal benefits, and even some select protections. Many different types of healthcare organizations are incorporated in different ways, depending on the type of organization, its location (to include what state it is located in), and the overall purpose of the organization. While a provider organization is most commonly used as an example in this textbook (such as a hospital, medical clinic, etc.), it should be noted that many other types of healthcare organizations also exist and are incorporated as business entities as well. Examples of such nonprovider organizations in the healthcare industry include managed care organizations, government and third-party payers, medical vendors/suppliers, and medical device/equipment vendors, just to name a few.

Sometimes the type of business entity is listed or shown in the marketing/branding materials for the healthcare organization. For example, there may be a local hospital named Colorado Springs City Hospital and down the road a dentist office named Dr. John Smith, DDS, PA. Both organizations are incorporated business entities—whether the actual business entity description is provided in the name of the organization or not. Table 2.1 demonstrates several types of business entities that may occur in the healthcare field and beyond, as established and implemented by the state in which the organization resides.

TABLE 2.1 Examples of business entities common in the healthcare industry

Type of business entity	Definition	Business entity example(s)
Sole proprietorships	Any individual without incorporation who offers (sells) goods/services.	A student graduated and started their own individual bookkeeping (financial accounting) service for outside individuals/organizations.
General partnerships (GPs)* Partnerships are able to include liability protection of partners based on their partnership type.	Two or more individuals who enter into an agreement to offer (sell) goods/services.	Two physicians entering into an agreement to work together and combine their specialty expertise in the treatment of patients. Unlimited, equal liability exists between individual partners in the GP model.
Corporations (also known as C corporations)	A business entity that is fully incorporated and therefore a distinction is made between it and its owners.	Examples include: Amazon Texas State University Dr. John Smith, DDS, PA
S corporations	A business entity that is fully incorporated yet has elected to received pass-through dividends and is taxed at the individual shareholders' tax rate/bracket (among other factors).	S corporations will closely resemble regular C corporation characteristics, except for their S classification.
Nonprofit corporations (also known as not-for-profit corporations)	A business entity that is fully incorporated yet has elected to possess a primary mission of community service, therefore reinvesting any/all profits back into the organization and also into the surrounding community—all in lieu of paying taxes.	Examples include: Colorado Springs Community Hospital Community Area Health Clinic Meals on Wheels National Volunteer Caregiving Network

Owners (providers, etc.) may choose to limit their individual liabilities for action(s) performed by their partners by further incorporating their partnership into one of the following categories:

- limited liability partnership (LLP)
- limited liability company (LLC) partnership
- limited partnership (LP)

Organization ownership should consult a legal and tax professional in determining the organizational structure selected for their new business. As demonstrated, various business entity structures exist (these often vary by state) and offer the organization's ownership member(s) options with regard to liability, treatment of profits (and losses), and other operational characteristics. In the end, the establishment of an incorporated business hypothetically creates a living, breathing business entity that can take on debt, possess a market reputation, and even establish creditworthiness—just like a human. Because of this business entity's existence, valid and reliable financial statements are required to properly document the organization's financial history, per GAAP procedures.

GAAP Concepts for the Healthcare Leader

According to GAAP, specific procedures and requirements are provided to guide the healthcare administrator's record-keeping activities and keep financial statements in proper order. Successful implementation of these GAAP concepts will allow for the organization to meet GAAP and FASB expectations and therefore assist when future accounting audits and other continuous quality improvement initiatives are conducted. In addition to delineating the specific financial statement formats, several GAAP concepts will be reviewed (see Table 2.2), and these influence a significant number of processes and practices in the development of valid and reliable financial statements.

TABLE 2.2   Summary of GAAP concepts important in healthcare administration

GAAP concept	Purpose
Consistency	Similar to reliability, the maintaining of regular, repeatable accounting practices and protocols within the healthcare organization's operational activities.
Going concern	The organization leaders have a fiduciary responsibility to make financial/operational decisions that further the organization's existence in the long-term future.
Historical cost vs. market value	Often used to delineate the values to record intangible and tangible assets on the organization's balance sheet, these two valuation methods define purchase price vs. market (supply and demand) value.
Materiality	A term used to properly define a matter that is of significance.
Solvency	Long-term viability (life) of the organization, often evaluated as the balance between an organization's unrestricted and restricted net assets (equity).

Helpful tip: Remember, by creating an official, incorporated business entity, the healthcare providers, medical and administrative staff, and the healthcare administrative leadership within the organization are working for an entity that exists almost as its own living, breathing organism. The healthcare entity can possess a market reputation, a financial creditworthiness record, and even take on debt. It can be liable for legal implications resulting from patient care experiences and/or medical provider actions.

TRY ON YOUR OWN

Imagine that you are a hospital administrator, working on the 15th floor of the building in your quiet office, sorting through financial reports in preparation for an upcoming meeting. Suddenly, you are notified of a potential act of negligence by one of the physicians treating a patient in the inpatient surgery unit (on the 4th floor). Would you (the healthcare administrator) want to be held liable—or even partially liable—for the acts of a single medical provider several floors below? What aspects of the business entity being incorporated help provide individuals protection from the actions of others?

GAAP concept	Purpose
Matching principle vs. conservatism	Two primary GAAP concepts regarding when to recognize (record) revenues and expenses related to any healthcare service or initiative.
Transparency (using financial statement notes)	A requirement for the healthcare leader to provide any/all information that is not truly evident or obvious from the values ($) on the financial statements themselves—often in the form of financial statement notes.
Financial period	An annual date that is regularly used for categorizing and generating financial statements and the related transactions falling within this time period.

In addition to these, other accounting principles and practices are defined by U.S. GAAP. While all GAAP procedures are vital to ensuring the creation of valid and reliable financial statements for any type of organization, the concepts covered in this chapter will consistently be emphasized and utilized throughout this textbook to generate the healthcare organization's financial statements.

Consistency

In healthcare operations, the industry likes to create processes that lead to best outcomes in patient care. Because of this, a consistent application of these best practice protocols is usually required for medical providers, unless an exception exists and is properly documented. The same applies for healthcare accounting practices—staying consistent with organizational processes and protocols to ensure the proper accumulation, recording, and presentation of accounting data in the form of financial statements. Consistency is necessary to support the creation of valid and reliable financial statements for the healthcare organization and includes important account and other industry data sets. Example include the following.

- Verifying the patient's date of birth (DOB) on the new patient paperwork and the DOB listed in the electronic medical record's billing system. This ensures the electronic claim will be sent without issue and the third-party payer will process the claim correctly. As a result, the organization's A/R (amount due to the organization for services provided) for that patient encounter will be received sooner, rather than later (as opposed to if it were to be a denied claim due to an initially incorrect DOB entered into the EMR system).
- Paying all invoices due (A/P) balances prior to their due date. Doing so will enable the healthcare organization to maintain a limited A/P (economic obligation) account balance, while also establishing creditworthiness with its medical and business supply vendors.

- Establishing organizational protocols so equipment depreciation and inventory methods are applied correctly to each piece of equipment and supply type/category. This action will allow for correct capture of depreciation and inventory expenses, per organizational protocols.

Consistency is easily summarized by working to maintain the status quo for any particular initiative and only changing routine processes and procedures if absolutely necessary. Documentation of such changes is required.

Going Concern

This GAAP concept demonstrates the organizational leader's requirement to make operational decisions based on the premise that the organization will be around for the long term. The primary goal of the organization's efforts is to provide quality care to the surrounding community for several years to come, versus simply trying to make as much profit as possible during the current financial period. Long-term planning is a priority for the organization, versus short-term gains when going concern is utilized. Even short-term losses may be necessary if they lead to achieving future projected long-term gains. A hospital will not benefit its surrounding community and associated stakeholders if it does not consider going concern when making operational decisions and is not around for years to come.

A prime example of hospitals (both for- and not-for-profit statuses) demonstrating going concern is their reactions and strategic plan deviations made to care for coronavirus (COVID-19) patients in their time of need. During the global pandemic, most states required all nonurgent (routine) healthcare procedures to be put on hold to allow for additional resources to be diverted to care for COVID patients. This led to many healthcare facilities experiencing a significant drop in gross revenues, as nonurgent, routine, and even outpatient care are a significant portion of any hospital's revenue in any given financial period. Further, the reimbursement for caring for COVID-19 patients has been shown to be much lower than the required resources to care for some of these high-acuity patients. However, the community hospitals and their leadership teams stepped up to these challenges by diverting from or even permanently altering their current strategic plans in order to care for the community. This decision was implemented regardless of the loss of revenue and the opportunity cost that was experienced, demonstrating going concern by the organization for the community. While the financial loss in this situation will be experienced for years to come, healthcare organizations possessed a going concern and made the decision to support surrounding communities for the long term, versus an attempt to continue normal operations during the global pandemic. Going concern is when short-term gains are forgone in an effort to establish long-term future organizational existence.

Historical Cost vs. Market Value

In healthcare financial accounting, historical cost is simply the documented purchase price of a *tangible* item. Physical, touchable, tangible items vary from disposable medical supplies to fixed assets such as expensive medical equipment, buildings, and even land. For most tangible assets, historical cost is the amount at which the asset is documented, regardless of what it may be worth in current-day market conditions. Therefore, most tangible assets on the organization's balance sheet are valued at their historical cost (purchase price).

Market value is what any tangible item would sell for when enacting current-day supply-and-demand market conditions. Therefore, normal market economic conditions are in play without any other confounding market variables. Many organizational resources (assets) are valued and presented on the financial statement using only the historical cost method. Any significant market value changes in an asset may be commented on in the notes to the financial statement (to be discussed later in this chapter). The actual dollar value for the asset on the statement itself will always remain the amount for which it was purchased (historical cost).

For example:

- Pre-coronavirus (COVID-19): N95 filtration masks were purchased at a typical historical cost ($x) and valued as supplies (organizational assets) while unused, waiting on the supply shelf.
- During the coronavirus (COVID-19) global pandemic: N95 filtration mask demand skyrocketed, and as a result, the historical cost (purchase price) for these supply items was significantly increased ($x + market demand amount) by the medical vendors. This higher price per mask was recorded as the historical cost for the item and was added to the organization's assets and corresponding supply expense accounts when purchased. However, if these same masks remained unused on the inventory shelf prior to COVID-19, they would still be valued at the original purchase price ($x).

The organization's *intangible assets* (such as short-term investments, etc.) will have their market value on the organization's balance sheet, but only after demonstrating historical cost (purchase price) of the asset on the balance sheet where its account value is listed. Market value changes (an increase or decrease) are to be noted in the financial statement notes at the bottom of the financial statement. Short- and long-term investments owned by the healthcare organization are an example. Any one investment will have a current-day purchase price (e.g., cost per share). This value will be recorded on the balance sheet under its respective account under the main asset account. However, investments such as stocks, mutual funds, and other related intangible assets do vary in current-day market value over time. These changes (as demonstrated by recording the current-day market value for any particular investment) are documented at the bottom of the balance sheet in the form of a financial note to the statement (more to follow later in this chapter). In the end, the original investment purchase price remains listed on the actual financial statement for each intangible asset's account value.

Materiality

In financial accounting, if something is material in nature, it is big. A material decision in the organization's strategic plan, a material accounting error identified by the organization's auditor—these are qualified by the material GAAP accounting concept.

Believe it or not, most financial auditors (CPA firms, etc.) are not looking for every single, tiny accounting error that may have occurred in the healthcare organization. Instead, they are searching for accounting processes and practices and errors to GAAP concepts that are material (of significance) in nature. Such errors usually alter the values for specific accounts significantly on the organization's financial statements. However, keep in mind that even a small accounting error—conducted over and over many times on a single day—can quickly become material in nature. This is another reason why the healthcare administrator must remain visible and engaged in all processes and protocols related to the accumulation of accounting data in the organization. It does not take much for a material error to arise during a typical healthcare operational routine.

Solvency

Like going concern, solvency relates specifically to the long-term viability (or life) of the organization. This is demonstrated by the balance between long-term debt obligations and short-term liquidity for daily operational expenses, as related to the amount of cash on hand to be maintained. The organization

TRY ON YOUR OWN

If you have purchased your home (and/or are currently financing it with a lender), the purchase price is the historical cost of your home. However, the housing market changes dynamically over time. Using an Internet browser, search for your home's (or a close relative's) current home market value. Is the market price higher or lower than the original historical cost of the home? What does this mean? How should the asset (the home) be valued on your individual balance sheet? What should be noted at the bottom in the financial notes section of the statement?

TRY ON YOUR OWN

You walk into your professor's office during open office hours to inquire about the grade you recently earned on a healthcare financial accounting exam. When reviewing your answers, your professor mentions "a material error made on how specific GAAP concepts were applied to the exam." Is this a good thing or bad thing? Explain.

has a choice in how it manages cash on hand. Choices related to how it manages its level of solvency include

- choosing to keep a lot of cash on hand to pay bills, prepare for unanticipated expenses, and so on; and/or
- choosing to keep a smaller amount of cash on hand and invest the remaining amount in an expansion project and/or external financial investments (stocks and bonds); and/or
- choosing to continue to increase financial obligations (loans) in order to meet short-term obligations, yet balancing debt with stockholder equity (for-profit organizations only).

The level of solvency to be maintained by the organization is determined by the healthcare leadership team and should demonstrate a plan to ensure the long-term viability of the healthcare organization. However, there is no specific answer or formula to inform the leaders of how much (or how little) cash to keep on hand, nor how much to invest. The opportunity cost of such decisions and the requirement to maintain a going concern for the healthcare organization will influence its level of solvency in short-term assets, as compared to its debt-to-equity status. This mixture of cash on hand versus an amount to be invested, as well as a comparison of how much debt the healthcare organization will endure versus its amount of equity maintained (for-profits only) demonstrates the GAAP concept of solvency and the need to thoroughly analyze long-term strategic goals.

Matching Principle

GAAP concepts establish and require the use of both the matching principle and conservatism—consistently. However, in the evaluation of any single financial transaction and/or financial decision for the healthcare organization, a zero-sum game exists. The more the organization implements the matching principle in any specific area of its accounting practices, the less conservative it will be on that same issue—and vice versa. In other words, there is an indirect relationship between these two GAAP concepts. They will never be able to both be fully implemented at any one time, for any single accounting practice, decision, and/or transaction.

To utilize the matching principle when recognizing revenues and expenses, the goal is to try to best match each expense incurred for any single service delivery with the revenue that is earned from that same initiative—in the same financial accounting time period. Whether speaking of a single medical procedure (which has its own associated revenue and expenses) or a much larger, organization-level strategic initiative like a hospital wing expansion project, the matching principle's goal is to assign the revenues earned and expenses incurred to a similar (or "matched") time period. This time period is usually a single operating month or possibly an annual financial period. The outpatient surgery center example below will demonstrate the differences between the matching principle and conservatism GAAP concepts, and the struggle to meet both simultaneously.

Matching Principle: Proposed Outpatient Surgery Center Example

Assume that a healthcare organization is evaluating a strategic initiative regarding whether to build a new freestanding outpatient surgery suite down the road from its main hospital location. In the decision-making stages of strategic planning sessions, a lot of variables will need to be addressed to determine the feasibility of such a project and to ensure its future success. Such decisions may involve researching and forecasting environmental variables such as the following:

- potential market demand for the range of outpatient surgery services to be conducted
- potential market competition within the surrounding area(s) that may generate ongoing competition with the proposed venture
- outpatient surgery reimbursement rates (by payer type) and a financial budget that demonstrates projected revenues to be earned
- a corresponding operating expense budget also to be included in the financial budget for the organization

As a result, the organization's leadership has a decision to make based on the estimated, additional revenues and expenses associated with moving forward with the outpatient surgical suite, or forgoing the initiative altogether. To demonstrate, a summarized budget is provided in Figure 2.1.

Projected center monthly gross revenue:	$50,000
Projected center monthly total expense*:	(8,500)
Projected center monthly net revenue:	+41,500

Additionally, the outpatient surgery center associated strategic planning (consulting) expenses (termed 'sunk costs') will be $30,000 and take 1 full month to plan, regardless of if a decision is made to build the center or not. This consulting expense amount is due in-full during month 2 the proposed center's timeline.

FIGURE 2.1   Monthly estimated revenue and expense budget for the proposed outpatient surgery center.

Utilizing the matching principle, the following revenue and expenses will be recorded (recognized) on the healthcare organization's monthly financial statements based on its decision on whether to move forward with the surgery center building initiative (see Table 2.3).

TABLE 2.3   Demonstration of the matching principle GAAP concept in the strategic planning of an outpatient surgery center

Revenue/Expense	Month 1 (actual)	Month 2	
		If center is built	If center *is not* built
Revenue recognized	$0	50,000 op rev	0
Expense recognized	0	–8,500 op exp –30,000 *sunk cost*	–30,000 *sunk cost*
Net revenue (profit/loss)	0	11,500 profit	–30,000 loss

Comparing the revenues and expenses of each decision, the cost of simply planning for the outpatient surgery center ($30,000 consulting fee) is going to occur and be an expense for the organization even if the decision not to continue with the outpatient surgery center is made. As a result, the monthly revenue is appropriately assigned to the month it is first able to be earned (Month 2, the center's first month of operation). It is not assigned to the second column under Month 2, because if the organization decided not to build the center, the revenue would not have been earned in this scenario. Likewise, the monthly estimated operating expense of $8,500 is also assigned to Month 2 under the first column, versus not recorded as an expense in the second column of Month 2—because there would be no operating expenses if the organization decided not to build/operate the center.

However, the $30,000 sunk cost of strategic planning for the decision of whether to invest in the outpatient surgery center is of concern when utilizing the matching principle. Here, the full $30,000 expense for evaluation and planning of the outpatient surgery suite initiative is properly matched to Month 2, regardless of whether it were to be built or not. This matching of the $30,000 strategic planning sunk cost to Month 2 of the organization's budget demonstrates GAAP's matching principle by recognizing it on either build/no build scenario for Month 2, incorporated with any revenues and expenses associated with that same time period (if any). Therefore, if the center were to be built, a net revenue of $11,500 profit would be experienced, while a net revenue of ($30,000) loss would be experienced if it were not to be built, according to the matching principle.

Conservatism

Healthcare leaders often take a very conservative approach in their strategic thinking and planning. The same goes for healthcare financial accounting GAAP processes. Use of the conservatism GAAP principle in accounting practices means

- un-anticipating any future revenues until they are received in cash, and
- anticipating any future expenses, even if they have not been paid in cash yet.

Such conservatism viewpoints in the field of healthcare management are often deemed overcautious, glass-always-half-empty, and sometimes even a negative perspective at the time they are made. However, as a GAAP principle and also operating in an already highly conservative industry such as healthcare, one has to apply the saying "don't count your chickens until they hatch" to all operational and strategic decisions in order to support the organization's financial well-being. Basic examples of enforcing the conservatism GAAP principle include the following.

- Delaying payment to a medical vendor for an invoice due (but not past the invoice's overall due date) to ensure enough funds are on hand to cover this payroll period's expense for your organization's employee paychecks—even though a direct deposit from Medicare for services rendered is expected to be received within the next 24 hours.
- Forgoing the upcoming weekend's health fair in the city park to provide free flu shots and support other charity care services to the local community stakeholders to protect the organization's healthcare workers and other team members from potentially dangerous, incoming weather (or possible infection from COVID-19).
- Simply recognizing any/all payable accounts on the organization's financial statements as future cash expenses to be paid from the organization's operational checking account as they become due—and adjusting plans based on their amounts and timing of due dates.

Conservatism: Proposed Outpatient Surgery Center Example (Continued)

In review of the proposed outpatient surgery center strategic initiative again, the conservatism GAAP concept can also be made when interpreting the budgeted revenues and expenses (see Table 2.4).

TRY ON YOUR OWN

Think of a time when you had a personal bill due (e.g., rent, cell phone bill, and/or a credit card invoice). Did this upcoming expense alter your plans/behavior in any way, prior to the bill(s) being paid? If so, you were most likely being conservative in your actions. If not, the chance of missing a future payment to a third party probably went up versus if you did act in a more conservative manner with regard to your personal finances.

TABLE 2.4 Demonstration of the conservatism GAAP concept in the strategic planning of an outpatient surgery center

Revenue/expense	Month 1 (actual)	Month 2	
		If center is built	If center *is not* built
Revenue recognized	$0	50,000 op rev	0
Expense recognized	–15,000 *sunk cost*	–8,500 op exp –15,000 *sunk cost*	–15,000 *sunk cost*
Net revenue (profit/loss)	–15,000	26,500	–15,000

Under the GAAP conservatism viewpoint, the organizational revenues are not anticipated or recorded in the respective time period in which they have been earned or received, as shown under Month 2, Column 1 (no change from our earlier matching principle example for revenue). The same goes for the $8,500 operating expense related to the first month's operation (also no change from our earlier matching principle for operating expenses). Because this example only reviews the first month of the center's actual operation (Month 2), these revenue and expense figures will not change between the matching principle and conservatism example.

However, the $30,000 strategic planning expense (sunk cost), which will be incurred by the organization whether it decides to build the surgery center or not, is now appropriately proportioned across both operating time periods (both Month 1 and Month 2). It also still totals $30,000 in strategic planning expenses as related to the initiative, completed during Month 2. This recognition of half of the sunk strategic planning costs ($15,000) during Month 1 and the other half ($15,000) recognized/recorded under Month 2, regardless of whether the center is built or not, demonstrates the conservatism GAAP principle by immediately anticipating expenses for both months as they occur. This happens all while un-anticipating potential revenue related to the healthcare organization's outpatient surgery center initiative.

While the total net revenue from the entire 2-year projected scenario does not differ between the matching principle and conservatism examples in Tables 2.3 and 2.4, the recorded expenses are different when considering the sunk cost of the consulting fees related to the initiative.

Transparency

The financial statements do a very good job of describing an organization's history using a dollar sign. However, there are times when additional information is required to provide full transparency. When the numbers do not clearly inform the healthcare leader of additional, important financial accounting information regarding the organization and/or a specific account value, the notes section of the statements are used (previously referred to in this chapter when addressing intangible asset valuation). Think of the notes section of the financial statements as an organized collection of free-text, written updates to the various formatted statement values. Per GAAP, this organized fashion often follows the categorization of notes by topic, following an A through E order as demonstrated in Table 2.5.

TABLE 2.5   Organization of notes to the financial statements

Financial statement note section	Financial statement note name	Items addressed
Note A	Summary of significant accounting policies	Basis of accounting Nature of operations Net patient service revenue Short-term assets (investments) Inventory Property and equipment Income taxes Charity care adjustments Temporarily and permanently restricted net assets
Note B	Accounts receivable (A/R)	What is the amount of pending A/R that is truly expected to be collected?
Note C	Long-term liabilities	What type of obligations make up this value on the organization's balance sheet, and what are their specific attributes?
Note D	Litigation	Are there any pending medical lawsuits filed against the healthcare organization?
Note E	Goodwill	What intangible characteristics add additional value (if any) to the healthcare organization, and how are they valued?

Note A—Summary of Significant Accounting Policies
Note A includes many subcategories of accompanying information, in addition to the financial statements themselves. Here, some basic yet important book-keeping information and other organizational processes are addressed to leave

Helpful tip: In healthcare financial accounting, one is rarely optimistic. Think of possible healthcare operational decisions and related outcomes involving both revenues and expenses. The healthcare leader always prepares for the expenses and works to meet such obligations now. The leader also does not count on the revenues being available for use until payment has actually been received. Using conservatism, prepare/expect the worst, and only celebrate the wins when the payment has been received and the ink has dried.

the healthcare leader no question regarding how the statements were developed and what GAAP-approved methods were used for specific activities. Table 2.6 provides a summary of Note A's subcategory polices. Many of these subpolicies will be covered in greater detail and utilized to create valid and reliable financial statements in future chapters.

TABLE 2.6 Explanation of Note A subcategories

Note A subcategory	Information summary	Example
Basis of accounting	Cash vs. accrual method?	The organization is utilizing the accrual basis of accounting in accordance with GAAP polices/procedures.
Nature of operations	Primary mission and purpose of the organization's actions and behavior.	The organization is a primary medical practice, and its mission is to provide quality and timely family medicine healthcare services to the surrounding community/population.
Net patient service revenue (NPSR) (addressed in Chapter 9)	Full-billed charges for services provided (gross revenue) is distinguished as a separate value from NPSR, which is a more accurate and realistic value intended to be collected by the organization for services provided.	The organization has numerous third-party payer contracts with managed care organizations that entail contractual adjustments from original, full-billed charges per procedure. Charity care is also deducted from gross revenue based on care provided to indigent patients. Estimated net realizable A/R values are also provided via the allowance for uncollectable accounts (AUCA)* for care provided and billed, but not yet adjusted for contractual adjustments and/or charity care adjustments.
Short-term assets (investments) (addressed in Chapter 5)	Historical cost of external investments by the organization versus any significant current-day valuation of these assets.	The organization has an original historical cost of $100,000 in XYZ stock since these funds were unbudgeted for use in the current financial period. At the current date/time, this investment has a current fair market value of $125,000 (+25,000).
Inventory (thoroughly addressed in Chapter 6)	What inventory method is used for inventory/supply valuation and costing (expensing)?	The organization utilizes the perpetual LIFO/FISH expensing and valuation method for expendable inventory/supplies.

Note A subcategory	Information summary	Example
Property and equipment (thoroughly addressed in Chapter 5)	What depreciation method is used for fixed assets and equipment?	The organization utilizes the straight-line depreciation method for all buildings and equipment. Historical cost less accumulated depreciation is therefore used to demonstrate current-day book value.
Income taxes	Is the organization a for-profit or a 501(c)(3) not-for-profit organization?	Per IRS Code Section 501(c)(3), the healthcare organization is designated as a not-for-profit organization.
Charity care adjustments (thoroughly addressed in Chapter 9)	What is the process for designating charity care percentages to the medically indigent?	The healthcare organization utilizes a formal, equitable process to designate a percent charity care eligibility from the patient's individual gross revenue (total charges) for services provided. All charity care evaluations are conducted by a medical social worker, and results of the patient's financial evaluation are located in the medical record.
Temporarily/ permanently restricted net assets (thoroughly addressed in Chapter 9)	What is the difference between the organization's temporarily and permanently restricted net assets (NA)?	The healthcare organization accepts a variety of philanthropic donations that are restricted based on time and/or purpose.

Note: The allowance for uncollectible accounts (AUCA) will also be covered in Chapter 5.

Note B—Accounts Receivable

In our healthcare industry, it is highly unusual for the organization to be paid at the time of service (when the care is provided to the patient). This is primarily due to how healthcare is often financed in our country using third-party payers such as commercial healthcare insurance companies, government healthcare payers, and so on. As a result, the healthcare organization provides a service to a customer (the patient) now and is most often paid later. This occurs once a medical claim is submitted to the third-party payer, processed, and approved, whereupon payment is sent to the organization. The healthcare organization is basically extending a line of credit to the patient for services provided since payment in full is not permitted at the time of service per the organization's preestablished contract with the third-party payer.

To be thoroughly addressed in Chapter 5 ("Real Account Valuation Methods"), the accounts receivable (A/R) notes section addresses the healthcare organization's specific practices and processes related to the use and calculation of the allowance for uncollectible accounts (AUCA) value on the organization's balance sheet.

- While A/R represents the total, gross revenue that has been billed to third-party payers for services already provided but not yet paid for, the AUCA is an account that lowers the total A/R, permitting a more *net realizable value* assessment of expected amounts due, based on an organization's internal process on how to calculate this amount.
- Additionally, other pending total charges for care already provided to patients by the organization may also be found uncollectable by means of the organization deeming certain patients and their related medical bills as charity care adjustments.

Figure 2.2 demonstrates how the AUCA is used to lower the organization's total A/R (again, made up of total volumes × charges provided but not yet paid for) to the net realizable A/R.

Total A/R	$250,000	Represents the total value (gross amount) charged for care provided, but not yet paid (pending)
Less (−) the AUCA	−50,000	Represents the estimated amount of pending A/R that is not expected to be collected (paid) due to estimated, future revenue deductions
Net realizable A/R	$200,000	The amount of the currently pending A/R that is estimated to be collectible after accounting for estimated, future revenue deductions (charity care and contractual adjustments)

Note: Significant FASB accounting updates regarding the provision for bad debts and related NPSR deduction standards are further addressed in Chapter 13 (Cognella Active Learning website).

FIGURE 2.2 Demonstration of the calculation of the net realizable A/R on a healthcare organization's balance sheet.

It is clear that a healthcare organization does not expect to collect 100% of its gross, full-billed charges for services provided to patients. At a very basic level (prior to recent and ongoing FASB updates), the AUCA helps provide a more realistic (net realizable value) of the pending A/R that has yet to be processed by the healthcare organization with regard to (a) contractual adjustments and (b) possible charity care adjustments. Once these figures are established (realized) by the healthcare organization and properly recorded, the AUCA is continuously updated with ongoing A/R estimated values based on ongoing pending A/R values resulting from ongoing patient care delivery.

Note C—Long-Term Liabilities

It is very normal for any healthcare organization to be encumbered with long-term liabilities in the form of bank notes (loans) and obligations such as bonds or mortgages to finance ongoing operational expenses and/or strategic initiatives such as organizational expansion and other market opportunities. While these accounts will be thoroughly addressed in Chapter 5, the account values on the organization's balance sheet simply reflect the amount of the pending liability (economic obligation) left to be paid by the healthcare organization.

Additional information on these large obligations is often provided in Note C in an attempt to further inform the healthcare leader on noncurrent (long-term) liability information such as the following:

- overall financial obligation length or duration remaining on the loan/liability
- current and/or variable liability interest rate
- amortization schedule of related principal/interest amounts

Understanding this information in addition to the balance sheet's long-term liability figures may assist the healthcare leader in decision making regarding monthly expenses and related cash flows. Otherwise, this information would not be interpretable with only the obligation's remaining value shown on the balance sheet.

Note D—Litigation

The provision of healthcare services is highly personal. It often involves high patient expectations, and patients expect optimal treatment outcomes. As a result, it is a common occurrence for incongruence to exist between the customer's (the patient's) initial expectations of the care to be provided and their actual perception (reality) of the care during and after accessing the healthcare system. Often, such a gap between expectations and perceptions of care results in the healthcare consumer and/or related parties taking legal action against a healthcare organization.

While the reasoning behind any healthcare lawsuit between a patient and an organization is beyond the scope of this textbook, it is evident that the transparency of any pending yet not finalized legal claims and/or actions against the organization must be clearly disclosed in Note D (litigation). Such transparency of potential actions (and the possibility of future malpractice, neglect, or other healthcare settlements) will help the leader interpret the risk

TRY ON YOUR OWN

You really want to buy that new car. But you already have a vehicle and are still financing it though your bank with remaining monthly payments. What additional information would you like to know about your current vehicle loan that may assist you in your decision of whether to trade in your current vehicle and purchase a new one, knowing you are on a very limited budget?

and possible related (future) legal expenses when making decisions regarding the organization's financial management and related strategic planning decisions. If no pending litigation against the healthcare organization exists at the time the financial statements are generated, this fact can simply be stated in Note D to demonstrate full transparency of any current-day, pending organizational legalities.

Note E—Goodwill

Goodwill represents an ongoing GAAP-permitted valuation of any healthcare organization's intangible asset(s) that add value to the facility's total assets (economic resources). These valuations are unrelated to financial investments. While thoroughly addressed in Chapter 5, the organization may possess the following attributes that add additional (intangible) realized value to the organization in a market valuation:

- positive, encouraging employee morale
- positive online market reputation and internal patient feedback comments/reviews
- a healthy creditworthiness reputation among the medical vendor community
- positive, recognizable brand awareness within the surrounding community

As a result, these intangible organizational resources add value to the organization's overall net worth and can be reflected as increasing the organization's asset section of its balance sheet. However, this occurs only if evaluated and reported in an objective manner. For instance, the healthcare administrator cannot individually estimate the organization's goodwill value on their own. Instead, an external, third-party medical actuary or medical marketing professional may complete this task as an unbiased evaluator. Documentation of such activity is to remain on file for auditing and other documentation purposes if claiming goodwill on the balance sheet.

In the end, the most valid and most accurate determination of any organization's goodwill account value would be the actual sale of the entire healthcare organization. Here, any value paid for the organization beyond that of its asset book value would be attributed to a positive goodwill valuation for the organization being acquired. Note E provides this additional information regarding how any goodwill valuation was obtained and any/all methods related to such an estimate.

Financial Period

A healthcare organization's financial period is an annual (yearly) period that represents any/all financial transactions and other operating events that fall within that single period. Many organizations choose to simply use the regular calendar year as the corresponding financial period for their financial statements (therefore, running January 1 through December 31). However, other organizations may choose to assign their financial period start/end dates based on their organization's inherent characteristics, such as operational workflow, annual/regular environmental conditions, and/or even organizational leader preference. Termed a fiscal year, it is important to note that such a strategy is also to follow the consistency GAAP concept, and therefore the start/end dates of any single organization's financial period should not be changed from year to year.

In Summary

Interpreted as basic, recommended guidelines for financial accounting process and procedures, GAAP helps the healthcare leader maintain established best practices and conformity expectations of the business community. This initiative helps ensure that all organizations are accumulating and communicating their financial statements and overall organizational status in a similar method. It is also important to understand that every organization is completely different in structure, status, and even service provided. As a result, GAAP procedures serve as guidelines, and financial statements will still vary in format and presentation between organizations.

The United States has adopted its own set of GAAP procedures (called U.S. GAAP), which differ in some areas compared to the international GAAP standards. This textbook will continue to apply U.S. GAAP concepts throughout all chapters, as this will be the financial accounting processes and practices expected of healthcare leaders for the perceived future. While a transition from the U.S. GAAP to the international GAAP practices has been suggested for quite some time, there are material changes related to such a proposed transition, especially for the healthcare industry. Therefore, a transition from U.S. GAAP to the international GAAP standard has not occurred.

Each GAAP concept is as critically important as the next, and it is recommended that use of these concepts continue to occur and be applied throughout all future chapters and related exercises. At times, some GAAP concepts compete against each other in various scenarios, and management will have to make a decision as to which one to utilize. It will be the healthcare leader's responsibility to ensure the best possible application of GAAP principles to generate valid and reliable financial statements.

Helpful tip: Throughout this textbook and related financial accounting questions, problems, and calculations, the *calendar year* will be used as the healthcare organization's *financial period* (January 1 through December 31). This practice is for the ease of demonstration of accounting practices and to help distinguish the differences among real and nominal account categories (to be addressed in Chapter 4).

TRY ON YOUR OWN

Research your current academic institution's financial period. When does it begin/end? To what operational characteristics in higher education can you attribute this organization financial period? Is there any argument to possibly transition the current financial period to the calendar year (January 1 through December 31)? Why or why not?

Chapter Questions

1. Conduct an Internet search for "AICPA illustrative financial statements." Provided by the American Institute for Certified Professional Accountants for small and medium-sized business organizations (both healthcare and non-healthcare applications), locate the financial statement notes for the sample company used in the example. What similarities and differences are you able to notice between this chapter's GAAP concepts and the sample statement notes?

2. Distinguish between the two GAAP concepts of conservatism and the matching principle. Using a hypothetical pharmaceutical drug company's development of a medication, review both principles as to the potential U.S. Food and Drug Administration (FDA) approval or disapproval of the developed medication and related laboratory expenses and future (if approved) sales revenue, as applied to both the matching principle and conservative accounting concepts. Are you able to demonstrate both principles with the sunk cost of a laboratory expense required for medication research and development?

3. Using the content of Note A to the financial statements, discuss how each section of this note furthers the transparency GAAP concept by adding additional information not easily seen on the actual financial statements.

4. Review any prior jobs you have worked in the past and assess that organization's potential (perceived) goodwill. Does your experience as an employee of that organization support a positive goodwill assessment for the organization, or did it detract from this intangible organizational asset value? Switching stakeholders, now assess that same organization's goodwill from the customer (not employee) perspective. Any differences here? Explain your perspective.

5. Using the real estate market as an example, discuss the difference between historical cost and market value of any home for sale in the United States. If this were your home for sale, what value would be shown on your personal balance sheet for the home (under the assets section)? What information would you like to add to the notes section of this statement if there is a significant (material) difference between the home's purchase price and current-day assessed market value? Where would this information be added to the balance sheet?

3

Applying the Financial Accounting Cycle to Healthcare Operations

Introduction

In this chapter we will introduce the financial accounting cycle, which follows GAAP concepts and procedures and assists the healthcare organization in generating *valid and reliable financial statements*. This cycle and related bookkeeping tasks are a significant contribution to the recording of accounting data within the healthcare organization. The final step of the cycle is the generation of the organization's financial statements for a current financial period, and then it starts all over again (cyclic process). Several helpful tips are included in this chapter to assist the learner in applying the financial accounting cycle to typical, everyday healthcare operations.

Learning Objectives

By the end of this chapter, the student should be able to:

- Illustrate and discuss the financial accounting cycle process.
- Interpret the basic and expanded accounting equations.
- Describe the difference between real and nominal account categories.
- List and discuss the debit and credit methodology, as applied to the expanded accounting equation.
- Discuss the requirements for a financial transaction to occur in typical healthcare operational activities.
- Explain the dual-entry process that occurs when recording and posting a financial transaction.
- Define a journal and a ledger and discuss their purposes.

Key Terms

1. Basic and expanded accounting equations
2. Real account category
3. Nominal account category
4. Financial accounting cycle
5. Dual-entry requirement
6. Debit and credit
7. Journal and ledger
8. Chart of accounts

The Basic Accounting Equation

The basic accounting equation is the initial formula utilized to begin the generation of financial statements. This equation involves three main accounts: assets, liabilities, and net assets. These three main accounts and their underlying subaccounts are all classified as "real" accounts and demonstrate the format of the balance sheet financial statement (to be fully introduced in Chapter 8). The basic accounting equation is shown in Figure 3.1.

$$\text{assets} - \text{liabilities} = \text{net assets}$$

FIGURE 3.1 Basic accounting equation.

Where,

- *Assets* are economic resources of the healthcare organization.
- *Liabilities* are economic obligations of the healthcare organization.
- *Net assets* are the net worth of the organization, calculated by subtracting economic obligations from economic resources.

In other words: what you have (assets) minus what you owe (obligations) equals what you are worth (net assets). There are many subaccounts located under each of these real accounts. Therefore, all subaccounts that fall under the asset account will sum to a total value (called total assets). The same applies to all the subaccounts located under the liability (total liabilities) and net asset real accounts. Finally, the left-hand side of the basic accounting equation (the total value of total assets) will always equal the right-hand side of the equation (the value of total liabilities plus that of total net assets). Figure 3.2 demonstrates

> Example of balanced equation: 500 assets – 200 liabilities = 300 net assets
> Therefore: 300 = 300

FIGURE 3.2 Demonstration of a balanced accounting equation.

Helpful tip: Net assets (NA) is synonymous with the term "equity." Additionally, because net assets represent the organization's net worth after accounting for what it has (assets) minus what it owes (liabilities), the term "net worth" is also used interchangeably throughout this textbook with "net assets." It is recommended that learners use the abbreviation "NA" when using the accounting equation and not "E" for "equity." This is because another main account (Expenses) begins with the letter "E," will be introduced later in the textbook, and will utilize the letter "E" for its abbreviation.

how the basic accounting equation is balanced when total assets minus total liabilities equals net assets.

Therefore, the basic accounting equation may also be abbreviated as follows:

$$A - L = NA$$

To make a lot of future accounting problems, interpretations, and even financial statements easier to interpret and synthesize, the minus sign in the basic accounting equation should be addressed so that all variables in the equation are of positive value. This action will prevent any assumptions with the equation—such as what to do if adding a positive (or negative) value to the –L main account, among other confusing tasks. Therefore, the –L variable in the equation will be moved to the right-hand side of the equation's equal sign. In effect, this changes the –L variable to an understood +L variable, as shown in Figure 3.3. This action now allows for an accounting equation with all positive account variables.

 $= NA$ original, basic accounting equation (move the -L to the other side of the equal sign)

$$A = L + NA$$ updated basic accounting equation with all positive variables

FIGURE 3.3 Demonstration of changing the –L variable to +L variable.

This updated accounting equation $(A = L + NA)$, shown with all positive values and no negative signs, is the general format of the healthcare organization's balance sheet financial statement. This important financial statement will be fully introduced and explained in Chapter 8. The accounting equation with all positive variables will still balance in the end, with total assets = total liabilities + NA.

Real Account (A, L, and NA) Classification

Helpful tip: Real account (assets, liabilities, and net assets from the basic accounting equation) values carry over to the next accounting period. Whatever value they end with at the conclusion of an accounting period is the value they begin with for the subsequent accounting period.

Previously addressed in Chapter 2, the healthcare organization's financial period is the time period of organizational activities and related operational transactions used to generate the organization's financial statements. Once the financial statements are generated, the organization's performance may be assessed. If the calendar year is used as the organization's financial period, the period will always begin on January 1 of every year and end on December 31 of every year. This is important to note, as the real account values carry over from the end of one financial period into the next. Asset, liability, and net asset accounts are also the main accounts that make up the balance sheet financial statement. This carryover characteristic of the A, L, and NA accounts also applies to all the subaccounts falling underneath each of these three main accounts.

Therefore, if you end the current financial period (the evening of December 31 of the current calendar year) with economic resources (assets) and economic obligations (liabilities), you will begin the next financial period (the morning of January 1) with that same value of assets and liabilities from the evening prior. Likewise, the ending net assets (organizational equity, or net worth) will also carry over to the beginning of the next financial period (January 1).

Chapter 5 will provide additional information regarding where the subaccount values (dollar amounts) falling under the main asset, liability, and net asset accounts originate. These dollar amounts are based on a variety of accounting principles (GAAP) and routine healthcare organization operations.

The Expanded Accounting Equation

To expand the basic accounting equation further, the nominal account classification needs to be introduced. This account category (and related total revenue and total expense account dollar values) is treated differently on the evening of December 31 for every accounting period, as compared to the real accounts (previously addressed).

Nominal Account (Rev and Exp) Classification

The other two main account categories used to create the healthcare organization's financial statements are revenues and expenses. These main accounts (often abbreviated as "Rev" and "Exp") are classified as nominal accounts and make up the healthcare organization's statement of operations financial statement. This statement is fully addressed in Chapter 9. Revenues represent the value (dollar amount) earned (or received as payment) for healthcare services provided to patients. Revenues also represent other dollar amounts earned/received by the healthcare organization for goods/services provided by the organization outside of patient care efforts. Expenses are values (dollar amounts) of payments made (or incurred) by the healthcare organization in order to provide healthcare services to patients and related operational initiatives.

The value of a healthcare organization's total revenue and/or expense accounts are highly dependent on the organization's chosen method of accounting—which will be addressed further in Chapter 4. Like A, L, and NA accounts, revenue and expense accounts both possess many underlying subaccounts. These subaccounts are totaled for both Rev and Exp in the same manner as total assets and total liabilities are calculated. The Rev and Exp main account values are then listed on the organization's statement of operations to demonstrate any profit or loss experienced by the organization over a specific time period (Figure 3.4).

When total revenues are greater than total expenses for any given time period, an organizational *profit* is experienced by the healthcare organization:

1/31/20X5	Revenues earned this month:	$40,000
	Expenses incurred this month:	23,000
	Organizational *profit*:	17,000

When total expenses are greater than total revenues for any given time period, an organizational *loss* is experienced by the healthcare organization:

1/31/20X5	Revenues earned this month:	$23,000
	Expenses incurred this month:	40,000
	Organizational *loss*:	(17,000)

FIGURE 3.4   Example of an organizational profit/loss (revenue – expenses) for January 20X5.

If the healthcare organization ends a financial period with more revenues than expenses, it will experience a profit. Likewise, if the organization ends the financial period with more expenses than revenues, it will experience a loss for the time period. What happens to this profit or loss is a nominal account

Helpful tip: Often, healthcare leaders will refer to an organizational profit as "being in the black." An organizational loss for a financial period is commonly referred to as "being in the red."

characteristic that makes revenue and expense accounts inherently different from the corresponding real accounts.

Nominal accounts (revenues and expenses) will demonstrate increasing dollar values as an accounting period progresses—and will then reset to $0 at the beginning of every new financial period (annually). In other words, if using the calendar year (01/01/20X5 to 12/31/20X5) as an organization's financial accounting period, revenues and expenses will each begin at $0 on January 1, 20X5, and increase in value as patient care is delivered. This is because revenue will be earned/received and expenses will be incurred/paid during regular healthcare operations and the delivery of patient care. Both nominal accounts will reach their maximum values on 12/31/20X5 at the end of that day's operations. Based on whether the organization experienced a profit or a loss for that year, the ending balances of total revenues and total expenses resemble the profit/loss calculations shown in Figure 3.4.

The healthcare organization's next financial period will begin the next morning, on 1/01/20X6, and because this is a new financial period, the revenue and expense accounts will both reset to $0. From that point forward, both revenue and expense account values will begin to increase in value again as patient care is delivered. These nominal (revenue and expense) accounts will again reach their maximum values by 12/31/20X6 and again reset to $0 that following day (the morning of 1/01/20X7). This continuous cycle occurs upon the completion of each annual financial period for the healthcare organization, therefore zeroing out the nominal accounts overnight and beginning the next financial period at $0 each.

Expanding the Basic Accounting Equation

Helpful tip: All real and nominal accounts are account categories, with many subaccounts falling underneath each. Each subaccount will possess the same real/nominal main account category characteristics as the main account they fall under.

To demonstrate the expanded accounting equation, simply add the real and nominal account formulas together. This essentially takes the balance sheet financial statement format (A = L + NA) and adds to it the statement of operations financial statement formula (Rev – Exp), as demonstrated in Figure 3.5.

A = L + NA	+	Rev – Exp
Real Accounts		Nominal Accounts
Balance Sheet format		Statement of Operations format
Values carry-over to next financial period		Values reset to $0 at beginning of the next financial period

FIGURE 3.5   Generating the expanded accounting equation by adding real and nominal accounts together.

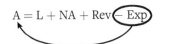

$$A = L + NA + Rev - Exp \qquad \text{Initial, expanded accounting equation}$$

$$A + Exp = L + NA + Rev \qquad \text{Expanded accounting equation with all same-sign variables}$$

Example of a balanced, expanded accounting equation:

$$500 \text{ assets} + 100 \text{ expenses} = 100 \text{ liabilities} + 300 \text{ net assets} + 200 \text{ revenue}$$

$$\text{Therefore: } 600 = 600$$

FIGURE 3.6 Generation of the expanded accounting equation.

Just as discussed with the basic accounting equation, the left side of the expanded accounting equation should always equal the right side of the equation. In other words, assets plus expenses should always equal liabilities, plus net assets, plus revenue. If the expanded accounting equation is ever not in balance, there is a data-entry error, and this is a clue to the healthcare administrator that a correction is needed in the bookkeeping processes and/ or a single accounting entry into the system. The sooner the healthcare leader identifies that the organization's accounting equation is not in balance, the easier it is to review prior accounting entries and identify the error causing the imbalance of the expanded accounting equation. Most often, automated accounting systems will disallow any journal entry into the organization's financial accounting system that do not balance. While this does ensure that a balanced journal entry is always in balance when entered into the system, it does not mean that the correct subaccount(s) was chosen when entering the transaction. As a result, further accounting audits and other quality control processes are still required.

General Bookkeeping: The Dual-Entry System

Utilizing the expanded accounting equation, the process of recording financial transactions for the healthcare organization will involve GAAP processes that help support consistency and accuracy of data accumulation, data entry, and financial statement formulation. To begin, we introduce the dual-entry debit/ credit methodology. This journal entry method will be utilized throughout the rest of this textbook and is directly associated with the expanded accounting equation from Figure 3.6.

Helpful tip: In financial accounting, everything must remain in balance. This means that the left side of the expanded accounting equation should always equal the right side of the equation. If at any time the equation does not balance, stop and look for the error. It is best to identify and correct an accounting entry error sooner rather than later.

Left-hand side of equation	Right-hand side of equation
Assets + Expenses = Liabilities + Net Assets + Revenue	
Debit: *increase*	Debit: *decrease*
Credit: *decrease*	Credit: *increase*

FIGURE 3.7   Debit/credit effects on the expanded accounting equation's main accounts.

As demonstrated in Figure 3.7, the equal sign in the expanded accounting equation becomes quite important in deciphering debit and credit effects on the accounts. In financial accounting (and financial management), the terms "minus" or "subtract" and "add" or "plus" are commonly replaced with the terms "debit" and "credit." That said, "debit" and "credit" can also mean to "add" or "subtract," depending on their use and the affected account.

Therefore, regarding left-hand side account categories (left of the equation's equal sign):

- If a transaction occurs in the healthcare organization and it calls for the value for either an asset or expense subaccount to be increased, a debit will occur.
- If an asset or expense subaccount account is to be lowered, a credit will occur.

The exact opposite occurs when crossing over the equal sign of the expanded accounting equation:

- To increase a liability, net asset, or revenue account value, a credit will occur.
- To decrease a liability, net asset, or revenue account value, a debit will occur.

Helpful tip: Debit does not always mean to decrease an account value, and credit does not always mean to increase an account value. It all depends on what main account is being manipulated due to the transaction and on what side of the equal sign the accounts being used in the journal entry are located.

The Financial Accounting Cycle

The financial accounting cycle will be utilized throughout this textbook and follows GAAP processes and procedures for all healthcare transactions (regardless of the type of healthcare organization). It is important to note that the cycle is also applicable to transactions related to other industries beyond healthcare organizations (non-healthcare, general business organizations).

This process begins with the identification of a healthcare accounting transaction and ends with the generation of valid and reliable healthcare organization financial statements for any given financial period (Figure 3.8).

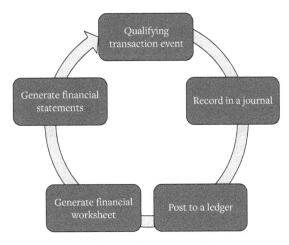

FIGURE 3.8   The financial accounting cycle.

Step 1: Identifying the Need for an Accounting Transaction

The first step of the financial accounting cycle is to identify the need for when an accounting transaction is to be conducted. Chapter 4 will specifically address cash and accrual accounting methods as applied to account transactions for various types of healthcare operational activities. However, there are some very basic requirements that must be met to queue the financial accounting cycle to begin and initiate the recording of an individual transaction. Therefore, the initiation of the financial accounting cycle occurs only if (and when) a transfer of either money, goods, and/or services takes place and objective evidence exists to support the transaction (see Table 3.1).

Objective evidence is used in typical healthcare operations to initiate the financial accounting cycle and often includes tangible (physical) paper documents such as the following:

- *invoices* (requesting payment for goods/services provided to the healthcare organization by outside entities)
- *cash receipts* (for goods/services received and paid for by the healthcare organization)
- any other paper document that captures a qualifying event as described in Table 3.1

TABLE 3.1 Requirements for a financial transaction based on healthcare organization activities

*Transaction involves	Description	Example
Transfer of money	Distributed out of the organization	Paying a bill for supplies already received
	Received by the organization	Receiving a patient payment for services already provided
Transfer of goods	Provided to the organization	Receiving a supply delivery
	Provided by the organization	Provider using a bandage in the treatment of a patient
Transfer of services	Provided by the organization	Provision of patient care
	Provided to the organization	Consultative services provided

For any of these transactions, objective evidence of the event is to be maintained on record by the healthcare administrator (accounting evidence). Such evidence may be a paper receipt, supplier invoice, or even a personal note to document the transaction.

The Chart of Accounts

Prior to moving forward in our financial accounting cycle process, an introduction to the legend, or indexing of all main account categories and their underlying subaccounts, is necessary. Here, GAAP provides main-account categories (assets, liabilities, net assets, revenues, and expenses) with their subaccounts falling directly underneath each category, with the subaccounts maintaining similar debit/credit and nominal/real account characteristics within each category. In other words, all subaccounts falling under the main account "Assets" are all asset accounts; all subaccounts falling under the main account "Liabilities" are liability accounts, and so on (see Figure 3.9).

Additional GAAP protocols include the use of account numbers to be listed next to each main and subaccount, as shown on the chart of accounts in Figure 3.9. Beyond the scope of this textbook but important to note is that additional digits (beyond the three-digit account numbers shown) can be utilized to assist with additional subaccount details and other classification measures. This is done by expanding the account numbers with additional digits beyond what is shown in Figure 3.9 and using a systematic coding methodology to provide additional information (for example, the location of the asset) regarding the account.

100	Assets	400	Revenue
101	Cash	401	Routine Services Revenue
102	Temporary Investments	402	Ancillary Services Revenue
103	Accrued Interest Receivable	403	Premium Revenue
104	Accounts Receivable (A/R)	404	Other Operating Revenue
105	Allowance for Uncollectible Accounts (AUCAs)	405	Rental Revenue
106	Inventory (Supply)	406	Tuition Revenue
107	Prepaid Insurance Expense	407	Interest Revenue
108	Prepaid Rent Expense	408	Non-Operating Revenue
109	Prepaid Interest Expense	500	Revenue Deductions
150	Land	501	Contractual Adjustments
160	Buildings(s)	502	Charity Care Adjustments
161	Accumulated Depreciation – Building(s)	600	Expenses
170	Equipment	601	Salary and Wages (S/W) Expense
171	Accumulated Depreciation – Equipment	602	Inventory (Supply) Expense
200	Liabilities	603	Utilities Expense
201	Accounts Payable (A/P)	604	Insurance Expense
202	Notes Payable (N/P)	605	Repairs Expense
203	Accrued Interest Payable	606	Rent Expense
204	Accrued Salaries and Wages (S/W) Payable	607	Depreciation Expense
205	Deferred Rental Revenue (Income)	608	Interest Expense
206	Deferred Tuition Revenue (Income)	609	Bad Debt Expense
220	Bonds Payable	610	Other (Miscellaneous) Expenses
300	Net Assets (Equity)		
301	Hospital Net Assets (NA)		
302	Revenue and Expense Summary		

Note: The description of the Revenue Deduction account category and associated sub-accounts will be addressed in Chapter 9.

FIGURE 3.9   The chart of accounts.

For the purposes of this textbook, a basic GAAP protocol concerns the assignment of the first-digit placeholder value, dependent on the main account category. This first-digit assignment follows the GAAP procedure as described in Table 3.2.

TABLE 3.2   GAAP assignment of the first-digit account number placeholder

If the account number's *first digit* begins with:	The account is categorized under the main account:
1	Asset
2	Liability
3	Net asset
4	Revenue
5	Revenue deduction
6	Expense

The chart of accounts serves as an important legend of all accounts utilized in this textbook. Appendix B is provided as a single-page chart of accounts template and should be earmarked or even printed and referenced for all future accounting transactions and associated questions/problems. Frequent use of the chart of accounts will assist in remembering the real and nominal account classifications, related debit/credit methods, and even help with the format of the balance sheet and statement of operations financial statements.

Step 2: Recording a Journal Entry

In review, when one (or more) of the events in Table 3.1 occur, a financial transaction is required. Moving to the next step in the financial accounting cycle, the qualifying transaction will be recorded in an accounting document called a journal, which is a chronological listing of all accounting transactions and their related subaccount names and dollar amounts. The journal consists of dates, the names of the specific subaccounts affected by the transaction, a description of the healthcare operation/activity, and the transaction dollar amounts.

Transactions are to be recorded in a journal by using correct subaccount names for all journal entries. This process will be utilized throughout the textbook and is proper accounting practice. At no time should a journal entry be recorded using a main account (category) name, as this lack of specificity is not appropriate and does not lead to valid and reliable financial statements. Each journal entry will follow a similar GAAP format, demonstrated by Figure 3.10.

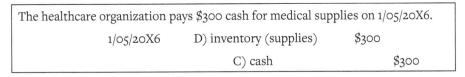

The healthcare organization pays $300 cash for medical supplies on 1/05/20X6.

1/05/20X6	D) inventory (supplies)	$300	
	C) cash		$300

FIGURE 3.10 Demonstration of a simple journal entry (only one debit and credit present).

As shown in Figure 3.10, the date of the transaction (payment in cash) is recorded in a journal at the time the transaction occurs (at the time of money/goods/service transfer). The organization's cash is being lowered (credited) because the transaction has a negative cash flow (payment for goods). In return, the organization is receiving medical supplies, which are increasing in value (a debit) because new supplies have been added to the organization's inventory (valued at historical cost). Review Figure 3.7 again to comprehend how lowering the value of cash is a credit and the procurement of medical supplies increases the value of the organization's inventory as a debit.

Additionally, the journal entry process involves what is termed dual entry, meaning that for every entry recorded in a journal, one or more accounts must be debited, and one or more accounts must be credited. Therefore, there must be at least one (or more) accounts debited and at least one (or more) accounts credited for a journal entry to be correct. This dual-entry requirement is necessary, per GAAP principles. When there is only one account debited and one account credited for any single journal entry, this is called a simple journal entry. If at any time one or more debits and/or one or more credits exist in any single journal entry, this is termed a compound journal entry (see Figure 3.11).

Helpful tip: All journal entries will follow the sample format shown in Figure 3.10. The account (or accounts) being debited will always be listed first/on top, while the corresponding credit (or credits) will always be listed under the debit(s) and intended to the right. The credits will also have their corresponding credit values indented to the right.

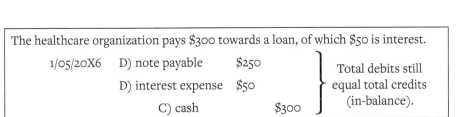

The healthcare organization pays $300 towards a loan, of which $50 is interest.

1/05/20X6	D) note payable	$250		
	D) interest expense	$50		Total debits still equal total credits (in-balance).
	C) cash		$300	

FIGURE 3.11 Example of a compound journal entry (more than one debit or credit present).

Finally, the total value of the account(s) debited must also exactly equal the total value of the account(s) credited for every journal entry. When total debits equal total credits for a journal entry, the entry is "balanced." If total debits do not equal total credits for any single journal entry, there is a data entry error present, and the journal entry should be fixed immediately.

Step 3: Posting to a Ledger

Per the accounting cycle in Figure 3.8, immediately after recording a transaction in the healthcare organization's journal, it is then posted to a ledger. The ledger is another accounting record (separate from the journal) that keeps all account debit and credit values in proper, side-by-side visible order, by account. The ledger consists of multiple T-accounts, which makes it easily identifiable (since it has "T" shapes all over it). Every subaccount used by the healthcare organization will have its own T-account with corresponding debits/credits that have been previously recorded in the journal.

Using the transaction example from Figure 3.10, the following ledger entries will be posted from the journal entry (see Figure 3.12).

inventory		cash	
300			300
Debit side	Credit side	Debit side	Credit side

FIGURE 3.12   Demonstration of a simple GAAP ledger entry when purchasing inventory with cash.

Helpful tip: The ledger consists of a lot of T-accounts (one for every subaccount that is listed on the healthcare organization's chart of accounts). While journal entries always have the debits listed on the top and credits listed below and indented to the right, the ledger will always have debit values posted on the left-hand side of the T-account and credits posted on the right-hand side of the T-account. This ledger format is used for any/all accounts listed in the organization's chart of accounts (regardless of what subaccount is being used).

Here, only the inventory and cash subaccounts are shown as an excerpt of the organization's entire ledger (which houses all of the chart of account's subaccount T-accounts). Since the debit and credit were already recorded as a journal entry in Figure 3.10, they are then posted to the organization's ledger (as shown in Figure 3.12) by posting any debit values on the left-hand side of an account's T-account and any credit values on the right-hand side of an account's T-account.

At this point in the accounting process, further details are to be introduced regarding the subaccounts that fall under each real account (assets, liabilities, and net assets). A review of each subaccount for assets, liabilities, and net assets is provided in Appendix C. Additional healthcare organizational transactions are also shown to demonstrate corresponding debit/credit transactions. It is recommended that each example transaction be memorized so future debits and credits are easily able to be identified when assessing typical operational activities for the healthcare organization. Appendix D provides flash cards for subaccounts often affected by common healthcare operations. It is recommended that these flash cards be used to memorize the debit/credit effects for these (and other related) template transactions.

In Summary: Completion of the Financial Accounting Cycle

To close the loop of the financial accounting cycle (Figure 3.8), two additional steps are involved: the generation of a financial worksheet (covered in Chapter 10) and generation of the statement of operations, statement of net assets, and balance sheet financial statements (covered in Chapters 8 and 9). The organization's annual financial period is represented by the financial accounting cycle in Figure 3.8, but financial statements can also be completed at interim time periods. These interim statements are generated during the organization's current financial period and are often monthly interim financial statements. Or these interim financial statements can be generated at any time when the healthcare administrator chooses to evaluate the organization's financial performance.

The financial accounting cycle begins on January 1 of every year and ends on December 31. Qualifying transactions are recorded in a journal and posted to a ledger, and a financial worksheet is generated to ensure dual-entry processes were properly followed. Finally, the final financial statements are to be generated. However, the cycle does not permanently end with the last step in Figure 3.8—the process is not only cyclic within a single financial period for interim (monthly) financial statements but also reoccurring, year after year. Therefore, once the final step is completed, the process starts all over again for the healthcare organization, as shown in Figure 3.13.

Once the annual financial statements are properly generated for the prior financial period (which often occurs in early January of the following year), the annual statements can then be analyzed and compared with the organization's prior financial statements. This action feeds into the concept of monitoring and evaluating healthcare organization financial performance, discussed in Chapter 12. As a reminder, when the cycle restarts to begin the next financial period (the morning of January 1), the nominal account values (all revenue and expense accounts) reset to $0, and the process starts all over again as patient care is delivered the morning of January 1, forward.

Helpful tip: The annual financial period in this textbook follows the calendar year (January 1 to December 31). However, interim financial periods, and therefore interim financial statements, can be generated at any point during the annual year when the healthcare leader wants to assess the formative (ongoing) financial performance of the healthcare organization.

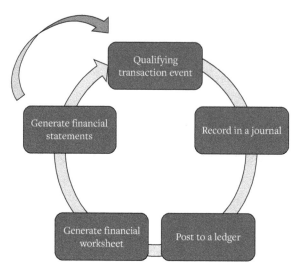

FIGURE 3.13 Reoccurring financial accounting cycle from one financial period to the next.

Chapter Questions

1. Derive the expanded accounting equation from the basic accounting equation. Specifically, demonstrate how the negative variables are eliminated to end with the final expanded accounting equation. Next, review how real (balance sheet) and nominal (statement of operations) main accounts are treated at the end of any annual financial accounting period.

2. For the following account increases/decreases, label with the appropriate debit/credit methodology. Do not forget to use the chart of accounts to help!

Subaccount value change:	Choose: debit or credit
Cash account increased	
Note payable account decreased	
A/R account decreased	
Unrestricted net asset account decreased	
A/P account increased	
A/P account decreased	
Accumulated depreciation account increased	

3. When reviewing the chart of accounts, how does one know what main (real or nominal) account each subaccount falls under? If the main account categories were not present on the chart of accounts, what other method could be used to identify asset, liability, net asset, revenue, and expense account categories (offered by GAAP procedures)?

4. What is the purpose of a journal? What is the purpose of a ledger?

    Next, circle the correct response (in ALL CAPS) below:
    - RECORD or POST to a journal
    - RECORD or POST to a ledger

5. Illustrate the financial accounting cycle process. Next, indicate on the process timeline where (and when) the organization's nominal accounts reset to $0 and also when the next financial accounting period begins.

6. Think of three hypothetical examples of healthcare operations that would constitute the initiation of a transaction in the financial accounting cycle for each of the three transactions requirements listed in Table 3.1.

4

Applying Cash and Accrual Accounting Methods to Healthcare Operations

Introduction

In this chapter we introduce the cash and accrual accounting methods used by various types of healthcare organizations. These methods will continue to be referenced throughout the rest of the textbook. A thorough understanding surrounding the recognition of revenues and expenses as related to the healthcare organization's operational activities is vital in becoming a competent healthcare leader. While only one accounting method will be adopted and utilized by any single healthcare organization, knowledge of both accounting methods assists with statement development and follow-on financial statement analyses.

Learning Objectives

By the end of this chapter, the student should be able to:

- Define both cash and accrual accounting methods and apply these methods to revenue and expense transactions for the healthcare organization.
- Record and post example journal entries for regular healthcare operation transactions using both cash and accrual accounting methods.
- Identify the importance of real and nominal account categories and their effect on journal entries related to healthcare operations.

Key Terms

1. Cash accounting (received, paid)
2. Accrual accounting (earned, incurred)

3. Accrued interest receivable
4. Accounts receivable (A/R)
5. Allowance for uncollectable accounts (AUCA)
6. Prepaid expenses
7. Accounts payable (A/P)
8. Accrued interest payable
9. Accrued salary and wages (S/W) payable
10. Deferred rent revenue
11. Deferred tuition revenue

Accounting Methods: Cash vs. Accrual

One of the most important concepts in any accounting course is delineating the difference between an organization's use of cash versus accrual accounting methods. Specific to the healthcare industry, it is very important to note the requirement for certain types of organizations to use one method of accounting over the other. Due to the nature of operations and extensive revenue deductions involved, it is standard for hospitals and other large, network healthcare organizations to utilize the accrual accounting method. Otherwise, most other organizations default to the cash accounting method. Each accounting method (cash vs. accrual) treats the recognition (recording) of revenue and expense transactions differently. An organization utilizes only one accounting method based on its organization type and accounting preference.

Additionally, a significant amount of healthcare organization transactions can be easily interpreted in error if a true understanding of both accounting methods is not achieved. Because the GAAP concept of consistency applies to the chosen accounting method an organization decides on (discussed in Chapter 2), switching from one method to another is not a routine practice and should not occur unless necessary. That said, there are times when a healthcare organization may want to view its financial statements in the alternative accounting method for temporary, strategic planning purposes. Automated (computerized) accounting software systems allow for this temporary switch in accounting methods (and return to their default method) for a better understanding of the healthcare organization's financial history.

The difference between cash and accrual accounting methods concerns only the nominal accounts (revenue and expense accounts) and timing—or when specific revenues and/or expenses are recognized (recorded as journal entries) on the organization's books. Organizations operating under the cash method of accounting only record revenues and expenses when there is a positive (revenue) or negative (expense) cash flow into or out of the organization. Accrual accounting is much more complicated.

Figure 4.1 demonstrates the differences in these two accounting methods in a highly abbreviated manner to assist with interpretation and follow-on application. Be sure to note the header of the figure that references "when" (timing), which distinguishes the primary difference between the two accounting methods.

RECORD (RECOGNIZE) REVENUES AND EXPENSES WHEN …

Accounting Method	Revenues	Expenses
Cash	received	paid
Accrual	earned	incurred

FIGURE 4.1   Cash vs. accrual accounting methods.

Cash Accounting Explanation

As shown in Figure 4.1, an organization utilizing the cash method of accounting records (and therefore recognizes) a revenue when cash is received, while an expense is only recorded (recognized) by the organization when a bill is paid. Examples of revenues received include cash payments, credit card payments, or other types of positive cash flow into the organization. Examples of expenses paid refer to the healthcare administrator writing checks or similar online electronic payments to external vendors and other agencies (cash outflows).

As a result, healthcare organizations that are utilizing the cash method of accounting are easily able to track their cash flows based on revenues (positive cash flows) received and expenses (negative cash flows) paid. More on this concept of positive and negative cash flows will be addressed in Chapter 11 ("The Statement of Cash Flows").

Accrual Accounting Explanation

Alternatively, healthcare organizations that operate using the accrual method of accounting recognize revenue immediately when it is earned by the organization, regardless of when (or if?) it is received from the patient or third-party payers in the future. Similarly, expenses are recorded immediately when incurred by the healthcare organization, regardless of when the bill for any good or service is actually paid. Therefore, revenues and expenses under this accounting method are not true representations of positive or negative cash flows but do support the GAAP matching principle (previously discussed in Chapter 2). By utilizing the accrual method of accounting, this helps ensure that revenues earned are appropriately matched in the same accounting period (or as close as possible) with the related expenses incurred for that same service provided.

Basic Application of Cash and Accrual Accounting Transactions

Consider the following example regarding healthcare revenue:

On 8/01/20X5, Dr. Smith conducted a physical for a high school football player to ensure that the student was healthy enough to play that season. The patient had third-party, commercial medical insurance offered through one of the parent's employers. As a result, the medical service (the football physical) was provided to the patient on 8/01/20X5 and has a billed charge of $200 set by the healthcare organization. However, the actual insurance payment of $105 for the service will not be received by the healthcare organization until 9/12/20X5.

- Using the *cash* accounting method, the following revenue journal entry will be recorded by the healthcare organization:

9/12/20X5	D) cash	$105	
	C) operating revenue		$105

Cash accounting revenue explanation: The journal entry is recorded (and therefore revenue recognized) only when the healthcare organization receives the payment. As a result, the revenue will be recorded in September (when eventually received from the patient's third-party commercial insurance carrier), even though the service was provided in August.

- Using the *accrual* accounting method, the following revenue journal entries will be record by the healthcare organization:

8/01/20X5	D) A/R	$200	
	C) operating revenue		$200
9/12/20X5	D) cash	$105	
	D) contractual adjustment	$95	
	C) A/R		$200

Accrual accounting revenue explanation: Under the accrual accounting method, the use of A/R by the organization still exists, yet this account is included on the books and therefore is shown on the organization's financial statements. As a result, the patient's date of service was August 1, and because the healthcare organization has provided a good or service and is waiting to receive payment for a service already provided, A/R is increased (while awaiting reimbursement). Also, the revenue is recorded when earned under this accounting method, which occurs immediately when the doctor provides the service to the patient (also on August 1).

Once the patient's third-party insurance carrier processes the claim and remits payment for the service, the cash is received on September 12, and the third-party discount (contractual adjustment) is applied to the account, per the healthcare organization's contract with the insurance provider (previously discussed in Chapter 1). Because the bill has now been paid and adjusted per the agreed-upon contractual, prospective FFS rate between the provider and insurance carrier, the A/R account is lowered. At this point the healthcare organization is no longer awaiting payment for the August 1 service.

Consider the following example regarding healthcare expenses:

For the same service scenario (Dr. Smith providing a football physical exam), let us assume the following additional details are available.

1. The healthcare organization ordered a bulk resupply of disposable items used for physical exams, which was received on 9/10/20X5 with an invoice totaling $250. Payment is due to the medical vendor within 30 days from the date of the invoice (delivery).
2. The healthcare organization paid the medical vendor's total $250 invoice with a check on 9/15/20X5.
3. A cost accounting analysis demonstrates that $10 worth of these disposable supplies are used by the healthcare organization each time a football physical is conducted.

- Using the *cash* accounting method, the following expense journal entry will be recorded by the healthcare organization:

9/15/20X5	D) inventory/supply expense	$250	
	C) cash		$250

Helpful tip: While the practice is owed payment for the service provided and not yet paid at the time of service, *no accounts receivable (A/R) exists on the books for the healthcare organization utilizing the cash accounting method.* This is because the A/R accrues over time as goods/services are delivered and the organization is awaiting reimbursement. However, it is proper practice for any business entity to track what customers (or patients) owe money to the organization, and how much. Therefore, the A/R account and associated dollar value is not represented on the organization's financial statements when operating under the cash accounting method. Instead, it is tracked off the books and only applied to revenue when payment is actually received.

Note: A credit to the cash account usually occurs after the transaction has been vouchered through the A/P organizational liability account. For clarity purposes, the cash account is directly credited in this chapter to better demonstrate cash accounting changes with organizational cash flow. The A/P voucher process is addressed in further detail in Chapter 5.

Cash accounting expense explanation: The bulk supply order to restock items used for football physicals was paid to a medical vendor on September 15. While this payment is for a variety of supply items that will support many separate patients in the future, the healthcare organization records the full payment of these supplies on the date of the payment (expenses recorded when paid by the healthcare organization). As a result, individual service expenses (supplies used for each football physical conducted) are not able to be matched to the revenue received for the procedure and the date of service. In other words, the GAAP matching principle is not able to be implemented under cash accounting.

- Using the *accrual* accounting method, the following expense journal entries will be recorded by the healthcare organization:

8/01/20X5	D) inventory/supply expense	$10	
	C) inventory/supply		$10
9/10/20X5	D) inventory/supply	$250	
	C) A/P		$250
9/15/20X5	D) A/P	$250	
	C) cash		$250

Accrual accounting expense explanation: Under the accrual accounting method, the use of A/P by the organization still exists, he use of A/P by the organization exists and this account is included on the books and demonstrated on the organization's financial statements. As a result, the patient received the service on August 1, and therefore the healthcare organization has associated supply expenses for that service, on that day. The cost of this single service supply ($10) was incurred on the date of service and therefore recorded as a supply expense (expenses are recorded when incurred by the organization, regardless of when paid by the organization). This individual supply expense is able to be matched to the service delivery date under the accrual accounting method.

Helpful tip: While the practice owed payment for the bulk medical supply order received on September 10, no accounts payable (A/P) exists on the books for the healthcare organization utilizing the cash accounting method. This is because the A/P accrues over time as goods/services are received by the healthcare organization from outside medical vendors, who are then awaiting payment. It is proper practice for any business entity to track what vendors are owed money for goods/services already delivered or received but not yet paid for—yet this A/P amount is not represented on the organization's financial statements when utilizing the cash accounting method. Instead, it is tracked off the books and only applied to expenses once payment is eventually issued.

Furthermore, the bulk resupply order also has journal entries to be recorded. The supplies were delivered on September 10 and not paid for when received (an invoice with trade credit terms was issued). The organization received the goods and will pay for them later (increasing the A/P account). It decided to pay this bill 5 days later (on September 15), therefore lowering the A/P liability account by paying the vendor's invoice with cash.

The application of cash and accrual accounting methods, while seemingly easy based on the information initially provided in Figure 4.1, are quite difficult. Healthcare leaders need to be able to understand the difference in cash versus accrual accounting methods, especially when interpreting financial statements and when analyzing financial performance of various organizations utilizing separate methods of accounting.

Cash Accounting Transaction Characteristics

Based on the examples above and characteristics associated with cash accounting transactions, some commonalities exist with cash accounting transactions that need to be further highlighted.

- Because a cash transaction is recognized (and therefore recorded) anytime cash is received or paid by the healthcare organization, the cash account will always be recorded in either the debit (receiving cash) or credit (paying cash) position.
- Because a cash transaction is recognized (and therefore recorded) anytime cash is received or paid by the healthcare organization, there will most likely be a revenue account credited when cash is received. Likewise, there will often be an expense account debited when cash is paid. The debit/credit opposite of these revenue/expense entries will always be the cash account.
- Anytime there is no cash paid or received by the healthcare organization, there is no cash accounting transaction (i.e., journal entry). Therefore, "no transaction" is the standard response when this situation is presented in this textbook.

Accrual Accounts and Related Transactions

The accrual accounting method is more thorough and transparent about healthcare operational activities by recording transactions when revenue

Helpful tip: A/R (an asset account) and A/P (a liability account) are two important accounts used in everyday healthcare operations and related financial transactions. As a result, organizations utilizing both cash and accrual methods of accounting must track and monitor who owes them what amount of money for goods/services already provided (A/R), and who they owe specific amounts of money to for goods/services already received (A/P). However, remember that only organizations utilizing the accrual accounting method have A/R and A/P present on their financial statements. These accounts and their related values at any point in time are pulled from the financial statements for organizations utilizing the cash accounting method—yet are still tracked internally for operational purposes.

is earned and when expenses are incurred. The following section demonstrates additional transaction information for the following accrual accounting accounts.

Helpful tip: It is important to note that all accrual accounts listed above fall under either the main asset or liability accounts—which are both real accounts and therefore carry over any ending value at the end of the organization's financial period. However, when calculating either revenue earned or expenses incurred with these accounts, the revenue and expenses accounts are still classified as nominal accounts (therefore resetting to $0 at the beginning of every new financial period).

- Asset accrual accounts
  - Accrued interest receivable
  - Accounts receivable (A/R)
  - Allowance for uncollectable accounts (AUCA)
  - Prepaid expenses
- Liability accrual accounts
  - Accounts payable (A/P)
  - Accrued interest payable
  - Accrued salary and wages (S/W) payable
  - Deferred rent revenue
  - Deferred tuition revenue

Accrued Interest Receivable

Similar to A/R but for hospital investments in external funds/initiatives, accrued interest receivable is utilized when the organization earns investment revenue over time yet is not consistently paid each month for interest earned. Rather, quarterly or semiannual payments are often arranged to reduce the frequency of interest checks written to the healthcare organization for monthly interest earned.

Example Accrued Interest Receivable Transactions
The hospital has a $250,000 external investment that earns 6.5% interest (annually) that began on 5/01/20X6. The investment is paid semiannually (or twice per year) on January 1 and July 1 of each year.

What is the *interest revenue* earned for the investment on *6/01/20X6*?

1. Calculate annual interest earned: $250,000 (0.065) = 16,250 annual interest/12 = 1,354 monthly interest revenue earned.
2. Count the number of months between 5/01/20X6 (start date of investment) to 6/01/20X6 = 1 month.
3. 1 month × 1,354 monthly rate = 1,354 interest revenue earned on 6/01/20X6.

What is the *interest revenue* earned for the investment on *9/01/20X6?*

1. Because interest revenue falls under the main revenue account, it is nominal. It will only reset to $0 on January 1 of every year.
2. Therefore, count the number of months between 5/01/20X6 (start date of investment) to 9/01/20X6 = 4 months.
3. Using the same monthly interest revenue interest earned amount from above: 4 months × 1,354 monthly rate = 5,416 interest revenue earned on 9/01/20X6.

What is the *interest revenue* earned for the investment on *3/01/20X7?*

1. Because interest revenue falls under the main revenue account, it is nominal. It will reset to $0 on January 1 of every year.
2. Therefore, count the number of months between 1/01/20X7 (remember, revenue is nominal and is reset to $0 on 1/01/20X7) to 3/01/20X7 = 2 months.
3. Using the same monthly interest revenue earned amount from above: 2 months × 1,354 monthly rate = 2,708 interest revenue earned on 3/01/20X7.

What is the *accrued interest receivable* value for the investment on *6/01/20X6?*

1. To determine the number of months the organization has accrued interest revenue on the investment but has yet to be paid (still receivable), ensure that a payment date is not crossed over in the calculation.
2. Therefore, count the number of months between 5/01/20X6 (investment start date) to 6/01/20X6 = 1 month (period since most recent payment date).
3. 1 month × 1,354 monthly rate = 1,354 accrued interest receivable value on 6/01/20X6.

What is the *accrued interest receivable* value for the investment on *9/01/20X6?*

1. To determine the number of months the organization has accrued interest revenue on the investment but has yet to be paid (still receivable), ensure that a payment date is not crossed over in the calculation.
2. Therefore, the number of months in which interest has accrued as a receivable but has yet to be paid will be from the most previous semi-annual payment date of the investment to 9/01/20X6. So, 7/01/20X6 (last payment date) to 9/01/20X6 = 2 months.

Helpful tip: If there are multiple payment dates for an amount due within the same accounting period, the accrued amount receivable will reset to $0 on each payment date. Therefore, if semiannual (2) payments per year are made, the accrued months will never be more than 6. Likewise, if quarterly (4) payments per year are made the accrued months will never be more than 4.

3. 2 months × 1,354 monthly rate = 2,708 accrued interest receivable on 9/01/20X6.

Accounts Receivable (A/R)

Due to the uniqueness of healthcare operations and the delivery of care in the United States, most often care is delivered right away (the date of service) and paid for later. The use of third-party payers is the primary reason for payment not being paid to the organization at the time of service. A/R is used to monitor who owes what money to the healthcare organization for care previously provided. Therefore, A/R applies to patients owing the healthcare organization for private, out-of-pocket amounts due, as well as copayments, coinsurance, and/or deductible amounts. It also represents the allowed amounts owed to the healthcare organization per contractual arrangements with these third-party payers. Once the payment is received by the healthcare organization it is then lowered or adjusted off the A/R balance since it is no longer receivable.

Example A/R Transactions

A hospital provides $50,000 of care to a patient on 6/07/20X6, and the patient's third-party medical insurance is billed. Based on the healthcare organization's contract with the patient's insurance carrier, the organization expects to be reimbursed 85% of what was initially billed (gross billed charge for the service provided).

What is the journal entry for the hospital on the date of service?

6/07/20X6:	D) A/R	50,000	
	C) operating revenue		50,000

The health insurance remits a payment of $42,500 as expected for the 6/07/20X6 date of service on 8/24/20X6. What is the journal entry for this transaction?

8/24/20X6:	D) cash	42,500	
	D) contractual adjustment	7,500	
	C) A/R		50,000

Here, the cash account is increased because the organization is being paid and experiencing a positive cash flow (payment received). Additionally, the organization has a contracted adjustment due to its relationship (contract) with the insurance carrier, and $7,500 is debited to the contractual adjustment account, which is classified as a revenue deduction account on our chart of accounts. Therefore, by debiting the contractual adjustment account (increasing the account in value), it is in effect lowering total revenue (revenue is decreased by debit entries, which is what is occurring by debiting the contractual adjustment account). Finally, in the end the organization is not expecting to be paid $50,000 anymore since this has been handled by the insurance company's remittance, and this amount is removed from A/R by a final credit of $50,000.

Note: Significant changes to healthcare accounting (especially hospital accounting) continue to occur based on FASB accounting standard updates (ASUs). Chapter 13 (Cognella Active Learning website) will address these healthcare industry accounting updates to date, beyond these basic journal entry examples.

Helpful tip: If the value of A/R were to be adjusted for charity care instead of a contractual adjustment, it would be for the amount (percentage) of charity care adjusted, substituting charity care adjustments in lieu of the contractual adjustment in the example above.

Allowance for Uncollectable Accounts (AUCA): The *"Estimate"* Account

To determine a *net realizable value* of the total A/R account, the actual amounts expected to be collected due to (a) contractual adjustments and/or (b) charity care adjustments are to be accounted for while the value of the service provided is pending in A/R (waiting to be processed by a third-party payer and/or a bill still due from a patient). Here, the AUCA is used to demonstrate the part of the amount billed yet not expected to be reimbursed for either contractual arrangements with third-party payers and/or charity care provisions.

Example AUCA Transactions

A hospital's total A/R (gross) is valued at $2,300,000 on 5/01/20X4. However, of this total A/R amount, the following are *estimates* projected by the healthcare organization for future adjustments (estimated uncollectables):

Contractual adjustments: 15% of existing A/R (gross)

Charity care adjustments: 18% of existing A/R (gross)

To show a true, net realizable value of the A/R account for what is actually expected to be received in cash payment (positive cash inflow), the AUCA is utilized.

What is the adjusting journal entry to estimate future write-offs from the current (gross) A/R value?

1. Calculate the estimated contractual adjustment value: $0.15 \times 2,300,000 = 345,000$
2. Calculate the estimated charity care adjustment value: $0.18 \times 2,300,000 = 414,000$
3. Record the journal entry while the total gross A/R value is pending and estimated amounts are available to establish a net realizable A/R value:

5/01/20X4:	D) contractual adjustments	345,000	
	D) charity care adjustments	414,000	
	C) AUCA		759,000

What does this action look like on the organization's balance sheet while the estimated adjustments are pending?

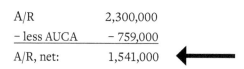

A/R	2,300,000
– less AUCA	– 759,000
A/R, net:	1,541,000

This is the net realizable amount of the pending A/R that is estimated to realistically be collected by the healthcare organization based on prior financial statement data.

Prepaid Expenses

When a hospital pays for a service in advance that will benefit a current and future accounting period(s), a prepaid expense account is utilized. There are two common prepaid expense accounts utilized in healthcare operations and referenced in this textbook:

- prepaid rent expense
- prepaid interest expense

All prepaid expense accounts are assets (they are not expenses, even though the word "expense" is in their account name) and therefore are classified as real accounts. Additionally, both prepaid accounts will decrease in value incrementally over time as the resources are utilized by the healthcare organization. Prepaid rent is only utilized when the healthcare organization pays for a lease (operational space/square footage) ahead of time for an extended, future time period. Prepaid interest is utilized when it pays for any ongoing liability's interest amounts ahead of time (usually prepaid in months).

Helpful tip: When you are estimating any future uncollectible A/R value, the AUCA is utilized. While an over- or underestimate may occur here in practical operations, this discrepancy can be adjusted when ongoing/future AUCA adjusting journal entries are made for future accounting periods pending A/R estimations.

Note: Significant changes to healthcare accounting (especially hospital accounting) continue to occur based on FASB accounting standard updates (ASUs). Chapter 13 (Cognella Active Learning website) will address these healthcare industry accounting updates to date, beyond these basic journal entry examples.

Example Prepaid Expense Transactions

A hospital leases a medical office down the road for $15,000 per month. The lease is prepaid for a full year, beginning on 8/01/20X8.

What is the *initial journal entry* for the hospital prepaying its rent?

1. Calculate the total prepaid amount that occurred on 8/01/20X8: 15,000/month × 12 months = 180,000 annual rent payment.
2. Record the journal entry for the first day of the lease:

8/01/20X8:	D) prepaid rent	180,000	
	C) cash		180,000

What is the value of the *prepaid rent* account on 3/01/20X9?

1. Prepaid rent is categorized as a real account; its value carries over between accounting periods. Therefore, determine how many months between 8/01/20X8 to 3/01/20X9 = 7 months.
2. 7 months × 15,000 per month = 105,000 rent expensed, to date
3. Determine the amount of prepaid rent remaining:

180,000	initial prepaid rent amount on 8/01/20X8
− 105,000	total rent expensed as of 3/01/20X9
75,000	amount remaining in prepaid rent account as of 3/01/20X9

What is the value of the *rent expense* account on the organization's statement of operations on 2/01/20X9?

1. Rent expense is a nominal account and is reduced to $0 at the end of each financial period (December 31 of every year).
2. The number of months between 1/01/20X9 to 2/01/20X9 = 1 month.
3. 1 month × 15,000 per month = 15,000 rent expense account value on 2/01/20X9

Helpful tip: As time goes by, the prepaid amount will lower incrementally, while the corresponding expense account will increase accordingly. After the prepaid amount has reached $0 at the end of its prepaid timeline, the entire initial prepaid value will then be fully expensed (and recorded as such). Also, once fully expensed and the prepaid account is $0, it may be time to purchase more of the prepaid asset if it is to be continually used/needed for ongoing/future healthcare operations.

Example Prepaid Interest Transactions

A 4-year, $25,000 hospital loan was initiated on 5/01/20X7 with 10% annual interest. Interest on the loan is prepaid on May 1 of each year.

What is the 5/01 journal entry to prepay the interest expense if it were to be recorded (adjusted) annually?

Every 5/01 for 4 years:	D) prepaid interest	2,500	
	C) cash		2,500

What is the value of *prepaid interest* on 7/01/20X7?

1. Calculate the monthly interest rate: 0.10 × 25,000 = 2,500 annual interest expense/12 = 208 monthly interest expense.
2. Determine the number of months between 5/01/20X7 to 7/01/20X7 = 2 months.
3. 2 months × 208/month = 416 total interest expense incurred to date.
4. Calculate the amount of prepaid interest remaining:

2,500	annual interest prepaid
− 416	interest expense on 7/01/20X7
2,084	prepaid interest remaining value

What is the *monthly adjusting journal entry for interest expense* during the life of this loan?

Each month:	D) interest expense	208	
	C) prepaid rent		208

Accounts Payable (A/P)

A/P allows the healthcare organization to track who it owes money to for goods/services previously received yet still not paid. Once the healthcare organization pays on its debt, the A/P (liability) account is lowered accordingly. Further discussion on the application of trade credit with healthcare and other business vendors is addressed in Chapter 6, as related to A/P.

Example A/P Transactions

A hospital receives a shipment of medical supplies on 6/01/20X6, and an invoice for $1,500 is attached.

What is the journal entry for the hospital on the date the goods were delivered (received)?

6/01/20X6:	D) supplies (inventory)	1,500	
	C) A/P		1,500

What is the journal entry for the hospital when it decides to pay the invoice in full on 6/15/20X6?

Helpful tip: Think of A/P as the exact opposite of A/R for the healthcare organization. Whereas A/R is an asset and increases when people owe the healthcare organization for goods/services previously delivered, A/P is a liability and increases when the healthcare organization receives goods/services from outside agencies and has yet to pay for them. From another viewpoint, the "owing" organization will carry the amount due on its A/P account ledger, while the "waiting to receive" organization will carry the amount due on its A/R account ledger. Therefore, A/R and A/P are exact opposites, based on the "owing" or "providing" organization involved in the transaction.

6/15/20X6:	D) A/P	1,500	
	C) cash		1,500

Here, the A/P (liability) account is lowered when it is paid to the supply organization. The amount is no longer due (in full) since payment was remitted. The same journal entry would apply for partial payments on amounts due for goods/services previously received by the healthcare organization at the corresponding partial payment amounts.

Accrued Interest Payable

Similar to A/P but for hospital liabilities (most often related to loans and/or bonds) owed to external entities, accrued interest payable is utilized when the organization accrues interest expense over time, yet is not consistently paying interest expenses each month. Rather, quarterly or semiannual payments are often arranged to reduce the frequency of interest checks written to the lending organization.

Example Accrued Interest Payable Transactions
The hospital loan of $250,000 requires 5.5% interest (annually) that began on 5/01/20X6. The interest on the loan is paid semiannually (or twice per year) on January 1 and July 1 of each year.

Note: The calculations below are for interest expense only (disregarding principal).

What is the interest expense for the loan interest on 6/01/20X6?

1. Calculate annual interest expense: $250,000 (0.055) = 13,750 annual interest expense/12 = 1,145 monthly interest expense incurred.
2. Count the number of months between 5/01/20X6 (start date of investment) to 6/01/20X6 = 1 month.
3. 1 month × 1,145 monthly rate = 1,145 interest expense incurred on 6/01/20X6.

What is the *accrued interest payable* for the loan interest on *9/01/20X6?*

1. Count the number of months between the last payment date (7/01/20X6) to 9/01/20X6 = 2 months.
2. Using the same monthly interest expense amount from above: 2 months × 1,145 monthly rate = 2,290 interest expense incurred on 9/01/20X6.

What is the *interest expense value* for the loan interest on *12/01/20X7?*

1. Count the number of months between 1/01/20X7 to 12/01/20X7 (because interest expense is a nominal account and resets to $0 every January 1st). This time period is 11 months.
2. 11 months x 1,145 monthly rate = 12,595 interest expense value on 12/01/20X7.

What is the accrued interest *payable* value for the loan interest on *12/01/20X7*?

1. To determine the number of months the organization has accrued interest expense on the loan interest but has yet to pay, ensure that a payment date is not crossed over in our analysis.
2. Therefore, the number of months in which interest has accrued as a payable but has yet to be paid will be from the most previous semiannual payment date of the loan interest to 12/01/20X7. So, 7/01/20X7 to 12/01/20X7 = 5 months.

3. 5 months x 1,145 monthly rate = 5,725 accrued interest payable on 12/01/20X7.

Salary and Wages (S/W) Payable

Healthcare organizations, along with many other businesses, do not pay their workers after each day of work. Instead, payroll is accrued and carried as a liability against the healthcare organization for services already delivered to the organization (the employees' labor efforts) yet not paid to date. Once a payday occurs, the liability (S/W payable) is paid down or lowered, while the actual S/W expense is recorded when incurred (daily or weekly, for example).

Example S/W Payable Transactions
A hospital pays its employees on the 15th of every month for S/W worked for the previous month.

If today is 1/12/20X3 and the employees have worked hours that total $14,500 in S/W, what is the corresponding journal entry?

1/12/20X3:	D) S/W expense	14,500	
	C) S/W payable		14,500

Because the S/W expense is to be recorded when incurred, the expense is immediately recorded on the books the day of occurrence (1/12/20X3). However, it will not be paid on this date, and therefore it is "owed" to the employees who performed the work (classified as a liability while unpaid to the workers). The hospital received a service (the employees' labor efforts) yet has not paid them to date. Therefore, it will increase the organization's liabilities (S/W payable) until finally paid in cash.

If today is 1/15/20X3 and the total S/W payable to date and owed to the employees totals $350,000, what is the corresponding journal entry to pay the employees?

| 1/15/20X3: | D) S/W payable | 350,000 | |
| | C) cash | | 350,000 |

Here the entire S/W payable account is paid down using cash (used to pay bills) for the work the employees previously provided to the hospital. While the S/W payable account value will immediately go to $0 (paid in full on the organization's payday), it will also immediately begin to incur additional S/W expenses as the employees report to work the following day.

Consider the following end-of-year scenario account values:

a) *On 12/31/20X3, the total amount due to employees for the current pay period is $14,500. What is the adjusting journal entry to account for the amount these employees worked but are not yet paid on 12/31/20X3?*

| 12/31/20X3: | D) S/W expense | 14,500 | |
| | C) S/W payable | | 14,500 |

b) *The hospital's employees earned the following S/W amounts during the given time periods:*

from 12/16/20X3 to 12/31/20X3: 10,200
from 1/01/20X4 to 1/14/20X4: 15,400

While both time periods fall within a single pay period, what is the S/W payable amount due to the employees on 1/14/20X4?

The S/W payable account is a real account (falling under the main liability account), and its end-of-year balances carry over to the next financial period. Therefore, the S/W payable amount due to the employees for both time periods = 10,200 + 15,400 = 25,600 (assuming no pay date fell within this date range).

c) *What is the amount of S/W expense on 1/14/20X4?*

The S/W expense account is a nominal account (falling under the main expense account). Therefore, it resets to $0 at the end of every financial period and accrues from there. So, only the 1/01/20X4 to 1/14/20X4 accrued amount will be classified as S/W expenses as of 1/14/20X4, which is 15,400.

Deferred (Unearned) Revenue

Deferred (also known as "unearned") revenue is not a revenue account—it falls under the liability (real) account on the chart of accounts. There are two primary deferred revenue accounts utilized throughout our textbook:

- deferred (unearned) rent revenue
- deferred (unearned) tuition revenue

Both liability subaccounts are used to record any amounts of money received by the healthcare organization for goods/services that have yet to be provided by the healthcare organization—as related to rent and tuition services; for instance, space that the healthcare organization may have available to lease to other entities and the offering of continuing education classes by the healthcare organization. When external entities prepay for these services and the space and/or educational classes have yet to be provided by the healthcare organization, they are owed by the hospital to those who initially prepaid. Therefore, these funds have been received and goods/services not yet delivered, constituting an obligation (liability) for the healthcare organization until it provides the intended service.

As time progresses and the healthcare organization slowly continues to provide the services that were prepaid, its obligation is incrementally lowered and earned at the same time. An adjusting entry is required to account for the amount of the deferred (unearned) revenue account being reclassified. The "other operating revenue" account is typically used for rent or tuition services, as this is not directly related to patient care but still part of the healthcare organization's mission.

Example Deferred (Unearned) Revenue Transactions
A hospital has unused space on its premises and leases it out to a local physician group for $15,000 per month. The physician group has prepaid for a full year on the lease on 8/01/20X8.

What is the *initial journal entry* for the hospital receiving the physician group's annual (prepaid) rent payment?

Helpful tip: Think of deferred (unearned) revenue as the opposite of a prepaid expense account. Whereas the prepaid expense (asset) account is used when the organization pays for goods/services that will benefit a current and future accounting period, the unearned (deferred) revenue (liability) account is used when the organization receives payment for goods/services it has yet to provide to the external entity.

1. Calculate the total amount that was received by the hospital on 8/01/20X8: 15,000/month × 12 months = 180,000 payment received.
2. Record the journal entry for the first day of the lease:

8/01/20X8:	D) cash	180,000	
	C) deferred rent rev		180,000

The cash account is debited because the hospital has received a payment. The entire amount is entered under the deferred (unearned) rent account because the organization has not earned any of this payment and owes an entire year of rent (space) as a service to the external physician group that prepaid the lease.

What is the value of the *deferred (unearned) rent* account on *3/01/20X9*?

1. Deferred (unearned) rent revenue is categorized as a real account, so its value carries over between accounting periods. Therefore, determine how many months between 8/01/20X8 to 3/01/20X9 = 7 months.
2. 7 months × 15,000 per month = 105,000 rent revenue earned, to date.
3. Determine the amount of deferred (unearned) rent remaining:

180,000	initial unearned rent revenue amount on 8/01/20X8
− 105,000	rent earned as of 3/01/20X9
75,000	remaining unearned rent revenue as of 3/01/20X9

What is the value of the *rent revenue* account on the organization's statement of operations on *2/01/20X9*?

1. Rent revenue is a nominal account and therefore reduced to $0 at the end of each financial period (December 31 of every year).
2. The number of months between 1/01/20X9 to 2/01/20X9 = 1 month.
3. 1 month × 15,000 per month = 15,000 rent revenue account value on 2/01/20X9.

In Summary

Healthcare leaders must have a solid understanding of basic accounting methods, per GAAP and accounting transactions generated from typical healthcare operations. This chapter introduces many basic concepts that describe the most basic healthcare transactions related to cash and accrual of accounting methods. Further analysis and utilization of these methods will continue throughout this textbook.

The expanded accounting equation combines the real and nominal account categories, while also creating a left and right side to delineate the debit and credit actions for all corresponding subaccounts falling under the real and nominal accounts. Any accounting transaction's affected accounts can then be recorded in the organization's accounting journal and then posted to the organization's ledger. It is from the ledger where account balances are pulled and displayed on their respective financial statements (this action will be further addressed in Chapter 10). By learning the correct journal entries for accrual and cash transactions, the healthcare leader will continue to work toward generating valid and reliable financial statements.

The following questions and additional materials are provided for additional application of accounting concepts regarding cash versus accrual accounting methods. Referenced in Chapter 3, Appendix D provides flashcards for many of these common healthcare accounting transactions with corresponding debit/credit journal entries. Leaders are encouraged to continuously review these flashcards to become accustomed to these common healthcare organization transactions and related journal entries.

Chapter Questions

1. Distinguish between the basic and expanded accounting equations and real versus nominal account categories. What financial statements are made up by each of these main accounts?
2. Describe the debit and credit methodology as applied to the expanded accounting equation.
3. Discuss the format for a simple journal entry. Next, discuss the format and purpose of posting to a ledger for any specific account.
4. Describe the cash and accrual accounting methods as applied to revenue and expense accounts.

Review of Common Healthcare Organization Transactions, *Accrual Accounting*

The following healthcare transactions occurred for Austin Community Hospital for the month of May. The hospital's beginning total assets were $350,000, beginning total liabilities were $100,000, and beginning total net assets were $250,000. Based on these transactions and the hospital's accrual accounting method, the corresponding journal entry recordings and ledger postings are shown.

Transactions for Austin Community Hospital, May 20X3:

1. The hospital took out a loan from its local bank for $50,000.
2. The hospital paid its employees $75,000.
3. The hospital received a check from an insurance payer for $10,000.
4. The hospital treated a patient, and their third-party insurance was billed $500.
5. The hospital received a shipment of supplies previously ordered that totaled $350.
6. The hospital paid the supply vendor invoice with a check totaling $350.
7. The hospital used $100 of inventory/supplies for patient care.
8. A monthly bank loan payment of $1,500 was made, of which $250 was for loan interest.

Austin Community Hospital General Journal:

Transaction #1:

D) cash	$50,000	
C) note payable		$50,000

Transaction #2:

D) salary/wages payable	$75,000	
C) cash		$75,000

Transaction #3:

D) cash	$10,000	
C) A/R		$10,000

Transaction #4:

D) A/R	$500	
C) operating revenue		$500

Transaction #5:

D) inventory/supplies	$350	
C) A/P		$350

Transaction #6:

D) A/P	$350	
C) cash		$350

Transaction #7:

D) inventory/supply expense	$100	
C) inventory/supply		$100

Transaction #8:

D) interest expense	$250	
D) note payable	$1,250	
C) cash		$1,500

Revenue/Expense Summary transactions (see ledger below):

D) revenue	$500	
C) rev/exp summary		$500
D) rev/exp summary	$350	
C) expense		$350
D) rev/exp summary	$150	
C) net assets		$150

Austin Community Hospital General Ledger (completed at real/nominal account level):

assets		liabilities		net assets	
(BB) 350,000			(BB) 100,000		(BB) 250,000
50,000		75,000			
	75,000		50,000		
10,000	10,000		350		
500		1,250			
350	350	350			
	100				
	1,500				
410,850	86,50	76,600	150,350		250,000
323,900			73,750		150
					250,150

revenue		expense		rev/exp summary	
	500	100		350	
		250			500
	500	350			150

Review of Common Healthcare Organization Transactions, *Cash Accounting*

The following healthcare transactions occurred for Austin Medical Group for the month of May. The hospital's beginning total assets were $350,000, beginning total liabilities were $$100,000, and beginning total net assets were $250,000. Based on these transactions and the hospital's accrual accounting method, the corresponding journal entry recordings and ledger postings are shown.

Transactions for Austin Medical Group, May 20X3:

1. The hospital took out a loan from its local bank for $50,000.
2. The hospital paid its employees $75,000.
3. The hospital received a check from an insurance payer for $10,000.
4. The hospital treated a patient, and their third-party insurance was billed $500.
5. The hospital received a shipment of supplies previously ordered that totaled $350.
6. The hospital paid the supply vendor invoice with a check totaling $350.
7. The hospital used $100 of inventory/supplies for patient care.
8. A monthly bank loan payment of $1,500 was made, of which $250 was for loan interest.

Austin Medical Group General Journal:

Transaction #1:

D) cash	$50,000	
C) note payable		$50,000

Transaction #2:

D) salary/wage expense	$75,000	
C) cash		$75,000

Transaction #3:

D) cash	$10,000	
C) operating revenue		$10,000

Transaction #4: no transaction

Transaction #5: no transaction

Transaction #6:

D) inventory/supply expense	$350	
C) cash		$350

Transaction #7: no transaction

Transaction #8:

D) interest expense	$250	
D) note payable	$1,250	
C) cash		$1,500

Revenue/Expense Summary transactions (see ledger below and Visual application/ QR code above):

D) revenue	$10,000	
C) rev/exp summary		$10,000
D) rev/exp summary	$75,600	
C) expense		$75,600
D) net assets	$65,600	
C) rev/expense summary		$65,600

Austin Medical Group General Ledger (completed at real/nominal account level):

assets		liabilities		net assets	
(BB) 350,000			(BB) 100,000		(BB) 250,000
50,000			50,000		
	75,000	1,250			
10,000					
	350				
	1,500				

410,000	76,850	1,250	150,000	65,600	250,000
333,150			148,750		184,400

revenue		expense		rev/exp summary	
	10,000	75,000			10,000
		350		75,600	
		250			

	10,000	75,600			65,600

Real Account Valuation Methods

Where Do the Numbers Come From?

Introduction

In Chapter 4 the two nominal accounts (revenue and expense) were addressed regarding how they are reported on the financial statements under both cash and accrual methods of accounting. This included not only when these two nominal account categories are recorded by the healthcare organization but also for how much (dollar value). Values for revenue and expense transactions were affected based on (a) the nominal account category's zeroing out process at the end of the financial period and (b) the method of accounting used by the healthcare organization (cash vs. accrual accounting methods).

In this chapter a thorough review of the real accounts (assets, liabilities, and net assets) is conducted to demonstrate methods of reporting these account figures (dollar values on the financial statements), as well as all subaccounts falling under each main real account category.

Learning Objectives

By the end of this chapter, the student should be able to:

- Discuss multiple asset valuation methods to report specific real accounts on the organization's balance sheet.
- Explain the difference between book and market value of tangible assets.
- Discuss multiple liability valuation methods to report specific real accounts on the organizational balance sheet.
- Calculate and interpret effective annual interest rates for various trade credit contractual agreements with medical supply vendors.

Key Terms

1. Historical cost
2. Book vs. market value
3. Fair market value
4. Net realizable value
5. Future profit
6. Trade credit
7. Effective annual interest rate

Asset Valuation

Asset valuation entails the reporting of all asset figures on the organization's balance at any single point in time to support the organization's financial position. This is an important task for the healthcare organization and its leaders' use of proper accounting practices (per GAAP) to ensure no misrepresentation or inflation of asset values are accidentally reported. Leaders are also responsible for not undervaluing the organization's economic resources at the same time. As a result, many asset valuation methods are available to support what dollar amount should be reported on the organization's balance sheet—based on the type of asset (subaccount) being reported. The following methods are among the most common utilized in a healthcare organization's asset valuation process.

Note: Chapter 13 (Cognella Active Learning website) offers additional FASB and other accounting entity updates for specific healthcare asset reporting procedures.

Historical Cost

The use of historical cost (easily defined as purchase price) is by far one of the easiest and most objective methods in assessing a tangible asset's value. This is also one of the most common methods to value an asset, primarily due to its inarguable viewpoint—the asset's purchase price. When an asset is purchased, this demonstrates the amount it was valued at on a specific date in true market conditions. To further explain the use of historical cost for tangible assets, two very basic economic valuation methods need to be defined.

- *Book value*: The fixed value at which an asset is reported "on the books" or financial records for the organization, regardless of external changes in market conditions.
- *Market value*: The value of an asset as tested at any one point in time (therefore a dynamic, ever-changing value) based on external changes in market conditions. Market value is based on supply and demand.

While a tangible asset may change in future market value as external market conditions fluctuate with time, the use of historical cost as the asset's valuation method locks in the purchase price of the asset as the reported value on the organization's balance sheet. This action (recording of historical cost) occurs regardless of market conditions concerning future changes in supply and demand figures. Again, due to its ease of reporting and inarguable dollar amount used to procure the asset at the time of purchase, historical cost valuation is a common and most objective asset valuation method. Documentation to support an asset's historical cost include receipts, invoices, and/or other objective evidence that document the original purchase transaction.

Chapter 7 will provide a detailed review of specific tangible assets (buildings and equipment) that are reported on the organization's balance sheet at their purchase prices yet have systematic, incremental adjustments to their historical costs based on a calculated wear-and-tear cost allocation procedure called depreciation. Figure 5.1 demonstrates how an asset (a piece of medical equipment) is be subjected to depreciation on an organization's balance sheet, reporting the wear-and-tear cost allocation as it accrues over time using the accumulated depreciation accrual account.

acct 124	equipment – ultrasound machine	40,000
acct 125	less (–) accumulated depreciation	(2,000)
	equipment – ultrasound machine, net:	38,000

FIGURE 5.1 Example of a tangible asset subjected to accumulated depreciation cost allocation on an organization's balance sheet.

While the organization's book value is currently reported as $38,000 "on the books" based on the asset's original historical cost, this does not mean that the device can be sold for this amount. In that situation supply/demand market economics would take over and dictate the current day's valuation of the asset in the current market environment. However, while on the organization's balance sheet as a tangible asset, the cost allocation depreciation method has accounted for a wear-and-tear amount of $2,000 to date (from Chapter 7) and therefore the net *book value* of the asset is $38,000 on the balance sheet. This asset's net amount after depreciation is often termed replacement cost.

Fair Market Value

Contrary to tangible assets' common use of historical cost as a valuation method on the balance sheet, other assets exist as organizational resources that are monetary in nature and often have fluctuating market values. Because of these value fluctuations that occur more frequently, the historical costing valuation method is not appropriate for these assets. Instead, the following assets are often valued using fair market value methods:

- stocks
- bonds
- other marketable securities (commercial paper, Treasury bills, money market accounts)

In some cases (such as purchased stocks), a current-day "mark-to-market" method may be used, which simply evaluates the current-day stock market valuation for that specific asset (investment). The date and valuation of the stock would then still be reported on the organization's balance sheet at its historical cost, while the mark-to-market (current day) value would be clearly reported in the notes to the financial statements (see Chapter 2, Tables 2.5 and 2.6). While the best test for this type of asset's valuation would be an actual sale of the asset in true marketing conditions, this action is not optimal for valuation reporting on an organization's balance sheet, especially if the organization is not interested in selling the asset. Instead, an attempt to identify that asset's sale by another business entity (such as the sale of the same stock in the market, current day) would allow for the best mark-to-market opportunity and should be reported as such. Otherwise, the sale of the next best, most similar stock or another like-asset is appropriate. In the end, the method used to value the asset in the market at any point in time will also need to be mentioned in the financial statement notes, along with the fair market valuation amount identified.

Net Realizable Value

In regular operational activities, the typical healthcare organization will provide a good or service to a patient, and reimbursement for these activities will not occur at the time of service. Instead, payment is often received days, weeks, and even months later. Primarily due to the use of third-party payers in the U.S. healthcare industry, this occurrence makes the organization's A/R asset account to appear inflated (or reported at too high of a value). This is because initially, the A/R is reported as gross revenue amounts (volumes × charges), prior to any revenue deductions. Therefore, the A/R account's net realizable value should be determined and reported on the organization's balance sheet in an attempt to provide a more transparent reporting value of what is realistically expected to be collected by the healthcare organization.

The net realizable value objective is to report what is actually expected to be collected from the total value of all charges related to patient care provided yet still pending reimbursement (payment). Figure 5.2 demonstrates the use of the net realizable value calculation as reported on a healthcare organization's non-GAAP statement of operations.

Note: The non-GAAP statement of operations and related FASB updates are discussed in Chapter 9 and Chapter 13 (Cognella Active Learning website).

Total A/R (volumes × charges):	1,450,000
Less (−) the allowance for uncollectible accounts	
– contractual adjustments:	(200,000)
– charity care adjustments:	(150,000)
= A/R, net:	1,100,000

FIGURE 5.2 Presentation of the net realizable value of the A/R asset account on an organization's balance sheet.

While the healthcare organization has provided and billed for a total of $1,450,000 in healthcare services delivered and is still awaiting reimbursement, 100% of this amount will not be collected due to revenue deductions unique to the healthcare industry: contractual adjustments and charity care adjustments. As a result, to be as fully transparent as possible on the organization's balance sheet, the amount that is estimated to be collected from the pending gross A/R value is calculated and deducted using the allowance for uncollectible accounts (AUCA).

Note: The AUCA and related material will be further reviewed in Chapter 8. Additional FASB updates regarding updated procedures surrounding bad debt and associated revenue deductions are also covered in Chapter 13 (Cognella Active Learning website).

While an ongoing estimate, this AUCA assists the organization in estimating the values of A/R not expected to be paid from contracted third-party insurance companies or indigent patients who are provided charity care services. Once the organization receives notice of the contractual adjustment amount and/or charity care amount, the actual revenue deduction can be taken, and this amount is adjusted from the estimated (AUCA) account for accuracy of reporting future estimated uncollectables. Healthcare leaders often use the prior financial period's data for estimating the current percentage of A/R to be adjusted. Using past write-offs (adjustments) for previous charity care and contractual adjustment values helps the healthcare organization estimate

Helpful tip: Remember, "net" is synonymous with "after." Therefore, net realizable value is a figure that has been adjusted somewhat or in some way. Here, it is gross (volumes × charges) revenue, minus revenue deductions, to "net" the net realizable amount of A/R. The net A/R is what is realistically expected to be collected in cash in the near future by the healthcare organization for services previously provided.

the net A/R value at the time a balance sheet is generated. This is an example of how historical (previous, or in the past) organizational financial statements can provide data to identify trends and patterns to assist with the generation of current-day, valid, and reliable financial statements.

Future Profit Valuation for Operational Decisions

The sale of an asset will most often result in the healthcare organization experiencing a net positive inflow of cash. However, the loss of the tangible asset will also result in the loss of use of that asset, as well as all services for which that piece of healthcare equipment was utilized. As a result, all the gross charges related to those services once provided by that piece of equipment will be lost because of the sale of the asset. If the asset is sold and the organization does not own it anymore, it is unable to perform services related to the asset and therefore will not bill for that bundle of services. It is the healthcare leader's responsibility to ensure the future profit valuation of the asset is analyzed prior to the decision to sell the asset. The expected cash flow from the sales transaction of an ultrasound machine is demonstrated in Figure 5.3.

---

a) Book value:

acct 124	equipment – ultrasound machine	40,000
acct 125	less (–) accumulated depreciation	(2,000)
	equipment – ultrasound machine, net:	$38,000 (book value)

b) Market value:
proposed cash offer from external customer: $25,000 (market value)

c) Future profit assessment:

Ultrasound machine billed charge per procedure:	$125
Ultrasound machine utilization estimate:	50 procedures/month
Ultrasound machine remaining useful life:	60 months
Estimated ultrasound machine future profit:	$375,000

FIGURE 5.3   Example of a tangible asset's future profits analysis.

In review, the calculated allocation of depreciation for the ultrasound machine and its remaining book value does not match its current market value. However, even if market value was proposed for the sale at $25,000, the healthcare administrator would also have to assess the remaining useful life of the asset still remaining (60 months), as related to the routine utilization of the equipment (estimated at 50 procedures/month, billed at an estimated $125/procedure). If the sale of the ultrasound machine were to occur, the $25,000 (book value) cash inflow from the sale would be much less than the projected future profits (again, estimated at $375,000) that would have been earned by the equipment if not sold and otherwise kept in regular operational use. This example demonstrates the importance of calculating an asset's estimated future profits and assessing that value as an opportunity cost if the equipment is sold.

Additional Asset Accrual Account Valuation

In addition to A/R and the AUCA represented on the organization's balance sheet under the accrual accounting method, the following additional accrual accounts possess reported values based on their monthly accrued amounts over any specific financial period:

- asset accrual accounts
  - accrued interest receivable
  - prepaid expenses (insurance, rent, interest)

Both accrual asset accounts have been previously described in detail (with examples) in Chapter 4 and in Appendix C. The healthcare leader is simply to recognize that the current value of each will be based on the monthly/annual accrued value for these accounts, respective to the time period(s) lapsed since their commencement (or most recent payment) date.

Liability Valuation

The valuation of economic obligations (or liabilities) of the healthcare organization is an important task for the healthcare leader. This process requires the leader to assess and interpret additional costs to the organization as related to regular cash outflows for a variety of activities related to receiving a good or service now and paying for it later. Termed "financing," the use of someone else's money to gain access to an organizational resource (an asset) to assist with healthcare operations includes several additional costs:

- regular principal payments (to lower the contracted/borrowed amount)
- regular interest expenses (the fee for the lender's service of providing the loan to the healthcare organization and associated risk with the activity)
- effective interest rates regarding trade credit contractual arrangements with external vendors
- employee salary and wage expenses earned by the organization's employees but not yet paid
- deferred (also known as "unearned") revenues such as cash received for tuition and rent revenue obligations for services that are yet to be provided by the healthcare organization

While the method of accounting used by the organization plays a significant role regarding when these expenses are incurred (versus paid), the future accrued expense obligations for liabilities will continue to exist for the organization. This accrual of liabilities and their associated accrual of costs is inevitable, even if they are not directly reported on the organization's balance sheet (for those organizations using the cash accounting method). Therefore, all healthcare leaders are responsible for maintaining a competent and detailed assessment of the organization's obligations, related fees for such obligations, and how they are valued.

Trade Credit Contractual Agreement With Third-Party Vendors

Supply vendors (both medical and nonmedical supplies) often establish trade credit agreements with their partner organizations based on the healthcare organization's overall reputation, creditworthiness, and even leadership team characteristics. The requirement for the healthcare organization and its vendors to work together as separate organizations is vital in the delivery of quality patient care. As a result, supply vendors are willing not only to extend a line of credit to the healthcare organization by not expecting payment immediately at the time of supply (or other goods/service) delivery but also to provide a discount to the healthcare organization if payment on the invoice is received from the healthcare organization sooner, rather than later.

Termed a *trade credit discount*, the supply vendor provides a discount incentive to the healthcare organization to assist with its own revenue cycle process. The sooner the payment for supplies delivered to the healthcare organization is received by the supply vendor, the sooner the supply vendor can turn around and purchase additional supplies from its wholesaler. The supply vendor will then sell these newly procured supplies to its respective healthcare organizations, which are in constant need of supplies for direct patient care.

The *trade credit discount formula* is shown below, simply serving as placeholder for the following interpretation of each variable:

$$x/y, \text{ net } z$$

Where:
  x = % discount offered off the total invoice amount
  y = number of days from the delivery date (and/or invoice date) in which the % discounted invoice amount may be paid to appropriately take advantage of the trade credit discount
  z = number of days from the delivery date (and/or invoice date) in which the entire invoice amount (without any discount) is required to be paid in full

Therefore, if a healthcare organization enters into a trade credit agreement with its medical supply vendor that states, "2/10, net 30," this means that a 2% discount will be deducted off the total invoice due amount if payment is received within 10 days of the invoice origination date (this is usually also the delivery date). Otherwise, if payment is received after the 10-day period, the full invoice amount is due in full on or before 30 days from the date of the invoice.

It is also important to maintain creditworthiness as a healthcare organization in the local community. The healthcare organization should work to continuously uphold an amiable relationship with all its supply vendors (both medical and nonmedical). Therefore, at no time should an invoice be paid after the final invoice due date (thereby qualifying as late or delinquent). If such instances were to arise, the inability to meet financial obligations related to the supplier's invoice should be communicated and a payment plan requested with the supply vendor to salvage the relationship between both organizations.

When Should the Invoice Be Paid?
Often, healthcare administrators are presented with a challenging decision regarding what bill to pay, and when, and in what order. This is often a decision based on both professional and corporate relationships, as well as trade credit contractual arrangement details. Both positive and negative cash flows will need to be analyzed by the healthcare leader in order to meet current and future organizational obligations. Incoming reimbursements from third-party healthcare payers, as well as upcoming expenses and their due dates, will never perfectly align and must be planned for using the conservatism GAAP concept. Chapter 11 will further address positive and negative cash flows and the navigation of due dates for various organizational revenues and expenses.

For example, one method to help create an objective order or priority of pending A/P accounts due to various medical supply and other vendors involves the calculation of effective, annualized interest rates. Here, the short-term time frame of how many days past a trade credit discount period are reclaimed to pay an invoice in full is analyzed against the effective interest rate incurred by the healthcare organization. In other words, when the healthcare organization is unable to pay the vendor's invoice within the early discount period, it incurs an additional cost (the discount dollar amount missed), in exchange for paying the invoice in full after the discount period. This extended payment period is basically an extension of the line of credit offered by the medical supply vendor to the healthcare organization. While the invoice amount due from the healthcare organization will never be technically late or delinquent, it will forgo the trade credit discount if not paid within the discount period.

It is always appropriate to take advantage of any trade credit discount offered by a supply vendor. If there is a 3/15, net 45 trade credit arrangement, pay the invoice in full, minus a

3% discount within the 15-day period. With many healthcare organizations' profit margins hovering around 2%–3% annually, the opportunity for any discount on any expense items like those of supplies/inventory is vitally important to succeed as an effective healthcare administrator. Because of this, when trade discount periods are missed by the healthcare organization, the percent discount missed is reported on the books as an interest charge. This is because the healthcare organization has chosen to pay an additional fee (the missed trade credit discount) for additional days to pay the vendor's invoice in full.

There are times when bills are not able to be paid within the trade credit discount period. Reasons for such actions should be reviewed and processes adjusted to enable discounts on future supply invoices to be properly exploited. That said, the decision as to when to pay the invoice in full after having missed the discount period deadline is also a question for many healthcare leaders. Should you pay right away, immediately after missing the discount period? Or wait until the full invoice due date gets closer? The example questions to follow assist in demonstrating the effective (annualized) interest rates associated with trade credit discounts.

Question #1: How much does it cost to miss the discount period and simply pay 1 day after the established discount period of 15 days (therefore, payment occurs on day 16) for a $300 supply order/purchase and a trade credit agreement of 3/15, net 45?

To calculate the effective, annualized interest rate of missing the discount period and paying the full invoice *1 day later*, we use the effective interest rate formula:

$$\textbf{\textit{annual interest = annualized interest paid/amount of original supply purchase}}$$

$$\textit{annualized interest rate} = 365/1 \text{ day after the discount period}$$

$$= 365(3\% \text{ of } \$300)$$

$$= 365(9)$$

$$= \$3,285$$

Where there are 365 1-day periods in a given year, and 3% of $300 annualized for this period = $3,285

$$\textit{Annual interest rate} = 3,285/300 = 10.95 \ (100\%)$$

$$= \textbf{1,095\% effective annualized interest rate}$$

In other words, choosing to pay 1 day after the discount period (and paying the 3% "interest" fee of $9 for this extra day) is an effective annualized interest rate of 1,095%. Paying this much interest on anything is probably not the best idea, especially in the healthcare industry. While the dollar amount may seem marginal, when annualizing the interest rate, the effective cost of getting 1 additional day to pay the invoice in full is not good practice.

Or the healthcare administrator can look at an alternative—paying closer to the invoice's final due date, again—only after already having missed the 15-day discount period.

Question #2: How much does it cost to miss the discount period and simply pay *30 days after the established discount period* (therefore, payment occurs on day 45) for a $300 supply order/purchase and a trade credit agreement of 3/15, net 45?

Again, using our annual interest rate formula:

$$\textit{annual interest rate} = \textit{annualized interest paid/amount of original supply purchase}$$

$$\textit{annualized interest} = 365/30 \text{ days after the discount period}$$

$$= 12.167(3\% \text{ of } \$300)$$

$$= 12.167(9)$$

$$= \$109.50$$

Where there are 12.167 30-day periods in a given year, and 3% of $300 annualized for this period = $109.50

Annual interest rate = 109.50/300 = 0.365 (100%)

= 36.5% effective annualized interest rate

Now, compare both calculated annual effective interest rates. Which would you choose: pay a 1,095% effective annual interest rate to get 1 additional day to pay the invoice in full, or pay a 36.5% effective annual interest rate to get 30 additional days to pay the same amount? While missing the discount opportunity is not a good idea in the first place (healthcare organizations should take any/all discounts offered to them), the calculation of the effective annual interest rate of 3% allows for an easy identification of when the full invoice (without the trade discount) should be submitted to the supply vendor.

As a result, even within the trade credit discount period, it is always best to pay the invoice as late as possible, without missing the discount period (if possible). If the discount period is not met, the additional effective interest rate realized by not paying within the discount period does "buy" the healthcare organization additional days in which to pay the invoice in full. However, the amount of the missed discount (observed as interest in these examples for auditing/reporting purposes within the organization) will not change in dollar amount once the discount has been missed. So, the healthcare administrator

Helpful tip: The healthcare administrator should attempt to have all service/supply contracts based on similar trade credit arrangements (percentage discounts, discount time periods, and full invoice due dates). Or try to have these trade credit arrangement variables as close to the same terms as possible. This similarity of invoice timelines/terms will assist in the interpretation of efficiency ratios (addressed in Chapter 12), while also enabling the healthcare leader to maintain a more systematic approach to weekly/monthly A/P practices and related organizational cash flows.

might as well capitalize on the full invoice due date period since the fee to pay after the discount period will be the same extra dollar amount (interest charge) when paying on day 16 or day 45 in this example. It is important to note that paying after the full invoice due date has not been addressed, as this scenario should not be an option for the healthcare organization operating in an effective manner.

Additional Liability Accrual Account Valuation

In addition to the liability valuation methods previously reviewed, the following additional accrual accounts (for organizations using the accrual accounting method) have been previously reviewed in Chapter 4:

- accrued interest payable
- accrued salary and wages (S/W) payable
- deferred rent revenue
- deferred tuition revenue

While these accounts still exist in healthcare organizations under the cash accounting method, they are not reported directly on these organizations' balance sheets. The healthcare leader who can understand, acknowledge, and interpret these accrual account effects on daily healthcare operations will be best prepared to make informed decisions regarding these and other liability valuations.

Net Asset Valuation

The final real account to discuss valuation methods is net assets—which is the easiest real account to assign a monetary figure. Net asset is simply the value that balances the basic accounting equation, as originally introduced in Chapter 3:

$$\text{Assets} - \text{Liabilities} = \text{Net Assets}$$

To review, what the organization has (economic resources) minus what it owes (economic obligations) equals the NA value to be reported on the healthcare organization's balance sheet. This value represents the organization's net worth at that specific point in time (when the balance sheet is generated). It is important to note that this value can significantly change throughout any given day based on the amount of accounting entries being made into the system.

Note: Updates to the presentation of net assets on the organization's balance sheet are further addressed in Chapter 13 (Cognella Active Learning website).

In Summary

Assessing a healthcare organization's real account values and properly reporting them on the balance sheet are important tasks required of the healthcare leader. The proper valuation method is to be chosen based on the question being asked and/or other reason(s) why an asset or liability needs to be assessed for reporting value. In the end, it all depends on what question is being asked and which valuation method makes the most sense for the healthcare organization. In its efforts, the healthcare organization must also be as transparent and as consistent as possible with its real account valuations. This practice allows the healthcare organization to report the most valid and reliable asset or liability subaccount to support the organization's financial statements and ultimately the financial management decisions related to these real account values.

Chapter Questions

1. You are a physician practice administrator, and one of your providers has suggested selling a medical device that is utilized frequently yet appears not to provide for sufficient reimbursement from several third-party healthcare payers. Discuss the asset valuation method and related implications you would use in this situation to address the provider's recommendation. What other information would you need to decide on this matter?

2. You are a hospital administrator, and your leadership team has suggested the sale of one of the ancillary therapy buildings associated with the hospital. They are requesting the current building's value as represented on the organization's current balance sheet to assess the potential sales price of this asset. What concerns would you have with this valuation method for the building, based on their proposal?

Helpful tip: The net asset account is not a drawer of cash. It is simply the value that balances the basic accounting equation. While it does represent the organization's net worth (equity), it is not technically monies available to be directly spent. Net asset account values and related subaccount characteristics are reviewed in greater detail in Chapter 8.

3. You are a practice administrator and are running into a cash flow problem for the current month. One of your supply vendor's invoices is coming closer to a payment due date and has the following trade credit terms:

2/10, net 30

The total amount due on the invoice is $1,400.85. Based on your organization's monthly budget and estimated cash flows, you are looking at paying this invoice on either day 12, 15, or 25.

a. Calculate the effective interest rate for each of these possible payment days.

b. Assuming the cash flow is positive enough to cover the cost of this invoice on any of these projected three dates, decide which date to pay the invoice and discuss why that date was chosen.

4. You are a hospital administrator and would like to renegotiate your current trade credit terms agreement (3/12, net 30) with your medical supply vendor for invoices that usually average $500/month. Your board members are requesting an updated trade credit agreement of 5/10, net 45 instead.

Discuss possible reasons how or why your organization may be able to utilize leverage in this situation to hopefully receive a more optimal trade credit agreement. Next, using the estimated monthly supply invoice balance provided—compare both current and requested trade credit agreements with regard to their effective interest rates for (a) paying within the discount period and (b) paying on day 20.

Accounting for Healthcare Inventory

Introduction

Inventory (also synonymous with the term "supplies") often constitutes up to an estimated 25% to 40% of any healthcare organization's operating budget. Classified as an organizational asset, inventory consists of any/all expendable items used during the provision of care in the organization, which also includes nonmedical supplies. Managing the organization's inventory status is a primary task of the healthcare administrator and involves the challenges of (a) not carrying an overstock of any one type of supply item(s) and (b) not experiencing a shortage of any one supply item(s). Cost management of these organizational assets is always focused on limiting the use of supply items to as little as possible per patient encounter, all while also ensuring that the quality of care does not suffer due to the conservative accounting principle initiative associated with healthcare inventory.

Learning Objectives

By the end of this chapter, the student should be able to:

- Identify the describe the importance of the inventory (supply) accounts as presented on the healthcare organization's balance sheet and statement of operations.
- Discuss the reasoning for using an inventory voucher system (A/P) when purchasing inventory/supplies.
- List the appropriate journal entries related to the acquisition and usage of inventory/supply items.
- Define and utilize inventory accounting methods for valuation and expensing (usage) of any single inventory item.

Key Terms

1. A/P voucher process
2. Periodic inventory method
3. Perpetual inventory method
4. Specific identification inventory valuation/expensing method
5. Periodic weighted average inventory valuation/expensing method
6. FISH inventory valuation and LIFO inventory expensing method
7. LISH inventory valuation and FIFO inventory expensing method

Inventory as an Organizational Asset

The healthcare organization's inventory consists of all expendable (one-time use) items that are used to achieve the organizational mission—the delivery of quality patient care. Falling into the revenue cycle operations for the organization, the inventory must be purchased, stored and readily available, and then eventually used in the delivery of care when needed/required. While the recording of inventory as an organizational expense and billing of the inventory as an organizational revenue differs based on the accounting method the healthcare organization is using (either cash or accrual accounting), the initial purchase of inventory will be quite similar for either method, as demonstrated below.

Example journal entry for the purchase of new inventory/supplies (bandages) when vouchered through A/P:

11/01/20X1	D) inventory (bandages)	$300	
	C) A/P		$300

Here, the organization has purchased inventory (bandages) from a third-party medical supply vendor. Because supplies are delivered to the organization and an invoice has also been provided, the organization does not pay cash at the time of delivery. Instead, a trade credit agreement exists between both organizations, and the supply amount due to the medical supply vendor is temporarily carried as an account payable (A/P, a short-term liability) during the invoice period. Eventually, the invoice will be paid using cash from the healthcare organization's operating account (cash). This voucher process is introduced as it is the most practical application of time-series events as related to the procurement of medical supplies and so on for any typical healthcare organization.

Why Process Through A/P When an Invoice Is Received?

It is common for organizations to not always use cash as an initial payment method for goods or services received. In fact, paying for anything with cash is highly discouraged, and the use of the A/P account allows the organization to temporarily voucher the pending amount due to an external organization. This means that the invoice is studied (audited) and processed according to organizational protocols to ensure it is a true operational expense. Otherwise, payment for items without vouchering through the A/P account and directly crediting the cash account for an immediate payment to the vendor could result in the organization paying for items not necessarily approved as true operational expenses. This includes potential fraudulent purchases made using organizational funds.

Healthcare leaders are encouraged to exercise an A/P voucher process that involves a thorough review of all the organization's pending invoices for these reasons, as well as other common third-party supply vendor issues that occur in everyday healthcare operations:

- accidental undersupply of an item that is not correctly represented on the original vendor invoice
- accidental oversupply of an item that is not correctly represented on the original vendor invoice
- accidental bill sent for an item that was never received by the healthcare organization in the first place
- ability to ensure that any trade credit discount opportunities are taken advantage of by the healthcare organization and are being upheld by medical supply vendor contractual agreements (previously discussed in Chapter 5)

Once any invoice issues are resolved and payment is approved by the healthcare organization's A/P voucher process, the associated journal entry to pay the supply vendor will lower the A/P liability account by paying the bill owed to the medical supply vendor with cash (a check is sent from the organization's operating account).

Example journal entry to pay a third-party medical vendor for inventory/supplies (bandages) when vouchering through A/P:

10/25/20X1	D) inventory (bandages)	$300	
	C) A/P		$300

Here, the supplies are received (in bulk) and paid for on credit terms with the medical supply vendor. A/P is increased because the healthcare organization has received the supplies but has yet to pay for them in cash.

11/01/20X1	D) A/P	$300	
	C) cash		$300

Now, the healthcare organization decides to lower its liability by paying the invoice that is due to the medical supplier. When choosing to voucher through A/P for organizations operating under the cash method of accounting, the organization tracks its A/P liabilities "off the books," while still utilizing the vendor's trade credit terms to fully verify the shipment/payment prior to sending a cash payment.

Recording Inventory as an Organizational Expense

In either of the two GAAP methods of accounting practices (cash or accrual), the inventory/supply usage will occur, and an inventory/supply expense will be recorded prior to any organizational revenue being earned or received. Before discussing further, it is important to review the differences in accrual and cash accounting methods, as related to when revenues and expenses are recorded for the organization.

Record revenues and expenses when …

Accounting method	Revenue	Expense
Cash	*received*	*paid*
Accrual	*earned*	*incurred*

As previously mentioned, the recording of the inventory (supply) item as an operating expense will be dependent on the organization's accounting method being used, per organizational policy. For instance, the cash accounting method will capture the entire inventory expense (full amount paid) at the time of purchase. However, if the organization is operating under the accrual method of accounting, the expense will be recorded much later—specifically, when each individual inventory item is used during the treatment of patients requiring that item.

Example journal entry to expense an inventory/supply (box of bandages) delivered to the healthcare organization on 11/15/20X1 under the cash accounting method:

11/15/20X1	D) supply expense (bandages)	$300	
	C) cash		$300

Here, the entire box of bandages is captured as an organizational expense on a single date, regardless of if/when the individual items are used in the future for patient care. This is a prime example of the cash accounting method, which captures the full organizational supply expense on the date of purchase. This occurs only after the purchase request has been processed through the organization's voucher system.

Under the cash accounting method, the supply expense account will always be debited and the cash account will always be credited when paying for an inventory/supply item. While an A/P voucher system may be used (and is highly recommended as an organizational best practice), the A/P ledger will not be included on the organization's financial statements when operating under the cash accounting method. Therefore, to ensure the accuracy of statements, any/all pending A/P accounts currently in the voucher process should be finalized and paid in cash prior to running updated financial statements for the healthcare organization. If not, vouchers pending in A/P should be added as a note in the financial statement for organizations operating under the cash accounting method to ensure this liability is accurately reported.

Alternatively, the same supply items will be recorded (journalized) as an expense much differently if the healthcare organization is operating under the accrual accounting method. Instead of expensing out the entire box of bandages all at one time when the cash account is credited to pay for the item(s), the operational supply expenses are recorded as debits only when individually utilized in the provision of patient care. This practice occurs regardless of when the invoice for those items was paid for by the healthcare organization. A basic example is provided below for use of individual bandages for this same supply purchase.

Helpful tip: Remember that the organization using the cash accounting method will keep an A/P ledger, but A/P is not presented on the organization's financial statements when cash accounting is used. Therefore, when the organization on cash accounting pays a bill with cash, it is assumed that the organization has run the supply purchase (expense) through its voucher process already.

Helpful tip: For the healthcare organization operating under the cash system of accounting, the A/P voucher process will consist of any/all pending invoices (bills) the organization has received and not yet paid. Because this account (A/P) is not presented on the organization's balance sheet financial statement while operating under the cash accounting method, it is important to address any/all pending invoices the organization has received prior to the generation of such statements. Otherwise, the received invoices that have yet to be paid at the time the financial statements being generated will understate the supply expenses. If not paid prior to running the financial statements, the A/P balance should be clearly notated in the notes to the financial statement(s) to demonstrate full transparency of pending liabilities.

Example journal entry to expense an inventory/supply (individual bandage) delivered to the healthcare organization and also used on 11/15/20X1 under the accrual accounting method:

11/15/20X1	D) supply expense (bandage)	$10*	
	C) inventory/supply (bandage)		$10

Note: The $10 (individual unit) supply expense value in this example will be addressed later in this chapter.

Due to the differences in the cash and accrual methods of accounting (per GAAP), an internal inventory of any single inventory/supply item must be maintained under both accounting methods. As a result, the accrual account-ing method tracks inventory usage better at the single-use, patient (and date of service) level.

Recording Inventory as an Organizational Revenue

During patient care, the healthcare provider will reach for an inventory item. This may include the use of a bandage for a bleeding patient, a syringe to admin-ister medication, and even the use of a paper gown for a surgical patient prior to a procedure. In all these examples, the supplies are intended for one-time use. These items have originally been purchased and stored as an organiza-tion resource (asset; specifically, the inventory/supply subaccount) by the organization. Then, when pulled off the shelf for use in the delivery of care, the organization will bill for the supply originally purchased beforehand—in addition to the other supplies and also provided at the time of service.

Note: In these examples the supply item is being used to demonstrate the use of inventory and recording of corresponding revenue for that single supply item to demonstrate cash/accrual accounting method practices. This individual revenue/ expense valuation of supplies disregards any bundled payment or other reim-bursement method sometimes used in managed care contractual arrangements. Further, enhanced cost accounting practices are required for bundled reimburse-ment methods and/or advanced reimbursement methods, which is beyond the scope of this textbook.

For healthcare organizations operating under the cash method of accounting, the revenue for that single supply item used to treat the patient will only be recorded when reimbursement is received (paid) to the organization. This payment is often received by a third-party payer, or possibly the patient at a much later time period. Because the cash accounting method only records revenue when cash is received by the healthcare organization, the actual cash inflow related to this item is clearly demonstrated by its associated journal entry.

Example journal entry to record revenue of an inventory/supply item (individual bandage) under the cash accounting method:

02/15/20X2	D) cash	$10	
	C) operating revenue		$10

Alternatively, this same inventory item is recorded as an operational revenue under the accrual accounting method as soon as it is billed to the third-party payer following the treatment of the patient, regardless of when payment is received.

Example journal entry to record revenue of an inventory/supply item (individual bandage) under the accrual accounting method:

11/15/20X1	D) A/R	$10	
	C) operating revenue		$10

Eventually, the pending A/R for this date of service and related supply billed to a third-party payer will be reimbursed with a check received in the mail or an EFT payment to the healthcare organization. The related journal entry for receipt of payment will occur as follows:

02/15/20X2	D) cash	$10	
	C) A/R		$10

The A/R account is credited (or lowered in value) when payment is received, because the reimbursement for the single supply item is no longer receivable. Because the A/R account is utilized in the accrual accounting method, the cash flows related to a supply use and its corresponding reimbursement are not associated with the supply's operating revenue transaction on the same date. This demonstrates the vital need for an organization utilizing the accrual accounting method to run a statement of cash flows. This statement enables the healthcare organization operating under the accrual method of accounting

Helpful tip: Under the cash accounting method, a revenue account will only increase (be credited) when payment is received for a service/item that was previously provided during patient care. This date of reimbursement is often many days (usually months) after the date of service, as demonstrated by the payment receipt date on the journal entry example here (as compared to the 11/15/20X1 original date of service). Based on electronic payment arrangements and other requirements set forth by some state laws, this electronic funds transfer (EFT) reimbursement often occurs within an estimated 45-day time period from the original date of service.

Helpful tip: Note that under the accrual accounting method, the revenue is recorded immediately when earned (on the 11/15/20X1 date of service), regardless of when (or if) payment is received by a third-party payer, the patient, or another entity. Additionally, because the revenue is recorded immediately when earned and used during patient care delivery, the service is provided, and the healthcare organization has not yet been reimbursed. Therefore, A/R is increased because the healthcare organization is awaiting reimbursement for a good/service already provided.

to properly track the flow of cash inflows and outflows—since they are not associated with specific revenue and expense journal entries as they are when operating under the cash method of accounting. This concept and statement of cash flows will be discussed in further detail in Chapter 11.

Healthcare Inventory Methods

The identification of specific, individual inventory/supply item expenses and revenues associated with usage during the delivery of patient care is important to the healthcare organization and varies based on type of inventory, its purpose, and especially the volume (quantity) of items used. Bulk purchases may exist on the books more often with the use of cash accounting methods (as previously demonstrated) because under this accounting method expenses are recorded on the books when paid.

Otherwise, the accrual accounting method identifies individual item values still unused, on the supply shelf (categorized as an organizational asset), and using any specific items consumed during patient care (categorized as an expense or usage). Therefore, the accrual accounting method provides valuable accounting information by maintaining the matching principle GAAP concept.

Inventory Valuation (Assets) Versus Expensing/Usage (Expenses)

Historical cost (purchase price) is often the easiest way to begin valuing the dollar amount of assets located on the healthcare organization's supply shelves, yet still to be used (categorized as inventory under the asset main account). Often, this method is also used to track the use of specific items as they are taken off the organization's supply shelf and used to treat patients (then categorized as inventory/supply expense under the expense main account). However, the time of purchase for inventory item(s) often results in dynamic market economics influencing any specific piece of inventory's purchase price as time progresses. These changes in price are often assumed to only increase—often because of supply/demand market economics, as well as general inflation of U.S. currency.

Several methods exist in order to identify the cost (expense) of using any one inventory item on a healthcare organization's supply shelf. These methods control for many of the same item types purchased either later in time or just recently—at varying market prices as previously discussed. Likewise, methods also exist to value the inventory remaining on the shelf, which are those items that are left unused and therefore remain classified as inventory/supply. Table 6.1 provides a summary of inventory valuation (on the shelf, still unused) and inventory expense (usage) costing methods.

TABLE 6.1   Summary of inventory valuation and expense (usage) costing methods

Inventory valuation method "still on the shelf"	⟷	Inventory expense (costing) method "going out the door"
Specific identification	Periodic	Specific identification
Weighted average	Periodic	Weighted average
FISH (first-in-still-here)	Periodic *and* perpetual calculations	LIFO (last-in-first-out)
LISH (last-in-still-here)	Periodic *and* perpetual calculations	FIFO (first-in-first-out)

   Periodic inventory methods will be described first, followed by the application of perpetual methods. For the purposes of this textbook, the periodic method will be utilized for all valuation/expense methods above, while perpetual will be applied only to the FISH/LIFO and LISH/FIFO inventory valuation/expense methods.

Specific Identification
Often several low-use, low-volume, high-cost inventory items are used in patient care. Often, these items are supplies that resemble implantable medical devices that are tracked to the individual patient level. Other items implanted into the body (such as hernia patches and artificial heart valves) are other examples. Usually, these low-volume items typically cost more than more routinely used disposable medical supplies. Because of these supply characteristics, they are most often tracked and accounted for by using their historical cost at the individual item level. For this reason, they are physically tagged with the purchase price at the time of purchase. This tagged historical cost (which does vary over time based on ongoing market economics), is used as the item's cost (expense) when pulled off the shelf and used during patient care. Those left on the shelf, still tagged with their original purchase price(s), are unused and remain recorded as inventory/supplies under the main asset account.

Periodic Weighted Average (WA)
As an alternative example to specific identification, the weighted average (WA) valuing and costing method works to assess the average value (or cost) or any single item, based on any/all items of similar kind purchased within that same financial period or time frame (usually the current or previous month).

Helpful tip: Notice that both specific identification and weighted average methods have synonymous valuation and expensing (costing) methods. Additionally, the FISH valuation method is synonymous with the LIFO expensing method (F matches with L), and the LISH valuation method is synonymous with the FIFO expensing method (L matches with F). In other words: "Never F-F or L-L, always F-L or L-F."

Helpful tip: Two main financial statements are impacted by (a) having an item sitting on the organization's supply shelf left unused (inventory/supply > asset [real account] > balance sheet) and (b) being pulled off the shelf and used in patient care (inventory/supply expense > expense [nominal account] > statement of operations).

These inventory/supply items are used in high volumes and are also low cost (opposite of those supplies/inventory used with the specific identification method previously mentioned). Examples may include bandages, utensils in a hospital cafeteria, and pills/medication.

Instead of tagging each individual inventory item (such as every single bandage) with its individual historical cost at the time of purchase, the average cost of that item is calculated using the total number of items purchased, the total dollar amount spent on that item for a time period, and the total number of inventory items used during any specific financial accounting time period.

Example of calculating the periodic WA of a single bandage, total supply expense, and remaining inventory value of bandages:

Fredericksburg Medical Clinic bandage purchases for 5/20X1:

May 1	beginning inventory	200	$2.50 ea.	= $500
May 9	purchase	150	$1.00 ea.	= $150
May 17	purchase	300	$2.00 ea.	= $600
May 25	purchase	250	$2.35 ea.	= $587.50

Total bandages used (expensed) in May 20X1 (given): **295**

Step 1: calculate the total number of bandages on hand and purchased in 5/20X1 = 900

Step 2: calculate the total amount spent on bandages in 5/20X1 = $1,837.50

Step 3: calculate the periodic WA amount for a single bandage in 5/20X1:

$1,837.50/900 = **$2.04** (WA per bandage purchased in 5/20X1)

Step 4: calculate the total bandage expense for 5/20X1 using the periodic WA method:

295 ($2.04) = **$601.80**

Step 5: calculate the total value of bandages left unused/on the shelf:

900 total inventory – 295 used = 605 remaining ($2.04) = **$1,234.20**

Note: WA inventory remaining and expensed is calculated using periodic WA only (versus perpetual WA). While perpetual WA calculations are normally completed using financial accounting software programs, it will not be addressed, in order to keep a focus on the manual process of inventory calculations.

Helpful tip: When calculating the WA of any single inventory item, the beginning inventory value and recent purchase total values are required, in addition to the total number of inventory units used (expensed) over a specific time period.

FISH—first-in-still-here: oldest items purchased remain on the shelf (unused supplies > assets)

LIFO—last-in-first-out: most recently purchased items are used first (supply expense > expense)

The FISH valuation method (what is valued as inventory/supplies > assets) matches with the LIFO expensing (or costing) method (what is being used to treat patients as inventory/supply expense). The primary methodology behind LIFO expensing is the act of choosing the historical cost (purchase price) of the items that were most recently purchased (the newest items on the self are the first to be used/expensed). In doing this, it leaves the oldest items left on the shelf, having been there the longest and remaining unused (first-in-still-here).

Using the periodic inventory system, the entire prior month of inventory purchases/sales are used to assess item valuation and expenses for this FISH/LIFO method—all at one time.

Example of calculating the periodic LIFO costing/expensing and FISH valuation and of bandages:

Fredericksburg Medical Clinic bandage purchases and usages for 5/20X1:

May 1	beginning inventory	200	$2.50 ea.	= $500
May 3	usage	75		
May 9	purchase	150	$1.00 ea.	= $150
May 10	usage	20		
May 15	usage	10		
May 17	purchase	300	$2.00 ea.	= $600
May 18	usage	90		
May 25	purchase	250	$2.35 ea.	= $587.50
May 30	usage	100		

Step 1: calculate the total number of bandages used in 5/20X1: **295**

Step 2: calculate periodic LIFO by starting at the end of the month (bottom of 5/20X1) and pulling inventory off the shelf as needed until 295 total bandages used is reached:

250	$2.35 ea. (from May 25 purchase)	= $587.50
45	$2.00 ea. (from May 17 purchase)	= $90
295	bandages used in 5/20X1	= **$677.50 total bandage expense using periodic LIFO**

Step 3: calculate the remaining value of bandages still left on the shelf using periodic FISH:

255	$2.00 ea. (remaining from May 17 purchase)	= $510
150	$1.00 ea. (from May 9 purchase)	= $150
200	$2.50 ea. (from May 1 beginning inventory)	= $500
605	bandages remaining unused (still on the shelf)	= **$1,160 total bandages remaining periodic using FISH**

Periodic LISH Valuation and FIFO Expensing (L-F)

LISH—last-in-still-here: most recently purchased items remain on the shelf (unused supplies > assets)

FIFO—first-in-first-out: oldest items purchased are used first (supply expense > expense)

Switching acronyms and gears, now the inventory supply and usage for Fredericksburg Medical Clinic can be calculated using LISH/FIFO valuation and expensing (costing) methods.

Example of calculating the periodic FIFO costing/expensing and LISH valuation and of bandages:

Fredericksburg Medical Clinic bandage purchases and usages for 5/20X1:

May 1	beginning inventory	200	$2.50 ea.	= $500
May 3	usage	75		

May 9	purchase	150	$1.00 ea.	= $150
May 10	usage	20		
May 15	usage	10		
May 17	purchase	300	$2.00 ea.	= $600
May 18	usage	90		
May 25	purchase	250	$2.35 ea.	= $587.50
May 30	usage	100		

Step 1: calculate the total number of bandages used in 5/20X1: **295**

Step 2: calculate periodic FIFO by starting at the beginning of the month (top of 5/20X1) and pulling inventory off the shelf as needed until 295 total bandages used is reached:

200	$2.50 ea. (from May 1 beginning inventory)	= $500
95	$1.00 ea. (from May 9 purchase)	= $95
295	bandages used in 5/20X1	= **$595.00 total bandage expense using periodic FIFO**

Step 3: calculate the remaining value of bandages still left on the shelf (inventory/supply > assets) using periodic LISH:

250	$2.35 ea. (from May 25 purchase)	= $587.50
300	$2.00 ea. (from May 17 purchase)	= $600
55	$1.00 ea. (remaining from May 9 purchase)	= $55
605	bandages remaining unused (still 'on the shelf')	= **$1,242.50 total bandages remaining using periodic LISH**

Perpetual LISH Valuation and FIFO Expensing (L-F)
LISH—last-in-still-here: most recently purchased items remain on the shelf (unused supplies > assets)

FIFO—first-in-first-out: oldest items purchased are used first (supply expense > expense)

Helpful tip: Keep in mind that FISH is synonymous with LIFO and LISH is synonymous with FIFO (F-L and L-F, make sure these first letters do not match). Therefore, by calculating the inventory going out the door (i.e., expenses/usages), this means that you now also know the inventory left on the shelf (i.e., supply/inventory). To calculate inventory being used (also known as expensing/costing), one is also simultaneously identifying the value of inventory remaining on the shelf (inventory valuation).

Transitioning to the perpetual method of inventory accountability (valuation and expensing/costing of individual inventory items), a significant approach to the given monthly inventory purchase/usage data is required. Under the recently discussed periodic inventory method (for WA, FISH/LIFO, and LISH/FIFO), the total number of inventory items for the entire previous month is calculated (previously 295 for both examples above) and then pulled off the shelf based on designated LIFO or FIFO methods—and remaining inventory valuated based on corresponding FISH/LISH valuation methods. Perpetual inventory differs from periodic in that an ongoing inventory assessment is conducted during the current month, rather than being able to look back at the previous month's entire inventory usage data all at one time. Instead, a line-by-line assessment of used/remaining inventory is conducted throughout (during) the month of provided inventory data.

Example of calculating the perpetual FIFO costing/expensing and LISH valuation of bandages:

Fredericksburg Medical Clinic bandage purchases and usages for 5/20X1:

May 1	beginning inventory	200	$2.50 ea.	= $500
May 3	usage	75		
May 9	purchase	150	$1.00 ea.	= $150
May 10	usage	20		
May 15	usage	10		
May 17	purchase	300	$2.00 ea.	= $600
May 18	usage	90		
May 25	purchase	250	$2.35 ea.	= $587.50
May 30	usage	100		

Step 1: starting with 5/01 (top/beginning of the month), begin a perpetual FIFO assessment line-by-line to expense out all 295 usage (expensed) inventory line items.

5/03 usage	75	75 @ $2.50 ea. (from May 1 beginning inventory)	= $187.50
5/10 usage	20	20 @ $2.50 ea. (from May 1 beginning inventory)	= $50.00
5/15 usage	10	10 @ $2.50 ea. (from May 1 beginning inventory)	= $25
5/18 usage	90	90 @ $2.50 ea. (from May 1 beginning inventory)	= $225.00
5/30 usage	100	5 @ $2.50 ea. (from May 1 beginning inventory)	
		+ 95 @ $1.00 ea. (from May 15 purchase)	= $12.50 + $95
	295	bandages used in 5/20X1	= **$595.00 total bandage expense using perpetual FIFO**

Step 2: calculate the remaining value of bandages still left on the shelf (inventory/supply > assets) using perpetual LISH:

250	$2.35 ea. (from May 25 purchase)	= $587.50
300	$2.00 ea. (from May 17 purchase)	= $600
55	$1.00 ea. (remaining from May 9 purchase)	= $55
605	bandages remaining unused (still on the shelf)	= **$1,242.50 total bandages remaining using perpetual LISH**

Perpetual FISH Valuation and LIFO Expensing (F-L)
FISH—first-in-still-here: oldest items purchased remain on the shelf (unused supplies > assets)

LIFO—last-in-first-out: most recently purchased items are used first (supply expense > expense)

Finally, the last method of inventory valuation and costing (expensing) involves a perpetual (ongoing) assessment of individual inventory (item) identification using the FISH/LIFO methods. Such actions are like the perpetual LISH/FIFO method, except now, throughout the month of May inventory items are assessed on a line-by-line (ongoing) basis with the newest/more recently purchased items being used first.

Example of calculating the perpetual LIFO costing/expensing and FISH valuation and of bandages:

Fredericksburg Medical Clinic bandage purchases and usages for 5/20X1:

May 1	beginning inventory	200	$2.50 ea.	= $500
May 3	usage	75		
May 9	purchase	150	$1.00 ea.	= $150
May 10	usage	20		
May 15	usage	10		
May 17	purchase	300	$2.00 ea.	= $600
May 18	usage	90		
May 25	purchase	250	$2.35 ea.	= $587.50
May 30	usage	100		

Step 1: starting with 5/01, begin a perpetual LIFO assessment line-by-line to expense out all usage (expensed) inventory line items:

5/03 usage	75	75 @ $2.50 ea. (from May 1 beginning inventory)	= $187.50
5/10 usage	20	20 @ $1.00 ea. (from May 9 purchase)	= $20.00
5/15 usage	10	10 @ $1.00 ea. (from May 9 purchase)	= $10.00
5/18 usage	90	90 @ $2.00 ea. (from May 17 purchase)	= $180.00
5/30 usage	<u>100</u>	100 @ $2.35 ea. (from May 25 purchase)	= $235.00
	295	bandages used in 5/20X1	= **$632.50 total bandage expense using perpetual LIFO**

Step 2: calculate the remaining value of bandages still left on the shelf (inventory/supply > assets) using perpetual FISH:

150	$2.35 ea. (remaining from May 25 purchase)	= $352.50
210	$2.00 ea. (remaining from May 17 purchase)	= $420.00
120	$1.00 ea. (remaining from May 9 purchase)	= $120.00
<u>125</u>	$2.50 ea. (remaining from May 1 beginning inventory)	= $312.50
605	bandages remaining unused (still on the shelf)	= **$1,205.00 total bandages remaining using perpetual FISH**

Which Inventory Method to Choose?

Often an important debate among healthcare administrators, the decision regarding which inventory method to utilize is quite important—especially because such decisions affect

- inventory (supply) account values under the asset main account on the organization's balance sheet, and
- inventory (supply) expense account values under the expense main account on the organization's statement of operations.

It should be noticeable in the inventory calculation examples that depending on which inventory method is chosen for any single inventory item within the healthcare organization, different total cost (expense) and inventory (asset) values will occur. While the actual number of inventory items used and left on the shelf (still unused) remains the same for every calculation, a slight manipulation of total expense and total asset account values may be exploited by the organization, based on the organization's preferences and organization needs.

Further, it is most important to choose an inventory method that best matches the current workflow and type of inventory item being assessed. It does not make sense to track very low-cost, high-use items (such as bandages, cafeteria forks, etc.) at a specific identification level. Likewise, high-cost, low-use inventory items (such as implantable devices and other one-time use inventory/supplies) should be tracked at a more item-specific level, using historical cost.

Regardless of which inventory method is chosen for any single supply item, the same dollar amount (historical cost) spent on the item in any given time period will also never change. In all of the chapter's LIFO/FIFO inventory examples, all values (both costing + valuation) for each method sum to $1,837.50. This is because the total amount spent on the inventory item during the month, as well as the number of items used during the month of May, did not change in any of the examples. The dollar values of the expense and asset accounts were simply trading amounts based on the inventory method utilized in each example.

In Summary

After human resources (labor/payroll), supplies/inventory are easily the next highest overall expense for the healthcare organization. Often approaching

Helpful tip: Note that for every inventory valuation/expensing method above, the total number of inventory items used (295) never changed, nor did the number of inventory items remaining on the shelf/unused (605). This is a good way to double-check your work when addressing inventory valuation/costs between methods. At the end of both expense and valuation calculations, add up the number of items used and the items left on the shelf to ensure they match the total number of beginning inventory items.

TRY ON YOUR OWN

Using the inventory/supply practical exercise located at the end of this chapter, cut out the example healthcare supply inventory items purchased and practice the periodic weighted average and periodic/perpetual LIFO/FISH and FIFO/LISH healthcare expensing (costing) and valuation problems by physically identifying those inventory items going out the door and those remaining on the shelf (which will be those left in the original pile of inventory).

50% of total operational expenses for any given time period, much attention should be devoted to the effective capturing of any/all organizational inventory (supply) expenses used during the course of patient care, while also establishing and correctly utilizing appropriate valuation and costing (expensing) inventory methods. This action will allow the inventory/supply asset and expense subaccounts to reflect correct and current values anytime a balance sheet and/or statement of operations is generated for further analysis and interpretation. While most healthcare accounting systems involve an automated software to assist in this process, it is important for the healthcare leader to master the manual inventory calculation processes to clearly understand the behind-the-scenes inventory processes for any single inventory item within the organization.

Additional healthcare inventory problems are provided at the end of this chapter to assist the learner in mastering inventory valuation/expensing calculations. Solutions are provided on the Cognella Active Learning website.

Chapter Questions

1. Discuss the A/P voucher process for any specific inventory item and why it should be utilized with healthcare inventory/supply management. Next, list the steps that you would incorporate into any specific type of healthcare organization (doctor's office, outpatient surgery suite, large acute care hospital) to ensure the A/P voucher process is effective in ensuring accuracy in healthcare supply management and associated payments to the medical vendor(s).

2. Describe the difference between periodic and perpetual inventory methods. Using healthcare inventory supply examples, discuss why or when a healthcare administrator would choose the periodic method for any one supply, as compared to the periodic method for another.

3. Discuss how the LIFO and FIFO inventory costing methods (and their corresponding valuation methods) directly affect the value of the supply/inventory accounts on both the balance sheet and the statement of operations.

4. Provide examples of inventory/supply items in a healthcare organization that are more suitable for using the periodic weighted average inventory costing/valuation method. Next, discuss why other healthcare

inventory/supply items would be considered for the specific identification costing/valuation method.

5. Describe how adding the total inventory expense for a single item to the total inventory value (for that same item) helps reconcile valuation/expensing calculations across multiple FIFO/LISH and LIFO/FISH analyses. What does it mean if any of these do not add up to the same value?

Healthcare Inventory Practical Exercise: Fredericksburg Urgent Care

This practical exercise is provided for the student to manually create two groups (piles) of inventory paper cutouts by conducting a physical (tangible manipulative) movement of inventory items out the door (inventory/supply expense account) and leaving unused items on the shelf (inventory/supply account). The individual cutout bandages have the historical cost (purchase price) for that individual item (bandage) and the date of purchase (month/day) shown on the bandages themselves.

Once the bandages are cut out using scissors, complete the inventory expense/valuation questions below.

1. Using the *periodic weighted average* costing method, determine the cost of using 5 bandages for patient care for the month of July for Fredericksburg Urgent Care.

   Next, calculate the remaining value of inventory left on the shelf.

   Reminder: A computer program/software is recommended for the calculation of perpetual WA costing and valuation. It will not be conducted here, since it is not part of the manual accounting process.

2. Using the *periodic LIFO* costing method, determine the total cost of using 3 bandages on 7/08/XX and 2 bandages on 7/27/XX for patient care in July for Fredericksburg Urgent Care.

   Next, calculate the remaining value of inventory left on the shelf. What is this valuation method that corresponds with LIFO costing?

3. Using the *periodic FIFO* costing method, determine the total cost of using 3 bandages on 7/08/XX and 2 bandages on 7/27/XX for patient care in July for Fredericksburg Urgent Care.

   Next, calculate the remaining value of inventory left on the shelf. What is this valuation method that corresponds with FIFO costing?

Helpful tip: When completing healthcare inventory expensing (costing) and valuation problems, use the total historical cost value for any single inventory item in a given time period to double-check your work in a specific calculation, as well as between problems. For example, in all the examples provided above, every calculated inventory valuation (left-on-the-shelf value) plus its respective costing (expensing) amount (what was used and went out the door) will always add up to $1,837.50. If at any time the total valuation and expense calculated values do not add up to the same total historical cost, there is an error present that needs to be corrected. The same double check can be done for the total number of items costed (expensed) and valued (as remaining assets).

Helpful tip: Line up all of the bandages in order of historical cost (purchase price) date—top to bottom. You are creating one column of bandages (cutouts) with early July at the top, through end of July at the bottom of the column. Reset back to this single, date-ordered column between each calculation/method below.

4. Using the *perpetual FIFO* costing method, determine the total cost of using 3 bandages on 7/08/XX and 2 bandages on 7/27/XX for patient care in July for Fredericksburg Urgent Care.

    Next, calculate the remaining value of inventory left on the shelf. What is this valuation method that corresponds with FIFO costing?

5. Using the *perpetual LIFO* costing method, determine the total cost of using 3 bandages on 7/08/XX and 2 bandages on 7/27/XX for patient care in July for Fredericksburg Urgent Care.

    Next, calculate the remaining value of inventory left on the shelf. What is this valuation method that corresponds with LIFO costing?

6. For all the calculations above, discuss what values you have calculated will show up on Fredericksburg Urgent Care's balance sheet, versus its statement of operations.

Healthcare Inventory Practical Exercise Cutouts for Fredericksburg Urgent Care

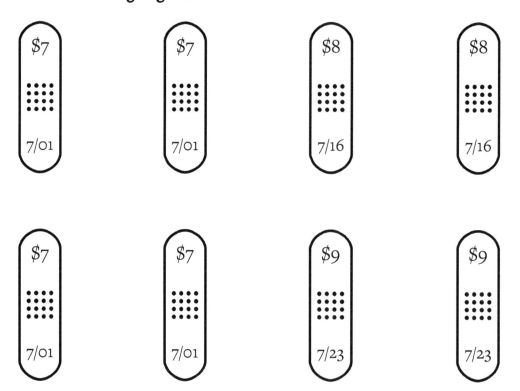

Additional Healthcare Inventory Problems

1. The following is inventory data regarding a single supply/inventory item frequently used at Fredericksburg Hospital from November 20X2:

11/01	beginning inventory	100	$0.50 ea.
11/03	purchase	50	$0.52 ea.
11/05	usage	75	
11/15	purchase	200	$0.55 ea.
11/18	purchase	70	$0.60 ea.
11/25	usage	100	
11/28	usage	20	
11/29	usage	5	
11/30	purchase	200	$0.62 ea.

Calculate both the ***inventory expense*** and ***remaining inventory*** account values for the month of November utilizing the following inventory costing/valuation methods:

   a. Periodic weighted average
   b. Periodic FIFO/LISH
   c. Perpetual FIFO/LISH
   d. Periodic LIFO/FISH
   e. Perpetual LIFO/FISH

2. The following is inventory data regarding a single supply/inventory item frequently used at Fredericksburg Hospital from December 20X5:

12/01	beginning inventory	250	$1.75 ea.
12/03	usage	15	
12/05	usage	50	
12/10	purchase	100	$2.50 ea.
12/15	purchase	50	$2.55 ea.
12/16	usage	75	
12/18	usage	20	
12/25	purchase	100	$2.56 ea.
12/26	purchase	20	$2.58 ea.
12/28	usage	10	
12/30	usage	55	

Calculate both the *inventory expense* and *remaining inventory* account values for the month of November utilizing the following inventory costing/valuation methods:

a. Periodic weighted average
b. Periodic FIFO/LISH
c. Perpetual FIFO/LISH
d. Periodic LIFO/FISH
e. Perpetual LIFO/FISH

3. The following is inventory data regarding a single supply/inventory item frequently used at Fredericksburg Hospital from July 20X0:

7/01	beginning inventory	105	$10.50 ea.
7/05	purchase	50	$10.55 ea.
7/06	usage	75	
7/08	usage	5	
7/10	purchase	50	$10.00 ea.
7/12	usage	10	
7/14	usage	5	
7/20	purchase	20	$11.00 ea.
7/25	usage	30	
7/28	usage	3	
7/30	usage	1	

Calculate both the *inventory expense* and *remaining inventory* account values for the month of November utilizing the following inventory costing/valuation methods:

a. Periodic weighted average
b. Periodic FIFO/LISH
c. Perpetual FIFO/LISH
d. Periodic LIFO/FISH
e. Perpetual LIFO/FISH

Accounting for Healthcare Depreciation

Introduction

The healthcare organization's building(s) and equipment will wear out over time. Reusable items in regular healthcare operations typically involve clinical and administrative equipment, as well as the buildings operated by the healthcare organization. These assets may be designated as both clinical and/or administrative in purpose. An assessment of the wearing-out process for equipment and buildings is to be conducted, and costs associated with this wear and tear are to be systematically allocated to respective depreciation accounts. As a result, the depreciation of the organization's buildings and equipment will only generate additional operating expenses for the organization. This chapter focuses on how to properly allocate the wearing out (depreciation expense) of buildings and equipment and the cost allocation of such activity. Capitalizing on the depreciation process in terms of strategic planning and future asset replacement is also addressed.

Learning Objectives

By the end of this chapter, the student should be able to:

- Define deprecation and its standard purpose in healthcare operations.
- Discuss the appearance of any item on a balance sheet being depreciated.
- Define and apply depreciation expense and accumulated depreciation account calculations for standard healthcare organizational assets.
- List two primary reasons why a healthcare organization would choose to depreciate mission-critical assets.

- Define the straight-line deprecation method and apply its formula to calculate depreciation expense and accumulated depreciation values for any given financial period.
- Define accelerated depreciation and the sum-of-years digits depreciation methods and apply their formulas to annual depreciation expense calculations.

Key Terms

1. Depreciation
2. Depreciation expense
3. Accumulated depreciation
4. Straight-line depreciation method
5. Accelerated depreciation method
6. Sum-of-years digits depreciation method

Depreciable Assets—Equipment

In healthcare, it is common for any organization to possess a significant amount of medical equipment. Such assets may be used for diagnostics, therapeutics, surgeries, or other services to deliver care to patients. Examples of medical equipment that should be monitored and depreciated over time on the books include the following:

- imaging devices (such as X-ray and ultrasound machines)
- robotic surgery equipment (such as da Vinci robotic surgical equipment)
- sterilization equipment (autoclaves)
- electrocardiogram (EKG) equipment and related devices

Also classified as equipment on the healthcare organization's books is the equipment that supports health service delivery and related operations but is not directly involved in clinical care like the items above. Examples of nonclinical equipment in the healthcare organization often resembles that of any typical business office, to include the following:

- paper, copy/scan/fax machines
- desks, chairs, trash cans, etc.
- computers (desktops, laptops, tablets, etc.)

While these equipment assets are typically purchased at different dates during normal operations for the organization, their historical cost (purchase price) is most often the value presented on the organization's balance sheet under the asset account. However, these examples and other equipment items in the healthcare organization do not hold their historical value for long. As time goes by and they are utilized in the delivery of care for patients (including the nonclinical equipment), these assets will begin to wear out, succumbing to the elements and related environmental conditions in the organization. The wear and tear can be assigned a dollar value, as it is understood that organizational equipment will lose its historical value over time. This allocation of total wear and tear for all of the organization's equipment during any single accounting period is able to be classified as an operational expense known as "depreciation expense—equipment" and is classified under the main expense account of the organization's chart of accounts.

Depreciable Assets—Building(s)

Similarly, healthcare organizations may also own their own building (or buildings) to assist in the delivery of care. Just like the organization's equipment, buildings may be designated as clinical care locations, administrative staff locations, or even both. Additionally, while the original, historical cost of the building is listed as the asset's value on the organization's balance sheet, buildings are expected to lose their value over time. Therefore, buildings will depreciate over time, and this wear and tear is assigned a systematic dollar value that is captured and reported on a regular basis under "depreciation expense—building(s)." This process is similar to the depreciation procedure conducted for the organization's equipment.

Accumulated Deprecation

To capture the wear-and-tear expense values for any organizational building and/or equipment, the accumulated depreciation account is used. This account is considered a contra-asset account, meaning that as it gets larger in value, it lowers (pulls value out of) the organization's original historic cost (value) on the balance sheet. Since the depreciation (wearing-out) process captures depreciation expense for any specific asset, this allows the organization's expenses to increase on the statement of operations, while also lowering the item's book value on the balance sheet. This process on the two financial statements occurs simultaneously. Figure 7.1 is a sample journal entry for a single monthly adjusting entry to capture accumulated depreciation for an X-ray machine.

| 5/31/20X6 | D) depreciation expense – x-ray equipment | $200 | |
| | C) accumulated depreciation – equipment | | $200 |

FIGURE 7.1 One-month depreciation adjusting journal entry example.

Emphasizing the main accounts under which the depreciation journal entry subaccounts fall, the depreciation expense account is a true operating expense. Operating expenses (including depreciation expenses) fall on the organization's statement of operations. As organization assets are depreciated, overall expenses for the organization are increased, and this lowers the organization's overall profit margin. As the organization captures more of the wearing-out value throughout the financial period, depreciation expense will continue to increase (accumulate) over time. At the same time, the accumulated depreciation account will increase over time as well. However, unlike the depreciation expense account (located under expenses), accumulated depreciation is classified as a contra-asset account, located under the main asset account on the organization's chart of accounts.

The accumulated depreciation account will continue to increase in value, which lowers the overall value of the asset account to which it is related (located directly above it on the balance sheet). This is also why accumulated depreciation is credited when recording a depreciation journal entry—because to lower an asset value, a credit is required, and this is what is basically happening here. The X-ray machine from Figure 7.1 would appear on the organization's balance sheet after the 1-month journal entry depreciation journal entry as shown in Figure 7.2.

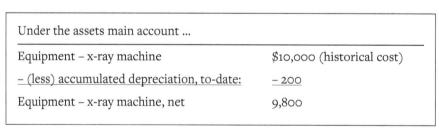

Under the assets main account …	
Equipment – x-ray machine	$10,000 (historical cost)
– (less) accumulated depreciation, to-date:	– 200
Equipment – x-ray machine, net	9,800

FIGURE 7.2 Example of accumulated depreciation on the organization's balance sheet.

As the equipment wears out over time, the assessed wearing-out value is captured under depreciation expense and also tallied under the accumulated depreciation (fund) account for that same asset. The depreciation expense account for any tangible asset (equipment and/or building) is always a regular operating expense, falling under the main expense account for the organization. This increase in expenses as a result of the wearing-out process of buildings and equipment lowers the organization's profit margin at the end of any specific financial period. Because expenses are nominal accounts and zero out at the end of the annual financial period, the depreciation expense account will start over at $0 at the beginning of the next financial period.

Contrary to the depreciation expense (nominal) account, the accumulated depreciation contra-asset account grows in value over time and lowers the value of the tangible building or equipment asset account associated with it on the balance sheet (as shown in Figure 7.2). However, the accumulated depreciation account falls under the main asset account for the organization—which is a real account and therefore carries over its values at the end of the financial period. Therefore, all accumulated depreciation accounts for buildings and equipment will continue to grow systematically and carry their end-of-period values into the next financial period.

Why Depreciation?

One may be wondering why one would capture the wearing-out value of any tangible asset owned by the organization—especially because this process increases the healthcare organization's overall operating expenses. There are several advantages to capturing depreciation expense and reporting the associated depreciation expense and accumulated depreciation on the organization's financial statements. While items that are typically depreciated are often mission-critical assets and are often high dollar value, any large capital asset that will need to be replaced should be depreciated by the organization. This leads to the benefits of depreciating such selected organizational assets.

Reason #1: Save for a rainy day.
All healthcare organizations possess equipment on their balance sheet, required to successfully deliver high-quality healthcare services. Buildings and equipment may also be owned by the organization (if not otherwise leased*), and if they are not available or are deemed inoperable, the organization must obtain another asset that performs similar tasks to meet operational needs. Purchasing a new building or equipment is a significant cost to the organization. Often these assets cost an amount beyond what any typical healthcare organization has in savings at any moment, especially if an unbudgeted (unplanned) purchase.

Ongoing changes related to operating and capital leases will be further discussed in Chapter 13 (Cognella Active Learning website).

Depreciation expense is recorded as an operating expense for the organization (a debit entry to the item's respective depreciation expense account). At the same time, the corresponding journal entry is recorded as a credit to the item's respective accumulated depreciation (contra-asset) account. The accumulated depreciation account continues to accept depreciation expense values over time, growing higher in value year after year (as a real account). When a piece of equipment or the building needs to be replaced, this systematic depreciation allocation of funds allows the organization to already have cash on hand in the accumulated depreciation account to purchase another similar asset. Otherwise, if cash was not on hand in the accumulated depreciation fund account for future replacement of mission-critical tangible assets, the organization would have to finance the needed replacement. This means taking out a loan and paying additional interest expenses for a new asset (a more costly replacement alternative).

Reason #2: Provide a for-profit healthcare organization tax shield.

Primarily applicable to for-profit healthcare organizations, but somewhat advantageous to those not-for-profits that want to ensure they do not look "too profitable," the capturing of wear and tear of depreciation expenses increases the organization's overall expenses on its statement of operations. Therefore, when depreciation is funded, the organization's overall expense account is inflated. However, this money is technically a "noncash" transaction, meaning that it never leaves the organization. In other words, there is no negative cash flow for depreciation expense transactions (it is an internally restricted fund account). It is expensed on the statement of operations and saved in the respective accumulated depreciation account for the future repurchase of large, mission-critical, expensive assets in the future.

In the end, the funding of depreciation helps healthcare organizations plan for the known wear and tear on their building(s) and equipment used in regular healthcare operations. The healthcare industry requires a significant amount of assets to complete its mission, and the use of allocating depreciation over time assists in the requirement to replace mission-critical assets. Additional benefits vary between for-profit and not-for-profit organizations, but it is highly common to depreciate items between both organizations to ensure the long-term viability of the organization.

Depreciation Methods

Multiple depreciation methods exist to calculate the value of depreciation expense for any single asset over a specified time period. From Figure 7.2, the X-ray machine had a net value of $9,800 after the depreciation expense of $200 was subtracted from its original, historical cost. GAAP procedures inform how to calculate the reoccurring $200 depreciation expense amount for any asset being depreciated. Further, this piece of equipment is only valued at $9,800 on the organization's balance sheet ("on the books"). This is because the concept of depreciation specifically involves cost allocation, not valuation. If the organization wanted to put the equipment up for sale in true market conditions, supply/demand and regular market economics influence the item's sale price. The historical cost and a systematic method to capture wear and tear as depreciable expense over the life of the equipment requires use of a depreciation method to allocate this organizational cost (book value only).

Method #1: Straight-Line Depreciation

The most common (and usually default) method of depreciation used in healthcare operations is the straight-line method. If there is no specific mention of what depreciation method was used, it is common to simply assume the straight-line method was utilized. Here, some important terms are to be introduced.

- *Useful life*: Every asset (buildings and/or equipment) has a useful life, which represents the average life span of the asset's purposeful use under normal operating conditions. This figure is most often reported in years to the healthcare organization on the date of asset acquisition.
- *Salvage value*: A dollar figure ($) that is provided to the healthcare organization on the date of acquisition that represents an estimated amount the organization should be able to receive when the asset reaches its useful life and is then sold. It is important to note that the asset can be sold and used for other purposes instead of what was originally intended (cut up into parts to sell or other completely different uses besides the asset's original purpose).

Both useful life and salvage value are important pieces of information that need to be obtained on the purchase date for any large asset that is indented to be depreciated. The healthcare administrator is not to estimate or fabricate these values, as they can directly affect the organization's financial statements. Instead, the medical equipment vendor, salesperson, or other third-party professional (such as a specialized healthcare marketer and/or healthcare actuary) are able to provide such figures in order to have an objective assessment of the asset's salvage value and projected useful life.

As with all depreciation methods to be reviewed, the straight-line method possesses a formula to assist with calculation of (a) total depreciation over the entire useful life of the asset and (b) accumulated depreciation values over any specified financial period(s), as shown in Figure 7.3.

1) historical cost − salvage value = total depreciation expense
2) total depreciation amount/useful life (in years) = annual depreciation expense
3) annual depreciation expense/12 = monthly depreciation expense

FIGURE 7.3   Straight-line depreciation formula.

Straight-line depreciation example #1:
A physician's office purchased an ultrasound machine for $12,000 (historical cost) on 3/01/20X3. Its useful life is estimated at 8 years, and it has a salvage value of $500. Therefore:

1. $12,000 − 500 = 11,500 total depreciation expense (over the entire useful life)
2. 11,500/8 years = 1,438 annual depreciation expense
3. 1,438/12 = 120 monthly depreciation expense

- Question 1: What is the *depreciation expense* on 5/01/20X3?
   Since depreciation expense is a nominal account, it resets to $0 at the beginning of every financial period for the organization. However, because this item was purchased on March 1, the amount of depreciation expense during the financial period will be from 3/01/03 through 5/01/03 (2 months).
   Therefore, $120 × 2 months = 240 depreciation expense, to date.
- Question 2: What is the accumulated depreciation on 5/01/20X3?
   Here, the answer is the same. This is because only 2 months have accrued since the purchase date (3/01/03 to 5/01/03), still totaling $240.

Helpful tip: For any depreciation method and related calculations, the total depreciation expense calculated will never be exceeded by the accumulated amount for the asset. Additionally, no asset will be depreciated beyond its useful life. Use these two rules to double-check depreciation calculations.

Straight-line depreciation example #2:
Using the same problem from example #1, multiple financial periods (years) are now involved to help demonstrate the effects on both real (accumulated depreciation) and nominal (depreciation expense) account values.
   A physician's office purchased an ultrasound machine for $12,000 (historical cost) on 11/01/20X3. Its useful life is estimated at 8 years, and it has a salvage value of $500. Therefore:

1. $12,000 − 500 = 11,500 total depreciation expense (over the entire useful life)

2. 11,500/8 years = 1,438 annual depreciation expense
3. 1,438/12 = 120 monthly depreciation expense

- Question 1: What is the *depreciation expense* on 4/01/20X4?

    Since depreciation expense is a nominal account, it resets to $0 at the beginning of every financial period for the organization. Therefore, begin counting the number of months to be expensed on January 1 of the year being solved for (20X4). So, 1/01/20X4 through 4/01/20X4 is 3 months.

    Therefore, $120 × 3 months = 360 depreciation expense, to date.

- Question 2: What is the accumulated depreciation on 4/01/20X4?

    Accumulated depreciation is a contra-asset account, falling under the main asset account on our chart of accounts. Assets are categorized as real accounts and therefore carry over their values from one financial period to the next (in other words, they do not reset to $0 on January 1). As a result:

    11/01/20X3 through 4/01/20X4 = 5 months accrued to date

    $120 × 5 months = 600 accumulated depreciation, to date

As demonstrated, there is a stark difference between the calculation of a nominal depreciation expense account versus a real accumulated depreciation expense account. An important key to identifying these differences in calculations is if/when the time period to be calculated crosses over a financial period.

Helpful tip: Reminder: In this textbook the healthcare organization's financial period will always match with the annual year (January 1 through December 31 of every year).

Method #2: Accelerated Depreciation

Less common than straight-line deprecation in the healthcare industry is a variety of accelerated (faster) depreciation methods. These methods are commonly used to speed up the depreciation process and related timeline. Whereas the straight-line depreciation method works to systematically accumulate the asset's depreciation fund account equally each month and/or year of its useful life, accelerated methods will depreciate the asset in higher values (depreciation expense) early in the asset's useful life, and then begin to decelerate as it gets older. Most often, accelerated depreciation methods are used for buildings or equipment that are to be utilized beyond what is considered normal operating conditions and therefore experience higher-than-normal wear and tear.

Of the several variations of acceleration depreciation methods, a focus on the three most frequently used are addressed. All three methods will utilize a standard depreciation formula, with slight variations based on the percentage of acceleration as chosen by the healthcare leader. An important note: *Salvage value is not utilized* (subtracted from historical cost) using accelerated depreciation methods.

The accelerated depreciation formula (ignore salvage value) is shown in Figure 7.4.

historical cost[1]/(useful life × DB ratio)[2]

Where:

[1] begin with the asset's purchase price and lower by the calculated annual depreciation expense amount

[2] keep the same denominator for each year's depreciation expense calculation

FIGURE 7.4   Accelerated depreciation formula.

Helpful tip: As a reminder, salvage value is not utilized in any accelerated depreciation calculation. By not subtracting salvage value from the historical cost of the asset, it is assumed that the asset will be depreciated (and therefore reach its estimated useful life) much faster than if it were being depreciated on a straight-line basis.

There are several ways to accelerate an asset's depreciation timeline. More aggressive acceleration ratios will result in the asset reaching total depreciation sooner. By using a ratio (fraction) as compared to the straight-line depreciation method, the following acceleration constants can be calculated and used in the denominator (depreciable base, or DB) of the accelerated depreciation formula from Figure 7.4:

150% of straight-line = 1/1.5, or **0.66** of depreciable base

175% of straight-line = 1/1.75, or **0.57** of depreciable base

200% of straight-line = 1/2.0, or **0.50** of depreciable base

Use the respective constant (decimal) above with the corresponding accelerated depreciation rate (%) in the DB denominator ([2]) of the accelerated depreciation formula.

Accelerated depreciation example:
The same ultrasound machine scenario will be used to assist in the demonstration of a 150% accelerated deprecation method and the formula from Figure 7.4.

A physician's office purchased an ultrasound machine for $12,000 (historical cost) on 3/01/20X3. Its useful life is estimated at 8 years, and it has a salvage value of $500. Therefore, the first 3 years of annual depreciation expenses for this asset are calculated as follows:

1. Year 1: $12,000/(8 × 0.66) = 12,000/5.28 = 2,273 annual depreciation expense
2. Year 2: 12,000 – 2,273/5.28 = 1,842 annual depreciation expense
3. Year 3: 12,000 – 2,273 – 1,842/5.28 = 1,493 annual depreciation expense

Compared to straight-line deprecation, the annual depreciation expense amounts will always be different (whereas with straight-line depreciation, annual depreciation expense is always the same). Even with this varying depreciation expense value each year, any single year's monthly depreciation expense can still be calculated by taking any annual amount and dividing by 12 (as usual). Finally, inherent in the accelerated depreciation formula is a very high annual depreciation expense early in the asset's salvage value, and then a systematic lowering of annual depreciation expense for each subsequent annual depreciation expense.

Method #3: Sum-of-Years Digits

Another form of accelerated depreciation involves the sum-of-years digits (SYD) method. Here, the objective is to accelerate the annual depreciation expense amounts early in the asset's useful life and lower these annual amount values as the end of the useful life approaches—while still utilizing the full useful life of the asset. With any SYD depreciation calculation, salvage value is not ignored and is therefore included in the SYD formula.

---

historical cost – salvage value = total deprecation (SYD fraction[1])

For each annual depreciation expense calculation after year 1, lower the numerator by 1 year.

[1]SYD fraction:

Numerator: begin with the total number of useful life years

Denominator: use the sum-of-years' digits of useful life years (a formula constant for all annual calculations)

FIGURE 7.5   Sum-of-years digits formula.

Helpful tip: Only the first 3 of the total 8 useful life annual depreciation expenses are calculated here. The purpose of any of the 3 accelerated methods (150%, 175%, or 200%) are to begin with a large annual depreciation amount and decline quickly to a final annual depreciation expense by the end of the last year of the asset's useful life. Therefore, if the above example were continued for all 8 years, the total of all 8 annual depreciation expense calculations should all sum to the original historical cost of the asset. This is a way to double-check your work upon completion of the calculation. Rounding to the nearest dollar will result in some discrepancies (usually equal to or less than a difference of $10 on most calculations).

SYD depreciation example:

The same ultrasound machine scenario will be used to assist in the demonstration of a SYD accelerated deprecation method and the formula from Figure 7.5.

A physician's office purchased an ultrasound machine for $12,000 (historical cost) on 3/01/20X3. Its useful life is estimated at 8 years, and it has a salvage value of $500. Therefore, the first 3 years of annual depreciation expenses for this asset are calculated as follows:

1. Calculate denominator SYD constant and determine the SYD fraction:
   This asset has 8 years of useful life. Therefore, the SYD of its useful life is $1 + 2 + 3 + 4 + 5 + 6 + 7 + 8 = 36$

   Therefore, the SYD fraction ([1]) for the first year is: (8/36)

2. Calculate each of the first 3 years of annual depreciation expense using the formula from Figure 7.5:

   Year 1: $12,000 − 500 = 11,500 (8/36)

   = 2,556 annual depreciation expense

   Year 2: 11,500 − 2,556 = 8,994 (7/36)

   = 1,749 annual depreciation expense

   Year 3: 11,500 − 2,556 − 1,749 = 7,195 (6/36)

   = 1,199 annual depreciation expense

Helpful tip: Just as with the accelerated depreciation method, the annual depreciation expense amounts calculated using the SYD method are also able to be added up and should equal the original depreciable base (again, disregarding salvage value). Remember that any rounding that occurs will result in this total being slightly different from the original depreciable base amount.

In Summary

Large organizational assets such as medical and business office equipment, and the building or buildings that house healthcare organizations, are all assets on the balance sheet subject to depreciation. Any organization that chooses to utilize depreciation methods for its equipment and buildings capitalizes on multiple financial accounting benefits, including internal fund accounts that serve as internal savings accounts for the replacement of these mission-critical assets. For for-profit healthcare organizations, the inflated operating expenses experienced by depreciating assets lowers the organization's overall profit margin, therefore lowering the organization's tax obligation. Accelerated depreciation methods are often utilized for equipment and buildings that will experience a higher level of operation than normal usage early in their useful life. The decision to depreciate an asset, and with what method, is ultimately made by the organization's leadership.

Additional depreciation expense and accumulated depreciation problems are provided at the end of the chapter to assist the learner in related straight-line, accelerated, and SYD depreciation calculations.

Chapter Questions

1. ABC Medical Clinic has a large, mission-critical piece of equipment used in treating several patients per day. Today it was noted that the machine is not functioning at its best operating ability and will need to be replaced soon. The equipment has not been depreciated throughout its entire useful life with the healthcare organization. Explain the healthcare administrator's options to fund a replacement for the asset without an internal depreciation fund and the implications of these remaining options.

2. Describe the characteristics of both real and nominal account categories. Next, discuss both depreciation expense and accumulated depreciation accounts, which account category they fall under (real versus nominal), and how these accounts behave at the end of any financial period.

3. Discuss why a healthcare organization's leadership team would decide to accelerate an asset's depreciation, versus simply using the straight-line method.

4. Describe how for-profit organizations can exploit an approved tax shield by choosing to depreciate organizational assets.

5. Delineate the difference between accelerated depreciation methods and the sum-of-years digits method regarding the use of salvage value in associated calculations.

Additional Healthcare Depreciation Problems

1. A medical device was purchased on 8/01/20X6 for $13,000 with a useful life of 10 years and salvage value assigned as 20% of the historical cost. Using the straight-line depreciation method, calculate the following:
   a. the total depreciation expense amount over the useful life for the equipment
   b. the annual depreciation expense for the equipment

c. the depreciation expense account value for the asset on 9/01/20X9

d. the accumulated depreciation account value for the asset on 9/01/20X9

2. A medical school has recently built a new building for $12,000,000 on 1/01/20X0 and would like to put it on a straight-line depreciation amortization schedule. Useful life was provided at 50 years and salvage value listed at $1,500,000. Calculate the following:

   a. the total depreciation expense amount over the useful life for the building

   b. the annual depreciation expense for the equipment

   c. the depreciation expense account value for the building on 12/01/20X3

   d. the accumulated depreciation account value for the building on 8/01/20X9

3. A reusable surgical instrument kit was purchased for $5,000 on 5/01/20X2 and will undergo very high utilization early on in its useful life. The practice administrator would like to utilize the 200% accelerated depreciation for the equipment. It was issued with a notification of 5 years of useful life and $100 salvage value. Calculate the following:

   a. the total depreciation expense amount over the useful life of the equipment

   b. all annual depreciation expense amounts for the equipment

   c. the accumulated depreciation account value for the equipment on 5/01/20X4

4. Using the information in question #3 above, recalculate a–c using the 175% accelerated depreciation method for the equipment.

5. A large healthcare organization installed a set of business office furniture and equipment to assist in a large volume of urgent claims and related processing for its organization's health insurance plan. This equipment totaled $25,000 and will be utilized by staffed employees at a very high level of operations early on and then lower in utilization as time passes. At the purchase of this equipment, it was estimated that its collective useful life is 7 years and salvage value is 10% of historical cost. Calculate the following:

   a. the total depreciation expense amount over the useful life of the equipment using the SYD depreciation method

   b. the annual depreciation expense amount for the first 5 years of the equipment's useful life

   c. the accumulated depreciation account value after the first 5 years of the equipment's useful life

8

The Balance Sheet

Introduction

Healthcare organizational leaders are responsible for maintaining the financial well-being of the organization to ensure its doors remain open and quality care is able to be provided. On any day, the organization's financial status will vary significantly—oftentimes dramatically. Bills will become due, electronic payments will be deposited via EFT, and all the while, medical providers will continue earning revenue and incurring expenses by delivering care to patients.

For operational reasons, the healthcare leader will want to conduct a financial litmus test on the organization's financial health (or status) at any single point in time. The balance sheet financial statement accomplishes this task. The purpose of the balance sheet is to provide a snapshot of the organization's financial position (status) at a single point in time. For this reason alone, it should be noted that the balance sheet will always be marked with a single date/time stamp. There will never be a date range on this statement, because it is demonstrating a cross-section view of the organization's financial position at a single point in time.

Learning Objectives

By the end of this chapter, the student should be able to:

- Discuss the purpose of the balance sheet for the healthcare organization.
- List and define the sections and subaccounts of the balance sheet.
- Demonstrate the requirement of the balance sheet to "balance."
- Describe the relationship among an organization's total assets, total liabilities, and net assets.

Key Terms

1. Current and noncurrent assets
2. Current and noncurrent liabilities
3. Asset, liability, and net asset subaccounts (several)

Statement Purpose

The healthcare leader will run a balance sheet to obtain the organization's financial status at any single point in time for a variety of reasons related to operational tasks and daily workflow. Below are examples demonstrating the need for an accurate, up-to-date balance sheet to assess the organization's financial well-being at any single point in time.

- The organization is requesting a note (loan), and the financing organization (the bank) requires the balance sheet for evaluating associated risk and established creditworthiness of the healthcare organization.
- The organization is requesting a trade credit contractual arrangement with its medical supply contractor. This extension of a line of credit associated with medical supplies/inventory payment due dates and associated prepayment discounts requires an assessment of the organization's ability to meet projected, future invoice amounts.
- The organization's board of directors is meeting today, and their operational decisions for the future of the organization will be based on its current financial status and then strategically looking forward. Questions may include the following examples.
  - Do we have enough cash on hand to meet the projected drop in workload as a result of current environmental conditions?
  - Is there room for the organization to expand its liabilities to finance a second location?
  - How much principal is left on the organization's long-term debt financing?
  - What is the organization's current unrestricted-to-restricted net asset (equity) ratio?

A second purpose of this statement is to clearly demonstrate the ongoing dual-entry process of accounting practices within the organization. The balance sheet demonstrates that the three main, *real accounts* on the statement are in balance. Organizational assets, liabilities, and net assets are the three real account categories on the balance sheet, and they will balance in the following manner:

$$\text{economics resources (assets)} - \text{economic obligations (liabilities)}$$
$$= \text{organizational net worth (net assets)}$$

Or, put more simplistically:

what you have (assets) – what you owe (liabilities)
= what you are worth (net assets)

However, it is important to remember the original, basic accounting equation from Chapter 3 and be sure to set all equation variables positive. Therefore, recalling the basic accounting equation with all positive real account variables establishes the basic format of the balance sheet (Figure 8.1):

total assets = total liabilities + net assets

abbreviated balance sheet formula: A = L + NA

alternative balance sheet formula: A = L + E
(remember "net assets" is also termed "equity")

Cincinnati General Hospital Balance Sheet 10/15/2021	
Total Assets	$50,000
Total Liabilities	20,000
Total Net Assets	30,000

FIGURE 8.1   Sample abbreviated balance sheet.

Notice that Cincinnati General Hospital's liabilities and net assets add up to the organization's total assets. The balance sheet balances. If for any reason the organization's A ≠ L + NA, most likely the accounting software would have already identified a data entry error, even prior to allowing the statement to be created in the first place. Otherwise, if the healthcare leader is ever presented with a balance sheet that (a) has more than a single date listed, and/or (b) does not balance, they should know the statement is inaccurate and requires attention prior to use for strategic, financial decision-making purposes.

Statement Format

The balance sheet becomes quite detailed as it is expanded and includes a variety of subaccounts and subtotals that delineate the types of asset, liability, and equity account values and their respective characteristics. The Cincinnati General Hospital example balance sheet the end of this chapter demonstrates the level of detail required for healthcare leaders to generate and interpret this statement on a regular basis. Table 8.1 describes the subtotaling sections of the balance sheet.

TABLE 8.1 Sections of the balance sheet, per GAAP

Section	Purpose	Notes
Current assets (also known as short-term assets)	Demonstrates asset subaccounts that typically can be liquidated within a 1-year period from the date of the statement.	• Current assets are also known as short-term assets. • Noncurrent assets are also known as long-term assets.
Noncurrent assets (also known as long-term assets)	Demonstrates asset subaccounts that typically can be liquidated beyond 1 year from the date of the statement.	• All asset accounts (falling under current and noncurrent categories) are listed in order of liquidity, per GAAP.
Current liabilities (also known as short-term liabilities)	Demonstrates liability subaccounts that typically can be paid within a 1-year period from the date of the statement.	• Current liabilities are also known as short-term liabilities. • Noncurrent liabilities are also known as long-term liabilities.
Noncurrent liabilities (also known as long-term liabilities)	Demonstrates liabilities subaccounts that can be paid beyond 1 year from the date of the statement.	• All liability accounts (falling under current and noncurrent categories) are listed in order of when they will be paid, per GAAP.
Restricted net assets	Those NA (equity) fund accounts that have been legally and ethically obligated for a specific purpose.	• This section of the balance sheet demonstrates the distribution of net worth at the time the statement is generated.

Section	Purpose	Notes
Temporarily restricted net assets	Those NA (equity) fund accounts that have been legally and ethically obligated for use only after a specified, future date.	• A percentage of net worth ownership is important for any for-profit organization that has sold minority shares of its net worth to third-party investors (< 50%).
Unrestricted net assets (also known as the general fund)	This account represents the experienced profit/ loss (revenue – expenses) experienced by the organization, accrued to date.	• The unrestricted fund is the net profit earned to date by the organization.
Revenue and expense summary	This account maintains a zero balance ($0) until the end of a financial period and is only used when "closing the books."	• This account is utilized when the organization "closes its books" and applies the net difference between total revenue and total expenses to NA (net worth). • Because this account falls under NA, it follows the same debit/credit methodology as NA. • See Chapter 10 for further information.

Cincinnati General Hospital Balance Sheet 10/15/2021		
Current Assets	$15,000	
Non-Current Assets	35,000	
Total Assets		$50,000
Current Liabilities	10,000	
Non-Current Liabilities	10,000	
Total Liabilities		20,000
Restricted Net Assets	10,000	
Temporarily Restricted NA	5,000	
Unrestricted NA	15,000	
Total Net Assets		30,000

FIGURE 8.2   Sample abbreviated balance sheet, continued with subtotals shown.

Helpful tip: If all the organization's asset account values equal the sum of its liability and net asset accounts, then naturally the subtotals of the balance sheet will do the same, as shown in Figure 8.2.

Asset Subaccounts

Organizational assets are composed of subaccounts that represent the economic resources that enable the healthcare organization to conduct its operations (the delivery of care). Naturally, one would expect an organization's total assets to be a very high number depending on the overall size of the organization. Assets are the resources that are required to assist the healthcare organization in conducting its mission-related activities.

Asset subaccounts are listed in order of liquidity on the balance sheet, with the most liquid assets listed first, and the less liquid assets following. Asset subaccounts are also categorized into two groups: current and noncurrent assets. Current assets (also known as short-term assets) are assets that can typically be liquidated within a 1-year period from the date of the balance sheet financial statement. Noncurrent assets (also known as long-term assets) are those accounts that will typically take longer than a 1-year period (on average) to liquidate.

Below is a description of each asset subaccount most utilized by any typical healthcare organization. It should be emphasized that many of these account definitions may seem quite basic; a thorough understanding of each subaccount is important to correctly apply the principles of GAAP in everyday operations. While this list is not all inclusive, most healthcare operations will involve the following asset subaccounts.

Cash

Cash is the most liquid organizational asset (being in its true form already) and represents dollar bills on hand, as well as monies being held by banking institutions that are readily available for spending (i.e., the organization's operational checking account or accounts).

Temporary Investments

These are organizational short-term assets in third-party ventures that can typically be liquidated within a 1-year period from the date of the balance sheet financial statement. Examples include money market fund accounts and other liquid investment accounts that may be termed within a 1-year period.

Accrued Interest Receivable

Related to any organizational investments with external firms, this account represents any interest earned by the healthcare organization in such investments but not yet received as of the date of the balance sheet financial statement.

Accounts Receivable

These are utilized to capture gross (volume × charges) revenue earned by the provision of healthcare services and not yet paid by the patient or third-party payer. This gross (unadjusted) A/R value also represents the organization's unreimbursed amounts billed for the delivery of care, including potential organizational write-offs such as contractual adjustments and/or charity care adjustments.

Allowance for Uncollectable Accounts

The AUCA account may be classified as a contra-asset, working against the A/R account directly above it on the balance sheet financial statement. It captures the estimated, future potential write-offs from the gross A/R account, as related to both contractual and charity care adjustment estimates.

Supply/Inventory

Supplies and inventory (synonymous terms) represent one-time use (disposable) medical and nonmedical supplies utilized by the organization to assist in achieving its mission.

Prepaid Expenses

Prepaid insurance, rent, and interest expenses are not true expense accounts, even though they have the word "expense" in their account names. Rather, the "prepaid" qualifier at the beginning of these account names classifies them as organizational assets (which therefore appear on the balance sheet), not expenses (which are presented on the statement of operations). These account values represent items/initiatives that the organization has paid for ahead of time and will benefit both current and future financial accounting periods.

Land

In its simplest form, land is the dirt the healthcare organization is built on. Land does not include land improvements. It is important to note that land does not depreciate.

Land Improvements

The value of all enhancements to the land the organization is built on (does not include dirt). Examples include pavement, parking lot striping, lighting, and landscaping.

Building(s)

The structure (four walls and roof) that constitute the healthcare organization's location(s) used for the provision of care. Buildings do depreciate.

Accumulated Depreciation—Building(s)

The to-date amount of depreciation that has accrued since the original purchase date of the structure(s).

Equipment

Tools/machinery (both medical and nonmedical) used to achieve the healthcare organizational mission. Examples include desks, trash cans, elevators, gurneys, IV poles, MRI scanners, and ventilators.

Accumulated Depreciation—Equipment

The to-date amount of depreciation that has accrued since the original purchase date of the equipment.

Liability Subaccounts

Healthcare organization liabilities are economic obligations that have yet to be paid by the healthcare organization to an external service provider or vendor. While the total value of liability accounts is initially subtracted from total assets to identify organization net worth (per the original, basic accounting equation: $A - L = NA$), the $- L$ variable in the equation is moved to the right side of the equal sign in the equation. This action makes all liability values positive (updated basic accounting equation: $A = L + NA$). Therefore, while liabilities are presented as a positive value on the balance sheet financial statement, it is a number that should be kept low in value, as opposed to the organization's total assets. The higher the value of organizational liabilities, the lower the organization's net worth (net assets).

As reviewed in Chapter 5, it is common for organizations, especially healthcare organizations, to have ongoing liabilities to ensure they have the resources required to conduct their mission. A challenge for the healthcare leader is to ensure that all organizational needs are met to ensure the highest quality of care, yet also contain the total amount of liability at any one time owed by the organization to external, third-party organizations providing such resources.

Accounts Payable

This account represents the total value owed to external organizations for any goods or services provided to the healthcare organization already, but not yet paid by the healthcare organization to the delivering organization/entity. Bills and other current liabilities with qualifying trade credit terms for medical supplies received and not yet paid for by the organization fall under this account until they are paid.

Notes Payable

Notes payable (N/P) constitute a loan to the healthcare organization from a single entity—the bank.

Accrued Interest Payable

This is the amount of interest for any organizational liability that continues to get larger as every month (or other financial time period) passes yet has not had its balance paid yet (per the liability's terms). This account represents accruing interest only, not the principal balance of the liability itself.

Accrued Salary and Wages Payable

The value of payroll (human resources) that has been provided by organizational employees to the organization but has yet to be paid to said employees. This account will grow higher in value as the organization's scheduled pay date approaches. It will then lower and begin to grow again in value as the next pay period begins to accrue and approach the next pay date (cyclic payroll process).

Deferred Rent Revenue

This liability account represents the amount prepaid by an outside organization or individual to the healthcare organization in return for the healthcare organization providing space as a lessor. An example would be a treatment room and/or office space being rented by a third party. Until the space has been provided over a specified time period, the prepayment by the third-party organization remains a liability to the healthcare organization (a "deferred revenue") and will only be reclassified as a revenue once it has been earned/completed over the established lease or rental period.

Deferred Tuition Revenue

Like deferred rent revenue, this account represents the value of prepayments received from students registering for continuing education/classes to be provided by the healthcare organization in the future. Once the continuing education has been delivered, this value is no longer prepaid by the students and has also been fully earned by the healthcare organization that completed the service delivery (education of the students). It is then moved from the liability ("deferred tuition") account to a true revenue account ("tuition revenue").

Bond(s) Payable

A bond is a loan from the community, not the bank. Often extending over a long time period (usually 10-, 20-, or even 30-year terms), the bond pays qualified investors a set percentage of interest every year during the life of the bond. When the bond terms on its final scheduled year, the last annual interest payment is paid to the investors, and their original investment amounts are also returned at this time.

Net Asset Subaccounts

Net assets (also known as "equity") represent the net worth of the organization at the date/time the balance sheet financial statement is generated. It is simply the organization's economics resources (assets) minus its economic obligations (liabilities). Naturally, a high value of net assets is intended for any specific type of healthcare organization. However, not all amounts under this main balance sheet account are accessible and able to be spent freely by the healthcare organization. This is especially the case if philanthropic donations are involved, which is very common for healthcare organizations of all types to gratefully accept.

There are no revenue or expense accounts on the balance sheet. This is because they are located on the organization's statement of operations. However, the net income earned by the healthcare organization (total revenue – total expenses) will affect the net asset account on the balance sheet. Figure 8.3 demonstrates this at a basic level.

From the organization's statement of operations for any specific time period:	
Total Revenue:	$150,000
Total Expenses:	75,000
Profit (or loss):	75,000
Effect on organizational net assets:	
Current NA value:	$473,000
+/– profit (or loss):	+ 75,000
= new NA value:	548,000

FIGURE 8.3   Effect of an experienced profit on organizational net assets.

Permanently Restricted Net Assets

These are donations received by the healthcare organization from a third-party donor that increase the organization's net worth. These donations involve a legal and ethical requirement (usually as prescribed by the donor) to be utilized only for a specific purpose. An example may be a donation received from a private donor who restricts its use to providing continuing education to current/future nursing staff in the organization.

Temporarily Restricted Net Assets

These are donations received by the healthcare organization from a third-party donor that increase the organization's net worth. These donations involve a legal and ethical requirement (prescribed by the donor) to be utilized only after or upon a specific date or time period. An example may be a donation received from a private donor that is restricted for use until after the donor has passed away.

Unrestricted Net Assets

This account represents the ongoing (cumulative) profit (or loss) experienced by the healthcare organization at any specific point in time. It should also reflect the total liquid and readily available funds under current assets that the organization may utilize at any time. This value is calculated by taking the profit (or loss) from any specific accounting period and applying it to the organization's prior profit/loss totals to date.

Revenue and Expense Summary

This account is basically a "holding tank" for specific debit/credit values used only when closing the books at the end of a financial accounting period (see Chapter 10, "closing the books"). Otherwise, unless the organization is currently engaged in the process of closing the books for the organization at the end of a financial accounting period, this account's balance is typically $0.

In Summary

The organization's financial position is constantly changing. A balance sheet is to be run at any time the healthcare administrator needs to evaluate the value of an organization's total economic resources, as compared to its total economic obligations. An assessment of organizational equity, including restricted (permanent and/or temporary) net assets, is also important for the administrator to see the distribution of the organization's net worth at any point in time to assist in an assessment of financial leverage. Because the statement represents a cross-section "snapshot" of the organization's financial position, the balance sheet is always labeled with a single date and time, and never a date range.

The balance sheet is one of the most common financial statements used by organizations to demonstrate overall financial position on a specific date. It is an inherent organizational goal to have more resources than obligations. However, in healthcare it is very common for organizations to take on financial obligations (liabilities) to access/obtain the organizational resources needed to enable the organization to meet its mission. Often, not-for-profit organizations will access such capital resources by increasing their liabilities in methods such as long-term loans, bonds, mortgages, and so on. On the other hand, for-profit healthcare organizations will often access capital by issuing shares of equity (NA) to third-party investors, in addition to increasing their liabilities.

The Cincinnati General Hospital balance sheet is provided as a template to review formatting and presentation of account values. The balance sheet follows GAAP protocols in order to allow for comparability not only between various financial periods within a single healthcare organization but also between different organizations. Balance sheet formatting and other FASB updates are provided in Chapter 13 (Cognella Active Learning website).

Chapter Questions

1. List at least three examples (other than the examples from the chapter) of daily, healthcare operational tasks that may require the organization's administrator to run a current balance sheet.
2. Discuss the differences between current (short-term) and noncurrent (long-term) assets. What about current and noncurrent liabilities?
3. One of your associates has emailed you an updated organizational balance sheet for you to print and take to a board meeting that (a) has a date range listed at the top of it and (b) does not balance. Write an email back to your associate team member discussing your concerns with the statement they provided.
4. Demonstrate how the formula for the balance sheet statement format is derived from the original accounting equation.
5. Since there are no actual debit/credit columns (figures) on the balance sheet, discuss what multiple columns mean on the statement and how one cannot simply add all values straight down the statement to get total assets, liabilities, and net assets without including some minor arithmetic first.

Example Statement Format

Cincinnati General Hospital Balance Sheet 10/15/2021		
Assets		
Cash	27,175	
Temporary Investments	5,500	
Accrued Interest Receivable	2,000	
Accounts Receivable (A/R)	191,345	
Less Allowance for Uncollectable Accounts	– 1,300	
A/R, net	190,045	
Supply/Inventory	14,000	
Prepaid Insurance Expense	2,890	
Prepaid Rent Expense	5,000	
Prepaid Interest Expense	275	
Total Current Assets		246,885
Long-Term Investments	15,900	
Land	250,000	
Buildings	250,000	
Less Accumulated Depreciation—Buildings	– 15,000	
Buildings, net	235,000	
Equipment	135,000	
Less Accumulated Depreciation—Equipment	– 14,000	
Equipment, net	121,000	
Total Noncurrent Assets		621,900
Total Assets	868,785	
Liabilities		
Accounts Payable (A/P)	5,675	
Notes Payable (N/P)	40,000	
Accrued Interest Payable	7,500	
Deferred Rent Revenue	35,000	

Deferred Tuition Revenue	750	
Total Current Liabilities		*88,925*
Mortgage Payable	100,500	
Bonds Payable	50,000	
Total Noncurrent Liabilities		*150,500*
Total Liabilities	*239,425*	
Net Assets		
Permanently Restricted NA	200,360	
Temporarily Restricted NA	79,000	
Unrestricted NA	350,000	
Revenue and Expense Summary	0	
Total Net Assets	*629,360*	

The Statement of Operations and Statement of Net Assets

Introduction

Healthcare organizations must make a profit to remain viable for their surrounding communities and solvent for the long term. Many service lines offered by various healthcare organizations are not optional—such as emergency care and the associated expenses for licensed community hospitals. Therefore, a main concern of the healthcare leader is whether the organization is earning a profit or incurring a loss over time. The statement of operations assists with this profit/loss assessment.

It is most important to treat all patients with the highest quality of care. However, knowing costs incurred and matching these associated costs with their respective revenues for any specific healthcare service is an important task to determine profits or losses for each service offered. Examples of costs to be analyzed at the service level include healthcare worker salaries/wages, medical supplies used, licensing fees, malpractice insurance costs, and even rental expense of the location where the service is provided (if applicable). While the identification of the fractions of these total service-level costs and other related cost accounting practices are beyond the scope this textbook, their accumulation contributes to the organization's overall profit/loss determination for any given time period. An organization-level analysis will be conducted to assess profits/losses for the healthcare organization, with an understanding that these figures are the ultimate result of many, many underlying individual medical services/procedures.

Note: This chapter addresses the statement of operations at a broad, general healthcare operations level for andragogical purposes. Some basic FASB Accounting Standards Updates to the healthcare organization's statement of operations have been included in this chapter. Other, more specific FASB Accounting Standards Updates are further addressed and updated annually in Chapter 13 (Cognella Active Learning website) to maintain the textbook's relevancy.

Learning Objectives

By the end of this chapter, the student should be able to:

- Discuss the purpose and format of the statement of operations.
- List and define the two common revenue deductions used in healthcare operations.
- Demonstrate the use of a non-GAAP statement of operations in healthcare operations.
- Describe the concept of bad debt, as applied to recent FASB Account Standards Updates and their changes to the healthcare organization's statement of operations.
- Discuss the purpose and format of the statement of net assets and the statement of changes in net assets.

Key Terms

1. Income
2. Gross patient service revenue (GPSR)
3. Net patient service revenue (NPSR)
4. Charity care adjustment
5. Contractual adjustment
6. Non-operating revenue
7. Fund account

Statement Purpose

To begin, the statement of operations has many other names, and all are utilized interchangeably throughout this textbook:

- statement of operations (often used by not-for-profit organizations)
- statement of revenue over expenses
- profit/loss statement
- income statement (often used by for-profit organizations)

Many names—yet the same statement. While for-profit and not-for-profit organizations sometimes prefer one statement name over another, this is not a GAAP requirement, nor is this practice truly consistent across the healthcare industry. Therefore, these statement names are deemed appropriately interchangeable across and within healthcare organizations.

The healthcare leader will run a statement of operations to obtain the organization's revenue and expense data for any given time period. By accumulating all revenues and expenses for the organization onto a single financial statement, the overall profit (or loss) for the organization can be determined. Unless specifically generated to evaluate a single day of operational activity, the statement of operations is going to cover a date range of operational activities and their associated revenues and expenses. As a result, it is considered standard practice for this financial statement to be labeled with a date range (usually never a single date).

Below are examples demonstrating the need for an accurate, up-to-date statement of operations to assess the organization's revenues and expenses over a specific time period.

- The healthcare leader is to brief the organization's board members on the current profits generated and their trending direction for the previous 6 months of operations.
- The organization's strategic plan includes the initiative to build an additional nursing wing, and future revenue and expense estimates are to be created using a current unit's financial data.
- The current environmental conditions (such as a global pandemic, etc.) are generating significant concern for the viability of the organization, and a more conservative approach to spending may be in order. These decisions will be based on current profit/loss information for the organization.

The purpose of this statement is to clearly demonstrate the organization's revenue earned/received and expenses incurred/paid by clearly showing the two main, nominal accounts (and all subaccounts) on the statement. Organizational revenues and expenses are presented on the statement of operations in this simple format:

Total Revenue − Total Expenses = profit (or loss)

or

Total Revenue − Total Expenses = Net Revenue

Unlike the balance sheet (Chapter 8), there is no "balancing" that occurs on the statement of operations. While it is possible that total revenue could exactly equal total expenses for any given time period for the healthcare organization,

Helpful tip: Often, the term "income" is used instead of "revenue." However, keep in mind that small changes to this term will quickly change its meaning (such as "net income," which refers to an amount of profit or loss that ultimately affects the organization's net asset value). In this textbook, "income" by itself is perfectly synonymous with "revenue."

this occurrence would occur very rarely. If the value for revenue is greater than the value for expenses in any given time period, this is deemed a profit. If the value for expenses is greater than revenue in any given time period, this is deemed a loss. Table 9.1 summarizes the potential outcomes of the statement of operation's total revenue and expense analysis, as well as common accounting language associated with these results.

TABLE 9.1   Statement of operations revenue and expense outcomes

Account values	Result	Often referred to as ...
Revenue > expenses	Profit	being in the black
Expenses > revenue	Loss	being in the red
Revenue = expenses	n/a	breaking even

It is important to also note that losses (being "in the red") do occur in the healthcare industry. Reasons for losses in the healthcare industry could be related to the specific type of healthcare organization, the type or range of healthcare services provided, and other operational workflow variables (including annual/seasonal workload changes). Dependent on a multitude of other variables, a primary volume-based reimbursement method does result in financial periods that produce low levels of profit and even losses for the month, quarter, and/or year. While this experience is not optimal for the healthcare leader and the overall organization, it should be addressed, and operational changes should be made to control for events leading up to the loss so it may be avoided in future financial periods. For additional perspective, many healthcare organizations regularly operate with a routine profit margin around 2% to 3% annually. Therefore, keeping costs down while continuing to provide quality patient care is crucial. With such small profit margins, little room is left for error by the healthcare leader—all the more reason to fully understand healthcare financial accounting and financial management so the organization can remain viable for the long term.

Statement Format

The statement of operations is presented in its most fundamental format in Appendix A and demonstrated again in Figure 9.1.

Helpful tip: The statement of operations assesses revenues earned/received by the healthcare organization, as well as expenses incurred/paid during the provision of such services. If at any time the value for total revenues equals the value for total expenses for a given time period, this demonstrates $0 profit and $0 loss, which is otherwise known as "breaking even."

Orlando Specialty Care	
Statement of Operations	
01/01/20X1 - 10/15/20X1	
Total Revenue	$500,000
Total Expenses	− 320,000
Net Revenue	180,000 (profit)

FIGURE 9.1   Sample abbreviated statement of operations.

Due to the intricacies of regular healthcare operations, this basic format is not suitable for full transparency of many healthcare organizations' operational effectiveness. As a result, the statement of operations will deviate somewhat from normal GAAP standards (unlike the other financial statements reviewed in this textbook that follow GAAP). This change (per FASB Accounting Standards Updates) is made by including additional information at the top of the statement, therefore adding more information to the healthcare organization's revenue section (and thus deviating from the regular GAAP statement of operations format).

Whereas the normal GAAP standard for the statement of operations begins with net service revenue, the non-GAAP statement of operations used in the healthcare industry will begin with gross service revenue. This change has been required and primarily applies to not-for-profit hospitals. However, most for-profit hospitals and other healthcare organizations have also adopted this non-GAAP statement of operations format to ease comparability between organizations and to further demonstrate how net service revenue is deduced from gross service revenue figures.

Presentation and Calculation of Net Patient Service Revenue

Specific to the healthcare industry and related healthcare financial accounting practices, the concept of net patient service revenue (NPSR) and how it is calculated is an important competency for the healthcare leader. It is already known that healthcare organizations—regardless of profit/not-for-profit status, organization type, and so on—do not expect to collect 100% of every total billed charge for the care provided. This is due to a variety of reasons specific to the healthcare industry and the nature of the service provided. As a result, two primary revenue deduction accounts are introduced to help provide a

TRY ON YOUR OWN

Using your personal, online checking account information, generate your personal statement of operations for a specific month (the first day of the month through the last day of the month). Did you end up "in the black" or "in the red" for the month? What about the next month? What happens if you create a statement that runs (covers) both months on a single statement of operations?

Helpful tip: There are no debit/credit columns on the statement of operations. Rather, the values shown on this statement represent the current (positive) value of each revenue and expense account. While revenues increase and expenses decrease the organization's net revenue, their values are shown as positive figures, demonstrating their existence on the organization's books during a specific time period.

more accurate revenue value that is more realistic in terms of collectability on accounts due from patients and third-party payers.

- *Charity care adjustments*: The deduction of revenue that is written off (adjusted) from the gross patient service revenue (GPSR) value for the accumulation of care provided to patients who are medically indigent (those who are unable to pay for their individual healthcare, as assessed/identified by the organization's charity care policy and related process).
- *Contractual adjustments*: The deduction of revenue that is written off (adjusted) from the *GPSR* value for the accumulation of discounts offered to third-party payer/commercial health insurance companies in return for the organization's ability to be contractually available to care for a large volume of eligible patients (provider "in-network" contractual status with the insurance company).

These revenue deduction accounts are presented in their most basic form to introduce the concept of using revenue deductions specific to the healthcare organization and to demonstrate how NPSR is calculated from GPSR. Figure 9.2 demonstrates at a very basic level how the healthcare organization accounts for these revenue deductions at the top of the non-GAAP statement of operations.

Gross Patient Service Revenue (GPSR)	(volumes × charges = gross revenue)
– (less) Revenue Deductions	(charity care and contractual adjustments)
Net Patient Service Revenue (NPSR)	Value of service revenue expected to be collected
	(GPSR – revenue deductions = NPSR)

FIGURE 9.2   GPSR to NPSR section of the healthcare organization's statement of operations (non-GAAP requirement).

For clarity and standardization, this textbook will begin all statement of operations financial statements with GPSR to demonstrate full transparency of the healthcare organization's full gross charges and associated revenue deductions. Further FASB Accounting Standards Updates related to the healthcare organization's statement of operations—beyond this basic introduction of the two standard revenue deduction accounts—are addressed in Chapter 13 (Cognella Active Learning website). Included in this online chapter resource and annually updated are the following updates/topics:

- proper reporting of charity care
- proper reporting of bad debt

- proper reporting of leases
- proper reporting of net assets

As the healthcare industry continues to adapt to changing environmental and economic conditions, future FASB Accounting Standards Updates (and other GAAP-related financial statement implications) will be continuously updated on the textbook's Cognella Active Learning website.

Table 9.2 summarizes the non-GAAP section of the statement of operations for review. This section is continuously updated by FASB Accounting Standards Updates. One primary example of ongoing updates to this section includes the provision for bad debts account and a transition to the use of both implicit and explicit price concessions as contra-revenue accounts. In the end, a journey to establish greater transparency regarding the intricacies of large healthcare (hospital) operations and related revenues and expenses continues beyond the publication date and scope of this textbook. For brevity purposes, the provision for bad debts is shown to demonstrate a deduction from NPSR as the industry's initial attempt to identify patient accounts and related revenues and the healthcare organization's knowledge of the patient's ability to pay for their healthcare services at the time service, or if the ability to pay for care was determined after the provision of care.

Helpful tip: *Gross* is very different from *net* in financial accounting. Remember that gross is usually the larger value; therefore, it means before any adjustments are subtracted. Therefore, "net" can often be synonymous with the term "after." Net patient service revenue means revenue expected to be collected after accounting for revenue deductions (charity care and contractual adjustments). Another example is net revenue, which means revenue remaining "after" accounting for (subtracting) expenses.

TRY ON YOUR OWN

Using your personal online checking account information from the previous exercise above, identify your personal gross revenue and then identify your personal net revenue for any given month of personal financial data.

TABLE 9.2   Non-GAAP revenue sections of the healthcare statement of operations

Section	Purpose	Notes
Gross patient service revenue (GPSR)	To accumulate any/ all revenues related to the provision of healthcare services. Where the non-GAAP statement of operations starts/ begins.	• Routine (operating) service revenue is revenue earned/received as a result of routine care for patients within the healthcare organization related to room/board and regular nursing care. • Ancillary (operating) service revenue is revenue earned/received for additional procedures or services ordered by a provider for specific patient care, in addition to routine service revenue.
Revenue deductions	Serve to capture deductions that lower GPSR to NPSR.	• Charity care adjustments • Contractual adjustments (explicit price concessions)

Section	Purpose	Notes
Net patient service revenue (NPSR)	The value of revenue related to patient care services after adjustments (revenue deductions). Where the GAAP statement of operations starts/begins (general business format).	• NPSR is the value of healthcare operational revenue earned/received after revenue deductions already adjusted from the GPSR amount.
Provision for bad debts	See FASB Accounting Standards Updates in Chapter 13.	• This amount is to be subtracted from NPSR (if a value is present). • Note "implicit price concession" updates in Chapter 13.
Premium revenue	A separate operating revenue account that demonstrates revenue earned/paid to the organization for contractual patient care arrangements based on at-risk or otherwise capitated reimbursement methods.	• If these contractual arrangements exist with the healthcare organization (usually with an external employer, etc.) this fixed, per-member-per-month capitated revenue is listed separately to demonstrate that it is not volume-based revenue and at risk for expenses to possibly exceed fixed, contracted revenue rate(s).
Other operating revenue accounts	Includes revenue accounts related to regular operational activities for the healthcare organization yet unrelated to direct patient care services.	• Rent revenue is revenue earned/paid to the healthcare organization for the provision of space (square footage) to an external entity being leased from the healthcare organization. • Tuition revenue is revenue earned/paid to the healthcare organization for the provision of professional education to internal employees and/or external attendees at continuing education sessions, etc.
Total operating revenue	= NPSR + premium revenue + other operating revenue	• Represents all revenues earned/paid to the organization for the provision of healthcare services to patients.

Additional Statement of Operations Sections and Accounts

Following the revenue section, the healthcare organization's operating expenses are listed (Table 9.3). Organizational expenses are to be 100% operations related, as there are no "non-operating expenses" on the statement of operations. Expense accounts are

TABLE 9.3 Expense sections of the healthcare organization's statement of operations

Section	Purpose	Notes
Operating expenses	Includes any/all expenses (costs) experienced by the healthcare organization. These accounts are used (listed on the statement) as needed (when such an expense type exists during the statement period).	• Salary/wage expense • Inventory/supply expense • Utility expense • Insurance expense • Repair expense • Rent expense • Depreciation expense • Interest expense • *Bad debt expense • Other (miscellaneous) expenses
Total operating expenses	Sum of any/all operating expense values for the statement's given time period.	• If there is no operating expense for a specific account above, it is either left off the statement altogether or listed on the statement as an account with $0 value for the time period.

*The bad debt expense account and related FASB updates are discussed in detail in Chapter 13 (online chapter).

listed/utilized as necessary. Therefore, if the healthcare organization does not have any rent expense (for example), this account is typically left off the statement altogether, or it can be listed with a $0 value if it is expected to be incurred in the near future.

FASB Accounting Standards Updates surrounding the bad debt expense account are further summarized in Chapter 13 of this textbook (Cognella Active Learning website). Such updates are related to the implicit price concession previously referenced in this chapter, which is an update made to the recent provision for bad debt deduction from NPSR. Ongoing challenges related to patients with high individual responsibility for payment continue to call for changes regarding how the healthcare organization reports expected collection amounts from patients with individual responsibility for their care. While one example relates to private-pay patients being billed for full (gross) charges for their care, the increasing prevalence of high deductible health plans has also created a need for healthcare organizations to report probable net A/R collection amounts (versus net A/R values that may still be considered also improbable to collect). In the end, the bad debt expense account remains a

Helpful tip: Operating revenues and operating expenses are all related to the provision of healthcare to patients. If it is patient care related, the account will be named accordingly by using "operating" and/or "service" in the account name.

true operating expense and used for patients who possess the ability to pay their bill at the time of service and then do not. It is suggested that leaders continue to review Chapter 13 for FASB Accounting Standards Updates, while also consulting with their organization's legal and/or tax professional regarding these ongoing changes.

Table 9.4 summarizes the final section of the statement of operations. Now that the healthcare organization's total operating revenues (Table 9.2) and total operating expenses (Table 9.3) have been presented, the net operating revenue is able to be calculated and reported. Additional non-operating revenues (discussed in the next section) are added to the net operating value. Unrestricted contributions (discussed later in this chapter) are also added into this calculation because these funds are liquid and available for use by the organization as deemed necessary by the organization's leadership. A final net income (profit or loss) is then determined as the last section of the statement.

TABLE 9.4   Final totals/sections of the healthcare organization's statement of operations

Section	Purpose	Notes
Net operating revenue	= total revenue – total expenses	• Represents the total profit (or loss) for the statement's financial period as related to operational activities (provision of healthcare services to patients).
Non-operating revenue (may instead be included with the other revenue accounts in Table 9.1)	Revenue related to the healthcare organization's earnings that are unrelated to healthcare operations altogether. Any non-operating revenues are added to net operating revenue.	• *Interest revenue* is revenue earned/paid to the organization for investments in external stocks/bonds or other marketable securities.
Unrestricted contributions (if needed)	Any unrestricted contributions received are added to net operating revenue.	• Philanthropic donations received by the healthcare organization from donors that are not restricted in any manner and may be used for any purpose as determined by the receiving healthcare organization.
Transfers to parent organization (if needed)	Any transfer of funds to a parent organization (for-profit or not-for-profit) will be deducted from net operating revenue.	• Transfers of funds within a large healthcare network comprised of subsidiary entities may occur for strategic and other financial reasons.

Section	Purpose	Notes
Net income	= net operating revenue + non-operating revenue + unrestricted contributions – transfers to parent organization	• For-profits often use the term "net income." Not-for-profits generally use "increase (or decrease) in net assets." • This figure represents the final over/under for the healthcare organization for the statement's financial period (includes both operating and non-operating activities).

Non-Operating Revenue

A non-operating revenue account is used for the healthcare organization to capture revenue earned or received due to outside investments in external stocks/bonds or other opportunities for non-operating interest revenue to be earned. While investing is not a main priority for the healthcare organization, it is a responsibility for the organization's leaders to manage these funds appropriately. Relating back to the previous liquidity and solvency accounting concepts from Chapter 3, the healthcare leader must ensure that such cash reserves are not held stagnant in operational checking accounts for an extended duration of time. This action will result in these funds losing value over time as a result of economic inflation and related opportunity costs.

Instead, the decision to move this large amount of unbudgeted cash to an external investment should be done in a highly conservative manner to protect the funds. Therefore, a low-risk investment will result in a low reward in the form of a low interest payment to the healthcare organization. However, this initiative is conducted to at least outpace the current economic inflation rate and/or other known variables. While the primary purpose of the healthcare organization is to provide patient care and not invest in the stock market, it is usual and customary for healthcare organizations to engage in external investment opportunities when large, unbudgeted amounts of unrestricted cash exist and will not be used in the financial period per the organization's current strategic plan.

The Statement of Changes in Net Assets and the Statement of Net Assets

The healthcare organization's net assets (NA), also known as equity and/or net worth, are the difference between the organization's economic resources (assets) and its economic obligations (liabilities). Net assets were addressed in Chapter 8. The organization's

Helpful tip: While a non-operating revenue account exists for the healthcare organization, it is important to note that there is not an account for non-operating expenses. This is because the healthcare organization should not incur any expenses that are unrelated to its primary mission—the provision of patient care services. Otherwise, such expenses would be considered highly questionable and should be investigated by the healthcare administrator.

net assets can be determined anytime a balance sheet is run on a specific date/time during a financial period. However, at the end of any annual financial period, the organization will look back and determine whether a profit or loss was experienced. This annual profit or loss, as identified on the organization's statement of operations, directly affects the organization's net worth—in other words, its net asset account value on the balance sheet. Therefore, the statement of operations provides the organization's profit or loss experienced over the prior financial period, and that profit (or loss) is then added (or subtracted) to the organization's net assets on the balance sheet.

The statement of changes in net assets demonstrates this change in net wealth (net worth, NA, or equity) for the healthcare organization. Two sample statements (one demonstrating a profit and one demonstrating a loss) are provided for the changes in Orlando Specialty Care in Figure 9.3.

Statement of Changes in Net Assets	
Orlando Specialty Care	
Statement of Changes in Net Assets	
01/20X1	
Beginning NA, 01/01/20X1	$300,000
+ 01/20X1 (profit)	+ 15,000
Ending NA, 01/31/20X1	315,000

Orlando Specialty Care	
Statement of Changes in Net Assets	
01/20X1	
Beginning NA, 01/01/20X1	$300,000
– 01/20X1 (loss)	– 15,000
Ending NA, 01/31/20X1	285,000

FIGURE 9.3 Abbreviated statement of changes in net assets examples demonstrating profit/loss effects.

Helpful tip: The statement of changes in net assets ties together the balance sheet and statement of operations by demonstrating overall changes in the organization's net worth. In other words, what you have (assets), minus what you owe (liabilities), plus any profit or loss experienced during the recent financial period.

As a result, a profit or loss experienced by a healthcare organization directly affects its net worth (NA) value over a time period—which is why the statement of changes in net assets always has a date range.

Statement of Net Assets

At any specific point in time, the healthcare leader may want to assess the organization's net worth and the specific types of net assets that make up its net worth. This requires a simple statement of net assets. This statement varies slightly from the statement of changes in net assets, as there no "changes" presented. Rather, a "snapshot" of the NA main account is provided on the statement of net assets. It consists of a simple format to demonstrate what constitutes the organization's net worth at a specific point in time. This is also why a single date is always shown on a statement of net assets.

Orlando Specialty Care Statement of Changes in Net Assets 01/31/20X1	
Retained earnings	$250,000
Unrestricted contributions	100,000
Temporarily restricted contributions	50,000
Permanently restricted contributions	200,000
Total Net Assets	600,000

FIGURE 9.4   Sample healthcare organization's statement of net assets.

Note: An FASB Accounting Standards Update regarding the not-for-profit healthcare organization's statement of net assets, as related to philanthropy and associated fund accounts, is provided later in this chapter and in Chapter 13 (Cognella Active Learning website).

Healthcare Philanthropy and Fund Accounts

It is very common for healthcare organizations (especially large hospitals and hospital networks) to accept donations (contributions) from private donors and other external entities or organizations. With the going budget challenges and estimated 2%–3% profit margins experienced in the healthcare industry on a regular basis, when a donor is willing to offer funding to a healthcare organization, it will be accepted. In return, private donors often receive applicable tax deductions and/or other possible financial benefits for their charitable contributions to not-for-profit healthcare organizations.

Helpful tip: It is common to forget which net assets statement possesses a single date versus a date range on it. Keep in mind that the statement of changes in NA requires a change to occur—between a start and end date. Therefore, the statement of changes in NA must involve several dates to demonstrate the profit or loss experienced on the corresponding statement of operations. The statement of NA (without any changes) is again a "snapshot" of the organization's net worth at a specific point in time, which therefore requires a single date.

It is important to also note that a donor's amount of tax deduction for philanthropy related to healthcare not-for-profits has changed over the years. For example, the Tax Reform Act of 1986 and more recently the CARES Act of 2020 have influenced charitable giving to healthcare organizations, and at various levels. In addition, such donations often come with legal and ethical requirements to be upheld by the receiving healthcare organization. These stipulations are often based on the donor's request(s).

Table 9.5 reviews the three types of donations (contributions) received by healthcare organizations and the contingencies related to such charitable events.

TABLE 9.5 Net asset account philanthropy categories and their legal/ethical requirements to be fulfilled

NA account category	Legal/ethical requirement	Example
Unrestricted contributions	None	A private donor gives to the healthcare organization and does not provide any stipulation as to the use of the funds.
Temporarily restricted contributions	The use of donated funds is not to occur until after a specific date in the future.	A private donor gives to the healthcare organization and requires that the funds be invested in a low-risk community bond to earn interest until the donor passes away. At that time the funds can then be spent in any manner needed.
Permanently restricted contributions	The use of donated funds is to occur only for purpose as prescribed by the donor at the time the donation occurs.	A private donor gives to the healthcare organization and requires that the funds be used only for nursing staff continuing education purposes.

Helpful tip: Why do people donate money to healthcare organizations? Beyond the fulfillment of their civic duties and helping those in need, the basis for philanthropic healthcare donations varies by organization type, as presented in Chapter 2. Often, donations to not-for-profit healthcare organizations offer tax deductions for the donor as an additional incentive.

Some donations to healthcare organizations may even be restricted as to time and purpose (therefore, both temporarily and permanently restricted contributions). It is easily assumed that such values received, as well as their potential donor restrictions, may begin to get complicated, considering the details involved and the continuing use of the organization's resources to meet ongoing financial obligations.

Fund accounts are utilized to assist the healthcare organization and its leadership team in keeping specific healthcare organizational dollars in separate categories based on purpose and overall initiative.

- Fund account: *A* separate, self-balancing account within the healthcare organization's main accounting system that allows the healthcare leader to distinguish monies with restrictions and/or specific budgetary purposes to be set aside from the regular, unrestricted operating account values.

Fund accounts can be viewed as separate, individual (self-balancing) internal initiatives of the healthcare organization and their corresponding values to be used only as intended. This separation and categorization of values keeps them separate from the organization's regular operating account funds. Depending on the scope of the initiative, such fund accounts may even have their own financial statements created to track the initiative's progress and status of the fund account's financial position, performance, and so on.

The breakdown of Orlando Specialty Care's statement of net assets in Figure 9.4 demonstrates that of its $600,000 overall net worth (net assets), over 58% of its equity is made up of philanthropic contributions (either unrestricted, temporarily restricted, or permanently restricted contributions). The retained earnings value ($250,000) represents the amount of profit (revenue over expenses) generated by the healthcare organization to date, which it keeps as its own net worth and can use however it chooses—in accordance with the organization's strategic plan.

FASB Accounting Standards Updates to the not-for-profit healthcare organization's statement of net assets have altered the way philanthropic contributions are presented. While the organization's total net asset value is listed as before, clarity regarding net assets with restrictions and those without is now required (Figure 9.5). Additional information on this financial statement

Helpful tip: Think of an organization's fund accounts like the File Explorer on a personal desktop/laptop Windows computer. When File Explorer is opened, several smaller files that make up the entire computer's hard drive are shown, and each file folder is a separate category of file types, user initiatives, reports, and so on. The same goes for fund accounts within the healthcare organization. Each separate fund account enables the healthcare leader to recognize that its values (funds) and related restrictions and/or initiatives are to be upheld separately and not intermingled with other organizational needs or purposes.

Previous NA Format	Updated NA Format
Unrestricted NA	NA without donor restrictions
Temporary Restricted NA	NA with donor restrictions
Permanently Restricted NA	

FIGURE 9.5 Demonstration of the change to a not-for-profit healthcare organization's statement of net assets.

change for not-for-profit healthcare organizations is provided in Chapter 13 (Cognella Active Learning website).

While it is common for healthcare organizations to accept donations, the healthcare leader needs to establish a constant, healthy balance between the organization's retained earnings (earned profits) and charitable contributions. The same balance of equity will also need to be maintained in for-profit organizations that often sell shares of stock to private shareholders (private investors) as an alternative method of raising capital. Further, for-profit organizations must continue to ensure that management and operational control is maintained by the healthcare organization's board, thereby maintaining majority control (> 50.0% ownership [shares] maintained by the organization). This practice will allow for private investors to own organizational shares at a minority status, while ensuring the organization maintains majority and operational control.

In Summary

It is important for the healthcare leader to consistently evaluate organizational performance (outcome) of all healthcare operations. An evaluation of overall organizational net worth and the ongoing changes in its net worth is essential in ensuring the ongoing viability of the organization and its ability to continue serving the surrounding community. For these reasons and many others, it is important for the healthcare administrator to be knowledge-able on the accumulation and communication of values on the statement of operations, the statement of changes in net assets, and the statement of net assets. All organizational members contribute to the values on these statements based on their actions, behaviors, and work ethic. Understanding how such processes and protocols assist in generating the performance figures for the organization on these financial statements will assist the healthcare leader and ensure the viability the organization.

Chapter Questions

1. List the additional section to the statement of operations to generate the non-GAAP statement of operations. What specific type of healthcare organization is required to demonstrate this additional section at the top of its statement of operations? Why is this now required? Is there any benefit to other healthcare organizations also demonstrating a non-GAAP statement of operations as well (even if not technically required by the policy)?

2. What is the difference between a charity care adjustment and a bad debt expense for a healthcare organization? Discuss what section of the statement of operations each account falls under and how the addition of a charity care adjustment or a bad debt expense affects the organization's overall profit/loss experienced.
3. What is the purpose of a statement of net assets? Describe the relationship between the statement of operations and the statement of net assets for the healthcare organization.
4. List the three categories of fund accounts used for philanthropic contributions to a healthcare organization. Provide an example of donation characteristics for each type of fund account.
5. Upon review of Chapter 13 (Cognella Active Learning website), discuss the updates/changes to the statement of operations and the statement of net assets for not-for-profit hospitals and how these changes (updates) better provide transparency on the healthcare organization's financial statements.

Example Statement Format

Orlando Specialty Care Statement of Operations 01/01/20X1–12/31/20X1		
Gross Patient Service Revenue (GPSR)	1,575,000	
Operating Service Revenue		
Routine Service Revenue		1,000,000
Ancillary Service Revenue		575,000
– (less) Revenue Deductions	(350,000)	
Contractual Adjustments		(250,000)
Charity Care Adjustments		(100,000)
Net Patient Service Revenue (NPSR)	1,225,000	
– (less) Provision for Bad Debts (if necessary)	(200)	
Premium Revenue	500,000	
Other Operating Revenue	40,000	
Rent Revenue		25,000
Tuition Revenue		15,000
= Total Operating Revenue	**1,764,800**	

Operating Expenses		
Salary/Wage Expense		850,000
Inventory (Supply) Expense		350,000
Utility Expense		25,000
Insurance Expense		40,000
Repair Expense		12,000
Rent Expense		10,000
Depreciation Expense		35,000
Interest Expense		14,000
Bad Debt Expense		50,000
Other (Miscellaneous) Expense		7,000
= Total Operating Expenses	**1,393,000**	
Net Operating Revenue	**371,800**	
Non-Operating Revenue	500,000	
Unrestricted Contributions	250,000	
Transfers to Parent Organization	(20,000)	
Net Income	**1,101,800**	

10

Creation of a Financial Worksheet to Generate the Financial Statements

Introduction

Referring to the accounting cycle from Chapter 3, preparation of the financial worksheet precedes the development of the healthcare organization's financial statements (Figure 10.1).

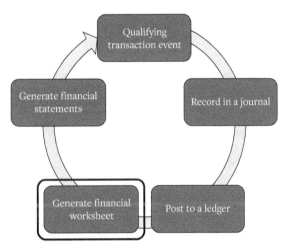

FIGURE 10.1 The financial accounting cycle.

The financial worksheet is the first step in determining whether the account values on the three primary financial statements are in balance. Again, this is to ensure that all three statements are in congruence prior to their actual creation. This chapter works to demonstrate the balancing requirement of the three statements, and it helps assist the healthcare leader by serving as a double-check step prior to investing the time and effort in the final step of the cycle. If the worksheet step does not balance, there is no need to move forward with the generation of the financial statements. Any accounting errors identified on the financial worksheet are to be properly addressed to ensure that the follow-on generation of the financial statements balance.

Learning Objectives

By the end of this chapter, the student should be able to:

- Relate the purpose of the financial worksheet to its position in the financial accounting cycle.
- Discuss the format (order) of the financial worksheet columns.
- Describe specific sections of the financial worksheet that assist in helping the healthcare leader confirm the use of proper GAAP accounting concepts/ practices.
- Illustrate the use of the financial worksheet and follow-on generation of valid and reliable financial statements.

Key Terms

1. Financial worksheet
2. Trial balance (preadjusted and adjusted)
3. Adjustment
4. Revenue and expense summary account

The Financial Worksheet

The financial worksheet assists the healthcare leader in ensuring that the following three financial statement values are in balance and confirming that it is appropriate to move forward with generating of the healthcare organization's financial statements:

- statement of operations
- statement of net assets
- balance sheet

This chapter also serves as a detailed review of the purpose of each statement involved, as well as how each relates to the others in the preparatory procedures involved with financial statement generation. The financial worksheet also displays sufficient information to assist the healthcare administrator in determining what account (and on what statement) may have an accounting error.

For the rest of this chapter, Figure 10.2 will be referenced quite frequently. However, due to the size of this Microsoft Excel attachment, screenshots of the financial worksheet sections will be utilized and referenced for each chapter section (Figure 10.2 in its entirety is shown at the end of this chapter). The Cognella Active Learning website provides access to this form in digital format, as well as additional resources to use in upcoming chapter questions/problems. Such digital (Microsoft Excel) resources include the following:

- template financial worksheet
- template financial statements
- template ledger

Financial Worksheet Section 1: Account Number and Account Name

This section of the financial worksheet, shown in Figure 10.3, should look very familiar. It is the chart of accounts listed vertically (top to bottom), in the same order as in Appendix B ("Chart of Accounts"): Assets, Liabilities, Net Assets, Revenue, Revenue Deductions, and Expenses.

Financial Worksheet Section 2: Preadjusted Trial Balance

A trial balance occurs any time all of the healthcare organization's current account values (subaccount totals taken directly from the ledger) are lined up in their respective debit/credit positions for each account and then totaled to determine whether all debits equal all credits. This action further double-checks the dual-entry rule in financial accounting and ensures that all journal entries to date have debit amounts that equal credit amounts (in the journal and from the ledger). These trial balance figures are the current values of each subaccount for the organization and are preadjusted (therefore, before December's adjusting journal entries have occurred).

Helpful tip: The accounts that appear on any organization's financial worksheet column are taken directly from the chart of accounts. If the account does not have any use and/or $0 value when the organization's financial worksheet is being generated, they can simply be left off (omitted) from the worksheet and follow-on financial statements, or listed with a $0 balance.

Acct. No.	Account Name	Acct. No.	Account Name
101	Cash	220	Bonds Payable
102	Temporary Investments	301	Hospital Net Assets (NA)
103	Accrued Interest Receivable	302	Revenue and Expense Summary
104	Accounts Receivable (A/R)	401	Routine Services Revenue
105	Allowance for Uncollectable Accounts (AUCAs)	402	Ancillary Services Revenue
		403	Premium Revenue
106	Inventory (Supply)	404	Other Operating Revenue
107	Prepaid Insurance Expense	405	Rental Revenue
108	Prepaid Rent Expense	406	Tuition Revenue
109	Prepaid Interest Expense	407	Interest Revenue
150	Land	408	Non-Operating Revenue
160	Building(s)	501	Contractual Adjustments
161	Accumulated Depreciation – Building(s)	502	Charity Care Adjustments
170	Equipment	601	Salary and Wages (S/W) Expense
171	Accumulated Depreciation – Equipment	602	Inventory (Supply) Expense
		603	Utilities Expense
201	Accounts Payable (A/P)	604	Insurance Expense
202	Notes Payable (N/P)	605	Repairs Expense
203	Accrued Interest Payable	606	Rent Expense
204	Accrued Salaries and Wages (S/W) Payable	607	Depreciation Expense
		608	Interest Expense
205	Deferred Rental Revenue (Income)	609	Bad Debt Expense
206	Deferred Tuition Revenue (Income)	610	Other (Miscellaneous) Expenses

FIGURE 10.3   Section of Figure 10.2 displaying the account number and account name.

Figure 10.4 demonstrates that the preadjusted trial balance balances at $1,940,250. If at any time a trial balance (including the preadjusted trial balance) does not balance, the healthcare leader should stop and work to correct an existing accounting data entry error occurring prior to or during the month of December, 20X5.

Acct. No.	Account Name	Pre-ADJ Trial Balance 12/31/20X5	
101	Cash	350,500	
102	Temporary Investments	120,000	
103	Accrued Interest Receivable	16,250	
104	Accounts Receivable (A/R)	345,000	
105	Allowance for Uncollectable Accounts (AUCAs)		4,500
106	Inventory (Supply)	67,000	
107	Prepaid Insurance Expense	5,600	
108	Prepaid Rent Expense	2,300	
109	Prepaid Interest Expense	400	
150	Land	167,000	
160	Building(s)	151,200	
161	Accumulated Depreciation – Building(s)		40,000
170	Equipment	55,000	
171	Accumulated Depreciation – Equipment		12,000
201	Accounts Payable (A/P)		3,450
202	Notes Payable (N/P)		6,000
203	Accrued Interest Payable		2,300
204	Accrued Salaries and Wages (S/W) Payable		12,500
205	Deferred Rental Revenue (Income)		4,500
206	Deferred Tuition Revenue (Income)		2,000
220	Bonds Payable		113,000
301	Hospital Net Assets (NA)		550,000
302	Revenue and Expense Summary		
401	Routine Services Revenue		786,000
402	Ancillary Services Revenue		240,000
403	Premium Revenue		50,000
404	Other Operating Revenue		40,000
405	Rental Revenue		14,000
406	Tuition Revenue		7,000
407	Interest Revenue		12,000

FIGURE 10.4   Section of Figure 10.2 displaying the preadjusted trial balance.

Acct. No.	Account Name	Pre-ADJ Trial Balance 12/31/20X5
408	Non-Operating Revenue	5,000
501	Contractual Adjustments	50,000
502	Charity Care Adjustments	65,000
601	Salary and Wages (S/W) Expense	220,000
602	Inventory (Supply) Expense	89,000
603	Utilities Expense	51,000
604	Insurance Expense	35,000
605	Repairs Expense	12,000
606	Rent Expense	6,000
607	Depreciation Expense	52,000
608	Interest Expense	15,000
609	Bad Debt Expense	22,000
610	Other (Miscellaneous) Expenses	7,000
	Total	1,904,250 1,904,250

Note: Any blank cells in the financial worksheet denote a $0 value.

FIGURE 10.4 (Continued)

Financial Worksheet Section 3: Adjustments

The next step in the creation of the financial worksheet is to post all ending values for any accounts experiencing a change in value, and by how much, for the month of December 20X5. If there is a value entered into an account's row under the adjustment column, this means that during the month of December, this account's cumulative increase or decrease is represented by the value entered in the respective debit/credit cell. In other words, these adjustment values are the net changes in subaccount account values (pulled from the organization's ledger) during the month of December (Figure 10.5).

Note that the adjustments column from the financial worksheet also balances—total adjustment debits ($138,600) equal total adjustment credits (also $138,600). This is due to the ongoing enforcement of the dual-entry requirement that ensures that all journal entries during the month of December have total debits that equal total credits.

Helpful tip: The trial balance is a useful tool for the healthcare leader in determining (from a broad viewpoint) that proper GAAP processes/protocols are being conducted within the organization and accounting system. The more often a trial balance is run (checked) by the healthcare administrator, the shorter the time frame of research experienced to identify an error.

Acct. No.	Account Name	Pre-ADJ Trial Balance 12/31/20X5		ADJ 12/20X5	
101	Cash	350,500			46,900
102	Temporary Investments	120,000		3,600	
103	Accrued Interest Receivable	16,250		350	
104	Accounts Receivable (A/R)	345,000		31,000	
105	Allowance for Uncollectable Accounts (AUCAs)		4,500		500
106	Inventory (Supply)	67,000			5,000
107	Prepaid Insurance Expense	5,600			600
108	Prepaid Rent Expense	2,300			500
109	Prepaid Interest Expense	400			250
150	Land	167,000			
160	Building(s)	151,200			
161	Accumulated Depreciation – Building(s)		40,000		5,000
170	Equipment	55,000			
171	Accumulated Depreciation – Equipment		12,000		3,000
201	Accounts Payable (A/P)		3,450		4,500
202	Notes Payable (N/P)		6,000	500	
203	Accrued Interest Payable		2,300	150	
204	Accrued Salaries and Wages (S/W) Payable		12,500	10,000	
205	Deferred Rental Revenue (Income)		4,500	500	
206	Deferred Tuition Revenue (Income)		2,000		
220	Bonds Payable		113,000	2,000	
301	Hospital Net Assets (NA)		550,000		
302	Revenue and Expense Summary				
401	Routine Services Revenue		786,000		50,650
402	Ancillary Services Revenue		240,000		15,000

FIGURE 10.5   Section of Figure 10.2 displaying the adjustments.

Acct. No.	Account Name	Pre-ADJ Trial Balance 12/31/20X5		ADJ 12/20X5	
403	Premium Revenue		50,000		
404	Other Operating Revenue		40,000		6,000
405	Rental Revenue		14,000		
406	Tuition Revenue		7,000		200
407	Interest Revenue		12,000		400
408	Non-Operating Revenue		5,000		100
501	Contractual Adjustments	50,000		3,500	
502	Charity Care Adjustments	65,000		2,500	
601	Salary and Wages (S/W) Expense	220,000		34,000	
602	Inventory (Supply) Expense	89,000		15,000	
603	Utilities Expense	51,000		4,000	
604	Insurance Expense	35,000		6,000	
605	Repairs Expense	12,000		900	
606	Rent Expense	6,000		600	
607	Depreciation Expense	52,000		6,000	
608	Interest Expense	15,000		10,000	
609	Bad Debt Expense	22,000		6,000	
610	Other (Miscellaneous) Expenses	7,000		2,000	
	Total	1,904,250	1,904,250	138,600	138,600

FIGURE 10.5 (Continued)

Financial Worksheet Section 4: Postadjusted Trial Balance

The postadjusted trial balance (TB) column on the financial worksheet simply displays the calculated net change to the original (preadjusted) trial balance, after calculating these account changes affected by the adjustments occurring during the month of December 20X5. It is not simply adding or subtracting straight across the respective account rows. Debit and credit balances need to be evaluated and the net change correctly posted to the corresponding debit/credit cell in the postadjusted TB column.

For example, consider account 101, Cash. This account's preadjusted TB was $350,500 (beginning debit balance). The adjustment for this account was then a credit entry of $46,900 (net change to the cash account during December 20X5). If the financial worksheet columns were viewed as simple T-accounts (as in a ledger), this activity would resemble the cash T-account in Figure 10.6 with an ending account balance of $303,600.

101, Cash

| 350,500 (pre-ADJ TB acct value) | 46,900 (ADJ amount) |
| 303,600 (ADJ TB acct value) | |

FIGURE 10.6   Example of a T-account for account 101, Cash, to demonstrate the account's net value change.

These calculations continue for all accounts, demonstrating the net change from the preadjusted TB, as affected by the December adjustments amounts, and showing the ending value of the accounts in the adjusted TB column. Figure 10.7 demonstrates another account's change in this process (salary and wage expense), yet in a slightly different manner from Figure 10.6 due to debit/credit balances in the respective T-account.

601, S/W Expense

| 220,000 34,000 (ADJ amount) | |
| 254,000 (ADJ TB acct value) | |

FIGURE 10.7   Example of a T-account for account 601, Salary/Wage Expense, to demonstrate the account's net value change.

Because the S/W Expense account began with a debit preadjusted TB value of $220,000, then experienced a net increase of $34,000 (also a debit entry to increase this account's expense value from the past month), these values are added together to show the new, adjusted TB value of $254,000 for S/W Expense.

Figure 10.8 demonstrates this net change on all applicable accounts for the adjusted TB column. The adjusted TB continues to properly balance at $1,976,450.

Acct. No.	Account Name	Pre-ADJ Trial Balance 12/31/20X5		ADJ 12/20X5		ADJ Trial Balance 12/31/20X5	
101	Cash	350,500			46,900	303,600	
102	Temporary Investments	120,000		3,600		123,600	
103	Accrued Interest Receivable	16,250		350		16,600	
104	Accounts Receivable (A/R)	345,000		31,000		376,000	
105	Allowance for Uncollectable Accounts (AUCAs)		4,500		500		5,000
106	Inventory (Supply)	67,000			5,000	62,000	
107	Prepaid Insurance Expense	5,600			600	5,000	
108	Prepaid Rent Expense	2,300			500	1,800	
109	Prepaid Interest Expense	400			250	150	
150	Land	167,000				167,000	
160	Building(s)	151,200				151,200	
161	Accumulated Depreciation – Building(s)		40,000		5,000		45,000
170	Equipment	55,000				55,000	
171	Accumulated Depreciation – Equipment		12,000		3,000		15,000
201	Accounts Payable (A/P)		3,450		4,500		7,950
202	Notes Payable (N/P)		6,000	500			5,500
203	Accrued Interest Payable		2,300	150			2,150
204	Accrued Salaries and Wages (S/W) Payable		12,500	10,000			2,500
205	Deferred Rental Revenue (Income)		4,500	500			4,000
206	Deferred Tuition Revenue (Income)		2,000				2,000
220	Bonds Payable		113,000	2,000			111,000

FIGURE 10.8   Section of Figure 10.2 displaying the adjusted trial balance.

Acct. No.	Account Name	Pre-ADJ Trial Balance 12/31/20X5		ADJ 12/20X5		ADJ Trial Balance 12/31/20X5	
301	Hospital Net Assets (NA)	550,000				550,000	
302	Revenue and Expense Summary						
401	Routine Services Revenue	786,000		50,650		836,650	
402	Ancillary Services Revenue	240,000		15,000		255,000	
403	Premium Revenue	50,000				50,000	
404	Other Operating Revenue	40,000		6,000		46,000	
405	Rental Revenue	14,000				14,000	
406	Tuition Revenue	7,000		200		7,200	
407	Interest Revenue	12,000		400		12,400	
408	Non-Operating Revenue	5,000		100		5,100	
501	Contractual Adjustments	50,000		3,500		53,500	
502	Charity Care Adjustments	65,000		2,500		67,500	
601	Salary and Wages (S/W) Expense	220,000		34,000		254,000	
602	Inventory (Supply) Expense	89,000		15,000		104,000	
603	Utilities Expense	51,000		4,000		55,000	
604	Insurance Expense	35,000		6,000		41,000	
605	Repairs Expense	12,000		900		12,900	
606	Rent Expense	6,000		600		6,600	
607	Depreciation Expense	52,000		6,000		58,000	
608	Interest Expense	15,000		10,000		25,000	
609	Bad Debt Expense	22,000		6,000		28,000	
610	Other (Miscellaneous) Expenses	7,000		2,000		9,000	
	Total	1,904,250	1,904,250	138,600	138,600	1,976,450	1,976,450

FIGURE 10.8 (Continued)

Financial Worksheet Section 5: The Financial Statement Data

Up to this point in our financial worksheet, we have

- listed all preadjusted trial balance figures for all accounts and ensured they balance,
- listed all adjustment balance figures for all accounts and ensured they balance, and
- listed all adjusted (or postadjustment) trial balance figures for all accounts and ensure they balance.

The second half of the financial worksheet simply lines up all respective accounts for the three primary financial statements. This consumes the three remaining columns on the financial worksheet. However, it is important to note the proper order of appearance of these statements as listed in the worksheet columns (left to right).

1. **Statement of operations:** Did Fort Collins General Hospital earn a profit or incur a loss at the end of 20X5?
2. **Statement of net assets:** What is the net change to Fort Collins General Hospital because of its profit/loss in 20X5?
3. **Balance sheet:** Do the financial statements (and all of their associated data) balance using the basic accounting equation (assets = liabilities + net assets) when the NA value is the updated (after accounting for the experienced profit/loss)?

The accounts needed for each of these three financial statements are simply pulled across from the adjusted trial balance and appropriately placed in the same respective debit/credit cells. It is important to note that most (but not all) of these actions will involve accounts that are all grouped similarly (either all as debits or credits), depending on which statement is being generated on the worksheet. For example, when populating the statement of operations data, all revenue accounts should be in the credit column of the adjusted TB, while all expenses should be in the debit column of the adjusted TB, and so forth. Exceptions to these basic debit/credit groups do exist for contra-asset accounts and revenue deduction accounts.

Figure 10.9 demonstrates the population of all three financial statement columns on the financial worksheet.

Statement of Operations 20X5	Statement of NA 20X5	Balance Sheet 12/31/20X5
		303600
		123600
		16600
		376000
		5000
		62000
		5000
		1800
		150
		167000
		151200
		45000
		55000
		15000
		7950
		5500
		2150
		2500
		4000
		2000
		111000
	550,000	1,061,850
	511,850	
836,650		
255,000		
50,000		
46,000		
14,000		
7,200		
12,400		
5,100		
53,500		
67,500		
254,000		
104,000		
55,000		
41,000		
12,900		
6,600		
58,000		
25,000		
28,000		
9,000		
714,500 1,226,350		
511,850	1,061,850	
1,226,350		1,261,950 1,261,950

FIGURE 10.9 Section of Figure 10.2 demonstrating the three financial statements' data.

- The organization had $1,226,350 in total revenue and $714,500 in total expenses. Therefore, a $511,850 profit was calculated. This amount was added back to the $714,500 value to show that it is truly the difference between total revenue and total expenses, equaling the larger $1,226,350 value again.
- The $511,850 profit was then credited to the revenue and expense summary account, directly underneath the $550,000 value on the statement of net assets column of the worksheet. This is because a profit increases an organization's total net assets (a credit entry is required to increase the NA account). The updated, new total net assets value sums to $1,061,850.
- Finally, the balance sheet columns demonstrate that A = L + NA. Important to note here that the net assets value used in this balance sheet column is the new/updated value, $1,061,850, not the original, preadjusted net assets figure of $550,000. If used in error, this will not allow the balance sheet columns to balance.

The entire financial worksheet (Figure 10.2) with all sections previously reviewed can be accessed at the end of this chapter and in Microsoft Excel format on the Cognella Active Learning website.

Financial Worksheet Additional Information and Closing the Books

Using the Fort Collins General Hospital financial data for 20X5, a profit was experienced in the final month of the year and the ending asset, liability, and net asset (equity) account values calculated. Because ending worksheet values are all classified as real accounts, the organization will begin the 20X6 financial period (on January 1, 20X6) with these same asset, liability, and net asset figures. While an interim financial worksheet can be generated at any time during a financial period, this example demonstrates the end of the calendar year, corresponding with the end of the organization's financial period.

Fort Collins General Hospital experienced a profit adjusted under the net assets column on its financial worksheet, and the debit/credit entries following this discovery correspond to ledger T-account entries. When posted to the ledger's T-accounts, an increase to the organization's net worth (a credit) occurs, while also debiting the revenue and expense summary account.

Up until this point in the textbook, this revenue/expense summary account has remained unused—until the organization reaches the end of a financial period and needs to close the books. Here, the revenue/expense summary is used to assist in closing the books by the following steps.

a) Closing out the nominal total revenue account by debiting its T-account for the total amount of revenue and storing the total revenue value in the revenue/expense summary account:

12/31/20X5:	D) revenue	1,226,350	
	C) revenue/expense summary		1,226,350

Revenue is closed out by debiting the revenue account in full.

b) Closing out the nominal total expense account by crediting its T-account for the total amount of expenses and storing the total expense value in the revenue/expense summary account:

12/31/20X5:	D) revenue/expense summary	714,500	
	C) expense		714,500

Expenses are closed out by crediting the expense account in full.

c) Adjusting the organization's total NA account according to the respective profit from the financial worksheet (which was $511,850 profit).

12/31/20X5:	D) revenue/expense summary	511,850	
	C) NA		511,850

Net assets are increased by the amount of the experienced profit by a credit.

Figure 10.10 demonstrates the revenue and expense T-account changes being posted from the a), b), and c) journal entries above.

What About a Loss?

Finally, keep in mind that a healthcare organization will not always experience a profit during any specific financial period. Often, healthcare organizations may go months or even years with losses due to operational shortfalls, environmental changes, market conditions, and government/policy updates, among many other factors.

As a result, if a loss is experienced (and therefore the total expense value is greater than total revenue value), the a) and b) journal entries in Figure 10.10 would still be the same with regard to their debit/credit entries. Revenues would still need to be closed out by a debit, and expenses would still need to be closed out with a credit. The revenue/expense summary account would also still be used as the storage area for these values, accepting the corresponding debit/credit entries, again from journal entries a) and b) above.

Helpful tip: The revenue/expense summary account is only utilized when the organization wants to close the books at the end of its annual financial accounting period. This will allow for total revenue and expense accounts to be reset to $0 (nominal accounts) and allows the profit/loss to be added/subtracted to the organization's beginning NA value. This NA value is then carried over to the next financial period (along with the other real account ending values: assets and liabilities).

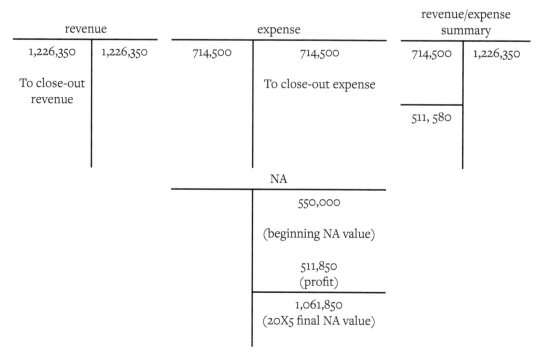

FIGURE 10.10 Adjusting entries to close out total revenue and expense values using the revenue/expense summary (temporary storage) account and increase the organization's net assets (equity, or net worth).

However, when considering a loss, the journal entry for c) would entail opposite debit/ credit entries. To lower the value of an NA account, a debit entry for the loss would occur. The corresponding credit would then be from the revenue/expense summary account, for the same amount of the loss so the journal entry balances. This journal entry and corresponding post to the ledger will lower the organization's beginning net asset value to account for the loss during the previous financial period.

Using a Completed and Balanced Financial Worksheet to Generate the Financial Statements

Once a balanced financial worksheet has been created, the healthcare leader can then work on the next, and final, step of the financial accounting cycle: the generation of valid and reliable financial statements. Conveniently, most of the data required on the financial statements is already displayed on the financial worksheet, except for subtotals of various statements sections, statement section titles, and other clarifying details outlined by GAAP and necessary FASB Accounting Standards Updates.

Figures 10.11, 10.12, and 10.13 demonstrate the three financial statements generated directly from the Fort Collins General Hospital financial worksheet. It is recommended

Fort Collins General Hospital		
Statement of Operations		
12/20X5		
Gross Patient Service Revenue (GPSR):		
	Routine Services Revenue	836,650
	Ancillary Services Revenue	255,000
		1,091,650
(Less) Revenue Deductions:		
	Contractual Adjustments	-53,500
	Charity Care Adjustments	-67,500
Net Patient Service Revenue:		970,650
(Less) Provision for Bad Debts		n/a
Premium Revenue:		50,000
Other Operating Revenue:		46,000
	Rental Revenue	14,000
	Tuition Revenue	7,200
	Interest Revenue	12,400
Non-Operating Revenue:		5,100
Total Operating Revenue:		1,105,350
Operating Expenses:		
	Salary and Wages (S/W) Expense	254,000
	Inventory (Supply) Expense	104,000
	Utilities Expense	55,000
	Insurance Expense	41,000
	Repairs Expense	12,900
	Rent Expense	6,600
	Depreciation Expense	58,000
	Interest Expense	25,000
	Bad Debt Expense	28,000
	Other (Miscellaneous) Expenses	9,000
Total Opearting Expenses:		593,500
Net Operating Revenue:		511,850
Unrestricted Contributions:		0
Transfers to Parent:		0
Net Income:		511,850

FIGURE 10.11 Fort Collins statement of operations in proper GAAP format from Chapter 9, end-of-chapter example format.

Fort Collins General Hospital	
Statement of Changes in Net Assets	
12/20X5	
Beginning Net Assets, 12/01/20X5:	550,000
December 20X5 profit:	511,850
Ending Net Assets, 12/31/20X5	1,061,850

FIGURE 10.12 Fort Collins statement of net assets in proper GAAP format from Chapter 9, Figure 3.

Fort Collins General Hospital		
Balance Sheet		
12/31/20X5		
Current Assets:		
	Cash	303,600
	Temporary Investments	123,600
	Accrued Interest Receivable	16,600
	Accounts Receivable (A/R)	376,000
	Allowance for Uncollectible Accounts (AUCAs)	-5,000
	Inventory (Supply)	62,000
	Prepaid Insurance Expense	5,000
	Prepaid Rent Expense	1,800
	Prepaid Interest Expense	150
		883,750
Non-Current Assets:		
	Land	167,000
	Buildings(s)	151,200
	Accumulated Depreciation – Building(s)	-45,000
	Equipment	55,000
	Accumulated Depreciation – Equipment	-15,000
		313,200
Total Assets:		**1,196,950**
Current Liabilites:		
	Accounts Payable (A/P)	7,950
	Notes Payable (N/P)	5,500
	Accrued Interest Payable	2,150
	Accrued Salaries and Wages (S/W) Payable	2,500
	Deferred Rental Revenue (Income)	4,000
	Deferred Tuition Revenue (Income)	2,000
		24,100
Non-Current Liabilities:		
	Bonds Payable	111,000
		111,000
Total Liabilities:		**135,100**
Net Assets:		**1,061,850**

FIGURE 10.13 Fort Collins balance sheet in proper GAAP format from Chapter 8, Table 1.

that the reader take the time to review the specific values on each statement and map them back to the financial worksheet. To review the financial statement formats, the following textbook references should be reexamined:

- Chapter 9, end-of-chapter example GAAP statement of operations (with the additional GPSR to NPSR information)
- Chapter 9, Figure 9.3: GAAP statement of changes in net assets
- Chapter 8, Table 8.1: GAAP balance sheet

Note: Total assets = total liabilities + net assets. These accounts balance at 1,196,950 on this balance sheet, while on the worksheet the balance sheet debit/credit columns balance at 1,261,950. The reason why these balancing numbers are different between the financial worksheet and this balance sheet is because the worksheet is a trial balance (sum of all debits compared to the sum of all credits), while the balance sheet reports all accounts in their respective main account format (assets, liabilities, and NA). As a result, the minus (subtracted) values in this balance sheet are those figures falling in the opposite main account debit/credit column on the corresponding worksheet's trial balance format. These accounts that are subtracted represent contra-assets and/or revenue deductions.

In Summary

This chapter concludes the financial accounting cycle by creating a financial worksheet to ensure that all the organization's accounting data balances and subsequent generation of valid and reliable financial statements can occur based on the financial worksheet's balanced financial data. An ongoing review of this chapter and the relationship of the financial worksheet figures and how they are reported on the corresponding financial statements is recommended to assist in understanding the purpose of each step of the accounting cycle process. Each action taken by the healthcare leader during the accounting cycle process is vital—and cumulative with regard to the ongoing generation of valid and reliable financial statements.

Chapter Questions

1. Discuss the purpose and format of the financial worksheet.
2. Identify sections of the financial worksheet that assist the healthcare leader in verifying proper GAAP procedures and balanced financial statements.

3. Describe the order of the columns on the financial worksheet (left to right) and why they must be in this order to complete the worksheet correctly.
4. Discuss the purpose of the revenue and expense summary account as related to closing the books.
5. Describe the effect of an organizational loss on the closing journal entries and ledger when using the revenue and expense summary, total revenue, and total expense accounts.

Acct No.	Account Name	Pre-ADJ Trial Balance 12/20X5	ADJ 12/20X5		ADJ Trial Balance 12/31/20X5	Statement of Operations 20X5	Statement of NA 20X5	Balance Sheet 12/31/20X5
101	Cash	350,500		46,900	303,600			303,600
102	Temporary Investments	120,000	3,600		123,600			123,600
103	Accrued Interest Receivable	16,250	350		16,600			16,600
104	Accounts Receivable (A/R)	345,000	31,000		376,000			376,000
105	Allowance for Uncollectible Accounts (AUCAs)	4,500		500	5,000			5,000
106	Inventory (Supply)	67,000		5,000	62,000			62,000
107	Prepaid Insurance Expense	5,600		600	5,000			5,000
108	Prepaid Rent Expense	2,300		500	1,800			1,800
109	Prepaid Interest Expense	400		250	150			150
150	Land	167,000			167,000			167,000
160	Buildings(s)	151,200			151,200			151,200
161	Accumulated Depreciation – Building(s)	40,000		5,000	45,000			45,000
170	Equipment	55,000			55,000			55,000
171	Accumulated Depreciation – Equipment	12,000		3,000	15,000			15,000
201	Accounts Payable (A/P)	3,450		4,500	7,950			7,950
202	Notes Payable (N/P)	6,000	500		5,500			5,500
203	Accrued Interest Payable	2,300	150		2,150			2,150
204	Accrued Salaries and Wages (S/W) Payable	12,500	10,000		2,500			2,500
205	Deferred Rental Revenue (Income)	4,500	500		4,000			4,000
206	Deferred Tuition Revenue (Income)	2,000			2,000			2,000
220	Bonds Payable	113,000	2,000		111,000			111,000
301	Hospital Net Assets (NA)	550,000			550,000		550,000	1,061,850
302	Revenue and Expense Summary						511,850	

FIGURE 10.2 Fort Collins General Hospital financial worksheet, 12/20X5.

Acct No.	Account Name	Pre-ADJ Trial Balance 12/20X5	ADJ 12/20X5	ADJ Trial Balance 12/31/20X5	Statement of Operations 20X5	Statement of NA 20X5	Balance Sheet 12/31/20X5
401	Routine Services Revenue	786,000	50,650	836,650	836,650		
402	Ancillary Services Revenue	240,000	15,000	255,000	255,000		
403	Premium Revenue	50,000		50,000	50,000		
404	Other Operating Revenue	40,000	6,000	46,000	46,000		
405	Rental Revenue	14,000		14,000	14,000		
406	Tuition Revenue	7,000	200	7,200	7,200		
407	Interest Revenue	12,000	400	12,400	12,400		
408	Non-Operating Revenue	5,000	100	5,100	5,100		
501	Contractual Adjustments	50,000	3,500	53,500	53,500		
502	Charity Care Adjustments	65,000	2,500	67,500	67,500		
601	Salary and Wages (S/W) Expense	220,000	34,000	254,000	254,000		
602	Inventory (Supply) Expense	89,000	15,000	104,000	104,000		
603	Utilities Expense	51,000	4,000	55,000	55,000		
604	Insurance Expense	35,000	6,000	41,000	41,000		
605	Repairs Expense	12,000	900	12,900	12,900		
606	Rent Expense	6,000	600	6,600	6,600		
607	Depreciation Expense	52,000	6,000	58,000	58,000		
608	Interest Expense	15,000	10,000	25,000	25,000		
609	Bad Debt Expense	22,000	6,000	28,000	28,000		
610	Other (Miscellaneous) Expenses	7,000	2,000	9,000	9,000		
	Totals:	1,904,250 1,904,250	138,600 138,600	1,976,450 1,976,450	714,500 1,226,350		
	Profit/Loss:				511,850		
	end-of-year NA update:					1,061,850	
	does it balance?:					1,261,950	1,261,950

FIGURE 10.2 (Continued)

11

The Statement of Cash Flows

Introduction

The healthcare industry possesses many characteristics that differentiate it from other U.S. organizations and their respective business operations. One of these unique differences is the sequence of activities that are involved with a patient encounter. Beginning with a patient accessing the healthcare system (for example, a routine doctor's office visit or emergency department treatment) through the charge capture, billing process, and follow-on reimbursement, this entire process is both complicated and important to the successful management of the organization.

The flow of funds into and out of the organization that specifically affect the cash account (either cash increasing or lowering in value) is of upmost importance regarding daily operations within a healthcare organization. This movement of cash is dependent on the sequencing of activities related to the delivery of care. It is in the healthcare organization's best interest to (a) receive payment for services provided to patients (cash inflow) as close to the patient encounter (date of service) as possible and (b) have enough funds (cash) on hand to pay external entities in their trade credit agreements. The challenge of working to receive payment for services provided and also ensuring that the organization possess enough cash on hand at the time bills are due is referred to as revenue-cycle management (RCM). RCM is an important competency and daily task for the healthcare administrator leading any healthcare organization.

Learning Objectives

By the end of this chapter, the student should be able to:

- Discuss the purpose of the statement of cash flows for the healthcare organization.
- Demonstrate the difference between the two similar statement of cash flows formats.

- Define the sections of the statement of cash flows and discuss examples of healthcare accounting transactions that may fall within each section.
- Discuss the importance of the statement of cash flows to identify hidden information not evident on other financial statements.
- Describe the relationship between revenue-cycle management and the statement of cash flows.

Key Terms

1. Operating activities
2. Financing activities
3. Investing activities
4. Cash (sales) receipt
5. Medical invoice
6. Revenue-cycle management (RCM)
7. Days-in-A/R

Statement Purpose

The statement of cash flows demonstrates detailed information that is not obviously evident or visible on the other primary financial statements previously addressed in this textbook. Transparency is an important accounting concept and consistent with GAAP procedures (Chapter 2). The statement of cash flows will work to clearly define organizational inflows of cash and outflows of cash as related to three main categories of healthcare transactions:

- operating activities
- investing activities
- financing activities

More specifically, there are "hidden" inflow and outflow cash activities that are not clearly displayed on the balance sheet and statement of operations for healthcare organizations utilizing the accrual method of accounting. If the healthcare organization is acknowledging revenues only when earned (regardless of if/when received), then revenues will be increased at the time of service (when earned), yet the actual cash account will remain unchanged for that specific accounts receivable amount until there is a payment received (either from the patient or their third-party payer). Likewise, if expenses are recognized when incurred (regardless of whether actually paid), then the expense account will be increased immediately, and the cash account will remain unchanged until the amount is paid by mailing a check or other payment method conducted by the healthcare organization.

Example: A healthcare organization's current short-term investment is purchased for $500, the amount shown under the short-term investment account on the organization's balance sheet under assets. The next month's balance sheet shows the organization's short-term investment account has increased to $550. Below are two ways the organization's short-term investment account could net to $550 yet remain unexplained on the balance sheet and statement of operations without the use of a statement of cash flows:

Helpful tip: Remember, under accrual accounting, revenues are recorded (recognized) immediately when earned (when the service is delivered by the healthcare organization), regardless of whether payment is received at the time of service or not. Expenses are recorded (recognized) immediately when incurred, regardless of when they are eventually paid by the healthcare organization.

Method #1:
The organization simply purchased an additional $50 of the investment over the past month.

Method #2:
The organization purchased an additional $250 of the investment and then sold $200 of the investment to net back to $550.

This variance in operational activities yet similar net account value can occur for just about any subaccount in the healthcare organization, including inventory/supplies, long-term investments, and even the cash account itself.

As a result, the statement of cash flows can be viewed as a hybrid statement (Figure 11.1), combining the information not truly shown by the balance sheet and statement of operations. Without the statement of cash flows, the healthcare organization operating under the accrual method of accounting is operating without the knowledge of inflows and outflows of cash for the organization.

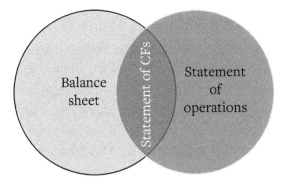

FIGURE 11.1   The statement of cash flows can be viewed as a hybrid statement between the balance sheet and statement of operations.

The statement of cash flows is based on the cash method of accounting. Therefore, while this is summarized at the end of this chapter, be aware that the healthcare organization utilizing the accrual method of accounting will have to regress to the cash accounting method for this statement to be generated.

Healthcare Organization—Operating Activities

Specifically, this statement will reflect the actual inflow of cash for the healthcare organization's efforts in the provision of care to patients as related to cash (or sales) receipts and payment toward a pending medical invoice.

- Cash (sales) receipt—occurs when a patient pays the healthcare organization at the time of service.
  - o This may be in the form of cash, credit card, or check.
  - o This payment may be applied to the patient's copay for that day's service and/or as prepayment toward their third-party insurance plan's coinsurance or deductible.

Example journal entries:

| 11/01/20X1 | D) A/R—pt. John Smith | $150 | |
| | C) patient service revenue | | $150 |

Patient billed for office visit and processed through third-party insurance

| 11/01/20X1 | D) cash | $25 | |
| | C) A/R | | $25 |

Patient paid insurance plan's designated copay at the time of service. Remaining A/R balance of $125 to be billed to the patient's third-party insurance.

- Medical invoice—issued by the healthcare organization to a patient and/or their third-party payer (in the form of a medical claim), requesting reimbursement according to the prospective payment contract with the insurance company.
  - o This invoice may also be directed to the patient who (a) receives a healthcare service not covered by their insurance plan (b) has had some or all the amount applied to their insurance plan's deductible, coinsurance, or unpaid copayment at the time of service.

o   Due to the nature of the U.S. healthcare system, this method of invoicing the third-party insurance and/or the patient after the service has been delivered is most common.

Example journal entries (continued):

2/01/20X2	D) cash	$100	
	D) contractual adjustment (ins)	$25	
	C) A/R		$125

Patient's third-party insurance payment later processed and a contractual adjustment (discount) applied per the prospective payment insurance contract with the healthcare organization.

The operating activities section of the statement of cash flows demonstrates the outflow of cash related to healthcare operating activities as well. These activities will represent any payments made for supplies, equipment, salary/wages, and other organization expenses related to the delivery of care.

Example journal entries:

11/01/20X1	D) inventory	$300	
	C) cash		$300
11/15/20X1	D) salary/wage expense	$17,250	
	C) cash		$17,250

In review, the statement of cash flows' operating activities section is devoted to the inflow and outflow of cash (cash received and cash paid) for any/all activities related to the provision of care to the organization's patients. If cash was not physically received or paid as related to healthcare operating activities, the values (cash flows) will not show up on this section of the statement.

Healthcare Organization—Investing Activities

Healthcare organizations are not primarily in the business of investing in assets beyond those required in the delivery of medical care (such as equipment, supplies, buildings, etc.). However, at times the healthcare organization may find itself in a position of excess cash on hand that is unbudgeted. Therefore, the last thing the organization wants to do is leave this large amount of money in the organization's operating (checking) account for a long period of time. Otherwise, inflation and other economic factors will slowly lower the value of this large, unbudgeted sum of money.

Instead, the healthcare organization is inclined to invest these funds in an external investment. It is recommended to invest conservatively—low risk and therefore low return—primarily to further enforce the conservative accounting concept. As long as the investment's interest rate outpaces the current market inflation rate, the value of the funds will remain stable when the investment terms and the funds are delivered back to the organization for use in operations.

Example journal entry:

| 11/01/20X1: | D) long-term investment | $15,000 | |
| | C) cash | | $15,000 |

Organization's purchase of an external investment of $15,000 to secure shares at X% interest for a predetermined amount of time in the future.

Likewise, in return for their original investment, the healthcare organization will receive payments in the form of stock dividends and/or interest payments (depending on the type of initial investment). This activity will result in a cash inflow—with the intent to hopefully offset the long-term weakening of the dollar over time due to ongoing inflation.

Example journal entry:

| 11/01/20X2: | D) cash | $750 | |
| | C) non-operating (interest) rev | | $750 |

Interest payment received for external investment originated on 11/01/20X1 ($15,000 original investment at 5% annual interest rate).

Healthcare Organization—Financing Activities

The third and final section of the statement of cash flows relates to the flow of money into and out of the healthcare organization regarding the organization accessing goods and services using someone else's money. This activity is most often conducted through the process of a loan (also known as a "note") with a banking institution or by issuing a bond. While there are various reasons why a healthcare organization would choose a note versus a bond to access funds to purchase organizational resources, it is assumed that the plan to utilize such funds provided by these financing methods will eventually generate organization revenues that (a) exceed the financing methods principal and interest payment requirements and (b) further assist the organization in achieving its strategic plan.

Example journal entries:

11/01/20X1:	D) cash	$25,000	
	C) N/P		$25,000

Bank loan procured at 4% simple interest rate for 5 years. Amount shown above is the loaned amount (principle) received by the bank when the loan originated.

10/31/20X2:	D) interest expense	$1,000	
	D) N/P	$5,000	
	C) cash		$6,000

Total payment to the bank of $6,000 is to pay the annual fee for using the bank's money over the past year (interest) and one fifth of the loan principle (amortized amount over 5-year loan period).

Statement Format

The statement of cash flows follows a simple format, demonstrating cash inflows and outflows for the organization based on each individual transaction's categorization (operating, investing, and financing activities). Each transaction, initially entered as a journal entry and posted to the organization's ledger, will be pulled and included in the total for each corresponding line (row) on the statement. Based on how the individual accounts are set up in the organization's financial accounting/software system, their inherent purpose will be programmed so the transaction value is listed (and summed) under the appropriate statement of cash flows category (row).

As demonstrated in the end-of-chapter example statement formats (Format A and Format B), the three sections of the statement of cash flows are presented (operating, investing, and financing activities). The net total for each of these sections is shown as the last entry under each section, labeled "net cash

Helpful tip: Be sure to differentiate between issuing and investing. While both start with the letter "i," it may help to remember that when an organization issues a bond, it is increasing its liability because it is in need of cash (cash poor). Investing (cash rich) involves the sheltering of excess/unbudgeted cash on hand by loaning it out to an external entity. This will generate interest revenue for the organization and protect the original (principal) amount of the investment from inflation. Issuing and investing are opposite activities.

inflow." The second column, offset from the first column of account totals, simply demonstrates the sum of the values above it.

There are two formats for the statement of cash flows—direct (example statement Format A) and indirect (example statement Format B), shown at the end of this chapter. The primary (and only) difference in these two statement formats is the inclusion of the itemized account values (increase or decrease) for all cash flows related to operating activities in the operating activities section of the statement for the indirect method (example statement Format B). Alternatively, these individual account value's increase or decrease may also be displayed at the very bottom of the statement. Here, they are summarized by their major revenue/expense account classifications within the abbreviated (shorter) cash flows from the operating activities section of the statement. In either example, the account values and overall financial statement figures are the same—the only difference is where on the statement the individual cash increases/decreases for operating activities are shown.

Revenue-Cycle Management

Any type of healthcare organization that is funded by prospective fee-for-service (FFS), volume-based, contractual arrangements with third-party payers endures a constant A/R and liquidity challenge. As discussed in Chapter 3, healthcare organizations are basically extending a line of credit to their customer (the patient) while third-party insurance claims are filed and pending for future reimbursement. As a result, expenses related to the care of the patient (salary and wages, medical supplies, utilities, etc.) are incurred immediately at the time of service yet are not reimbursed until much later. This balance between expenses incurred (and bills due) and available cash on hand outlines the importance of the organization's RCM process and related procedures. This activity has a direct influence on the organization's statement of cash flows and the operating activities section.

There are numerous continuous quality improvement initiatives that any typical healthcare organization can conduct to further streamline its revenue cycle and enable the transition from a pending A/R value to cash inflow. The goal is to create as short a time period as possible between the two events (date of service and date of reimbursement). The organization can proactively work to shorten its days in the A/R time period for those pending charges for care delivered. Table 11.1 offers insight into these potential tasks and related opportunities as examples to ensure a quick turnaround of medical claims.

TABLE 11.1   Examples of an outpatient clinic's patient checkup tasks and revenue-cycle initiatives

Event	Revenue-cycle initiatives
Patient must complete new patient paperwork prior to the medical appointment.	• Ensure the patient receives the proper clinic forms and completes them prior to their arrival for care on the date of service. • Possibly include the option for the patient to download/type their responses to these forms, versus handwritten responses (for increased legibility). • Possibly include the option for typed responses to be automatically input into the organization's EMR system (to further prevent transcription errors).
Patient must arrive 15 minutes early to check in for their first appointment with the organization.	• Involve the use of phone system/EMR technology to ensure the patient is contacted the day prior to remind them of their scheduled appointment. • Offer an option to reschedule ahead of time, versus the organization absorbing a "no-show" and losing the opportunity to care for another patient in that time period. • Offer information regarding organization location, direction, public transportation options, and other wayfinding resources.
Patient's HMO plan referral must be received from the patient's primary care physician prior to the appointment date.	• The organization should track those patients with gatekeeper third-party insurance plans for formal (usually electronic) referrals and ensure they are for the correct service(s) to be provided on the scheduled date of service. • An automated follow-up process should be implemented to ensure the referring physician's office is contacted about any missing referral(s) for the patient prior to the date of service. • Likewise, the organization's medical provider(s) must also be aware that only the referred service may be conducted on the scheduled date of service, unless otherwise approved by the patient's health plan.
The service is to be billed electronically by the organization to the patient's third-party insurance company.	• All services rendered by the organization should have claims spooled and sent electronically to the organization's medical claims clearinghouse that same evening, ensuring that any/all internal edits are identified and corrected prior to closing the clinic down for the day.

Think of a time when you or a loved one has accessed the healthcare system for a nonroutine medical procedure and/ or treatment (either at a hospital, physician's office, outpatient surgery center, or other healthcare organization). What specific steps were required of your family member to ensure that the visit was able to be scheduled and completed correctly and timely? What recommendations would you offer to the organization as a healthcare financial accounting student to further streamline its revenue-cycle process? Fill in the chart below to demonstrate your understanding of these simple yet highly influential tasks to help the organization's statement of cash flows.

Any services provided yet not reimbursed are to be tracked on the organization's "days-in-A/R" report for analysis and resubmission.

- Claims denied for reimbursement are to be followed up on the day they are received to ensure that an appeal for proper reimbursement with additional information is submitted timely.
- Days-in-A/R report is to be analyzed by payer type and payer name to ensure all contracts are being followed by both the organization and the third-party insurance company.

Personal Example of a Patient Encounter and Revenue-Cycle Improvement Opportunities	
Patient/family member tasks or actions required to ensure the visit occurred as scheduled without any interruptions of service delivery:	Recommended healthcare organization revenue-cycle initiatives to further streamline the process and shorten its days-in-A/R period:
1.	1.
2.	2.
3.	3.
4.	4.
5.	5.

In Summary

The statement of cash flows is a valuable resource for the healthcare leader, and especially the healthcare organizations operating under the accrual method of accounting. For these organizations, the inflow and outflow of actual cash is not captured under revenue or expense accounts. To see this inflow and outflow of cash, the statement of cash flows must be generated, which reverts to the cash method of accounting (for this one statement). Direct and indirect statement methods are available to the administrator for reasons of preference, presentation requirements, and ease of interpretability.

Depending on the time period in which the statement is generated, cash inflow and outflow subsections and overall total may net to a positive or negative value. Such values are to be interpreted carefully, as it is common for organizational characteristics and workflow to significantly affect any one section (or multiple sections) of the statement of cash flows during any particular time period. Overall, a positive cash flow is required to keep the organization viable and able to support the surrounding community's needs.

Based on organization type (for-profit or not-for-profit) and its strategic initiatives, positive or negative net increase cash on this statement may be used to further influence the organization's strategic plan and related financial management decisions.

Chapter Questions

1. What type of accounting method (accrual or cash accounting) requires the statement of cash flows, and why?
2. What financial statement previously addressed provides the same cash inflow/outflow activity information as the statement of cash flows for those organizations that use the cash method of accounting?
3. Discuss the importance of revenue-cycle management (RCM) and its relationship to the statement of cash flows.
4. What is the difference between the direct and indirect method formats in the statement of cash flows?
5. Explain why the following accounts increase (add) to the value of the statement's operating activities in Example Statement Formats A and B at the end of this chapter:
   a. depreciation expense
   b. increase in deferred revenues
6. Explain why the following accounts decrease (subtract) from the value of the statement's operating activities in Example Statement Formats A and B at the end of this chapter:
   a. increase in A/R
   b. decrease in A/P
7. Discuss the difference between financing and investing activities. Provide an example for each activity for any type of healthcare organization.
8. In your own words, define revenue-cycle management. Next, outline the steps involved for a patient accessing the healthcare system, for receiving a healthcare service, and then the follow-on billing procedures for the healthcare organization to receive payment.

Helpful tip: For the direct method, cash inflows/outflows for operating activities are listed as major classes within the statement itself, while Schedule A (at the bottom of the statement) reconciles the net cash flow for this section of the statement by listing each inflow/outflow operating activity.

Example Statement Format A

Huntsville Hospital Statement of Cash Flows—*Direct Method*

Operating (unrestricted) account

20X1

Cash Flows From Operating Activities

Cash received from patients and third-party payers	$10,201
Cash received from other operating activities	2,334
Cash received from non-operating activities	500
Cash payments for salaries/wages	(4,560)
Cash payments to suppliers	(1,300)
Net cash inflow (operating activities)	7,175

(see Schedule A below)

Cash Flows From Investing Activities

Cash payment for purchase of plant assets	(650)
Cash payments for purchase of long-term investments	(239)
Cash received from selling of assets	75
Cash received from selling of investment account(s)	50
Net cash outflow (investing activities)	(764)

Cash Flows From Financing Activities

Cash received from bank note (loan)	3,000
Cash payment for bond interest	(450)
Net cash outflow (financing activities)	2,550
Net increase/decrease in cash:	8,961

Schedule A:

Net income	13,353
Depreciation expense	1,700
Increase in accrued interest receivable	(2,000)

Increase in A/R	(4,560)
Increase in supply/inventory	(400)
Decrease in prepaid expenses	50
Decrease in A/P	(1,300)
Decrease in accrued expense payable	(68)
Increase in deferred revenues	200
Gain on sale of long-term investments	(300)
Loss on sale of plant assets	<u>500</u>
Net cash flow from operating activities	7,175

Example Statement Format B

Huntsville Hospital Statement of Cash Flows—*Indirect Method*

Operating (unrestricted) account

20X1

Cash Flows From Operating Activities

Net income	13,353
Depreciation expense	1,700
Increase in accrued interest receivable	(2,000)
Increase in A/R	(4,560)
Increase in supply/inventory	(400)
Decrease in prepaid expenses	50
Decrease in A/P	(1,300)
Decrease in accrued expense payable	(68)
Increase in deferred revenues	200
Gain on sale of long-term investments	(300)
Loss on sale of plant assets	<u>500</u>
Net cash flow from operating activities	7,175

Cash Flows From Investing Activities

Helpful tip: For the indirect method, cash inflows/outflows for operating activities (previously represented by Schedule A from the direct method) are now listed directly within the statement itself. As a result, there is no need for a Schedule A in this statement format.

Cash payment for purchase of plant assets	(650)
Cash payments for purchase of long-term investments	(239)
Cash received from selling of assets	75
Cash received from selling of investment account(s)	<u>50</u>
Net cash outflow (investing activities)	(764)

Cash Flows From Financing Activities

Cash received from bank note (loan)	3,000
Cash payment for bond interest	<u>(450)</u>
Net cash outflow (financing activities)	2,550
Net increase/decrease in cash:	<u>8,961</u>

Evaluating Financial Position and Performance of the Healthcare Organization

Introduction

The goal of healthcare financial accounting is to create valid and reliable financial statements for the healthcare organization. These statements are tools to demonstrate the financial status and overall performance of the organization for any specific time and/or time period. The four statements covered in this textbook (Figure 12.1) possess data that can then be interpreted using healthcare financial management analyses. These analyses pull financial data from the statements to assist with future projections, often in the form of budgets and other pro forma tools used by the healthcare organization leadership.

- Balance Sheet
- Statement of Operations (also known as the Income Statement, Profit/Loss Statement, or Statement of Revenue over Expenses)
- Statement of Net Assets (and Statement of Changes in Net Assets)
- Cash Flows Statement

FIGURE 12.1   Healthcare financial statements reviewed.

Further stressing the primary purpose of healthcare financial accounting, this bookkeeping process precedes any decisions being made by the organizational leaders. These decisions are responses to questions that often arise related to the future of the organization and are based on its current financial status, such as the following.

- Do we have enough cash on hand to meet the upcoming pay period for our employees?
- If we needed a short-term bank loan right now, would we qualify?

- How long does it take for us to get paid once we file an electronic claim to a contracted, third-party payer?
- Is our organization's financial status trending in the positive direction?

Answers to these and other operational questions are responded to by utilizing the organization's financial accounting processes and practices and generated financial statements. The financial statements provide the data for financial management analyses to assist in the future decision-making processes for the organization. The healthcare financial management discipline, as based on the data received from healthcare financial accounting initiatives, was initially introduced in Chapter 1.

Learning Objectives

By the end of this chapter, the student should be able to:

- Discuss the important relationship between healthcare financial accounting and healthcare financial management.
- List and describe the purpose of liquidity, profitability, efficiency, and solvency financial ratios.
- Interpret the preferred directionality (trending) of various financial ratios.
- Understand how a strong knowledge in healthcare financial accounting assists the healthcare leader with healthcare financial management initiatives for the organization.

Key Terms

1. Healthcare financial accounting
2. Healthcare financial management
3. Benchmark (internal and external)
4. Directionality
5. Liquidity ratio category
6. Profitability (effectiveness) ratio category
7. Efficiency ratio category
8. Solvency ratio category
9. Opportunity cost
10. Noncash expenses

The relationship between financial accounting and financial management is reviewed in Table 12.1. below.

TABLE 12.1   Distinction between healthcare financial accounting and healthcare financial management

Distinguishing characteristic	Healthcare financial accounting	Healthcare financial management
Timing/time period	Provides historical information up to current day (retrospective, backward).	Provides decision-making information from current day forward (prospective).
Decision making occurs?	No	Yes
Utilizes GAAP?	Yes	Yes
If errors present?	Financial statements with accounting errors will affect future management decisions made based on the incorrect accounting data.	Financial management decisions made will affect the future revenue/expenses of the organization, which will then result in future accounting data being recorded based on such decisions.
Statement analysis of organization position and performance	Provides the bookkeeping data (account values) for use in financial management analyses.	Utilizes established ratios and other formulas to pull information out of the financial statements' data for use in decision making for the organization's future.

Due to the relationship of healthcare financial accounting and healthcare financial management, some basic financial management tools are briefly reviewed to assist in the demonstration of the use of this textbook's healthcare financial accounting cycle and follow-on financial management analyses. As applied to healthcare financial management and healthcare financial management courses/curriculum, organizational position and performance analyses demonstrate the importance of correct and consistent accounting efforts (in accordance with GAAP) and the requirement to establish valid and reliable financial statements. While common financial ratios are addressed in this chapter, many other financial ratios and analyses exist beyond the scope of this textbook.

Introduction to Financial Ratios

Before reviewing the various categories and specific financial analysis ratios commonly used to evaluate the healthcare organization's financial status and performance, some discussion surrounding the interpretation of ratios and their use in the decision-making process is warranted. To begin, a ratio is a fraction (consisting of a numerator and a denominator) and is representative of a financial analysis at a specific point in time. Further, the ratio is also termed a financial benchmark, which means that it can be used in a comparative analysis with other benchmark values for the organization and beyond. Benchmark (ratio) values may be used to compare the organization against itself (referred to as internal benchmarking), as well as to other organizations' financial statement benchmark values (known as external benchmarking). While every healthcare organization operates in a completely different environment and possesses several different types of strategic and management initiatives, GAAP does help enable these various organizations' financial statements to maintain specific comparative appearances and values, permitting external benchmarking to be possible.

Directionality is another important consideration when interpreting financial statement benchmark values. For instance, should the ratios, over specific time periods, be trending upward (higher) in value or downward (lower) in value? This trend line direction of the ratios across one or multiple financial periods is extremely important for the healthcare administrator to comprehend and provides the leader an opportunity to explain their interpretation(s) to the other leaders within the organization. As an example, if one is analyzing the directionality of liquidity ratios, an expected directionality would be for this ratio pattern to remain somewhat stable, or close to the team's preestablished expectation of liquid (current) assets remaining readily available for use. Likewise, ratios that evaluate profit (performance) are intended to increase, and those assessing liabilities (debt) are expected to decrease over time (granted that additional obligations such as notes or bonds are not initiated within that same financial period).

There are hundreds of possible financial statement ratios available to be used in interpretation of the healthcare organization's financial position and performance. That said, one does not simply conduct every single ratio possible when analyzing their respective organization's financial statements. Instead, only those ratios that are useful in answering management decisions and ongoing monitoring of specific strategic initiatives are run and interpreted by the healthcare leadership team. Otherwise, conducting all possible financial ratios will ultimately result in too much information (also termed "analysis paralysis"). In the end, only run the ratios needed to get the important questions answered.

Financial Statement Analysis—Liquidity

The balance sheet provides the organization's financial position at any specific point in time. Multiple balance sheets may also be assessed, often on the same date across multiple financial periods (e.g., 12/31/20X1, 12/31/20X2, 12/31/20X3, and so on). Now that an understanding of the purpose and overall formatting of a balance sheet has been addressed (Chapter 8), one should also be questioning what elements within the statement demonstrate a "healthy" financial position, versus one in financial duress. This statement is the tool that provides the data to answer this question, and a multitude of financial ratios exist in the field of healthcare financial management to assist in evaluating organizational position. While financial ratios often fall within the discipline of financial management, a few are reviewed here to further emphasize proper statement GAAP format and also emphasis statement purpose (see Table 12.2).

TABLE 12.2   Financial ratios to assist in evaluating organizational position

Ratio category	Ratio	Formula	Reason to assess?	Trend direction?
Liquidity	Current ratio	current assets/ current liabilities	"Do we have enough cash and/or near-cash assets to cover our economic obligations that are due within the next 1-year period?"	Stability preferred versus a constant upward/downward directional trend line.
Liquidity	Quick ratio	(cash + marketable securities + A/R)/current liabilities	"Do we have enough cash and/or near-cash assets to cover our economic obligations that are due now?"	Stability preferred versus a constant upward/downward directional trend line.
Liquidity	Days cash on hand	[(cash + marketable securities)/ (operating expenses - bad debt expense - depreciation expense)] / 365	"How many days are we able to operate with the cash and cash equivalents already on hand and still meet regular operational expenses?"	Stability preferred versus a constant upward/downward directional trend line.

Both the current and quick ratios are commonly used to assess organizational liquidity, or how much cash and/or near-cash assets are readily available to meet short-term, current obligations. While one would commonly think that too much cash (or near-cash assets) on hand is never a bad thing, being too liquid as an organization does come with an opportunity cost—for example, failing to invest these funds in more lucrative strategic initiatives that would earn the healthcare organization additional revenue. In other words, while cash will hold its current value (notwithstanding ongoing inflation effects), it could otherwise have been invested in another project that could possibly yield an even better return on investment for the healthcare organization.

TRY ON YOUR OWN

Calculate your individual (personal) current ratio. Do you have twice the short-term assets (current economic resources) as compared to your short-term liabilities (current economic obligations)? If no, what are actions (changes to the ratio numerator and denominator) as related to financial decisions in your life that might enable you to reach this goal?

On the other hand, having too little cash on hand will not permit the organization to meet its short-term obligations either—also not a good situation for the organization. The balance between how much and how little cash (or near-cash assets) to keep on hand is a strategic decision assessed by using liquidity ratios. Judgment of the healthcare administrator and other organizational leadership is often highly influenced by the external environment (and other related factors) and is important in interpretation of organizational liquidity.

Regarding the days cash on hand ratio, notice that the denominator possesses the constant 365 value, yielding an answer (value) to the ratio formula that represents an actual number of days the organization is able to handle all regular operational expenses. This value assumes no further payments (or positive cash flow) will be received in the meantime. Additionally, it is important to note that both bad debt expense and depreciation expense account values are adjusted (or subtracted from) this ratio's formula denominator. This is because both of these operating expenses are actually noncash expenses. This means that while they are included as true operating expenses (and therefore lower the organization's experienced profit margin on the statement of operations), there is no true cash outflow related to these accounts, and therefore they contribute to a positive cash flow for the organization.

Financial Statement Analysis—Profitability

Profitability is a postassessment (summative review) of the healthcare organization's cumulative efforts in conducting its strategic mission (financial effectiveness in the treatment of patients). In other words, an effective organization is one that (a) meets all healthcare needs of its respective patient population and (b) experiences more revenues than expenses within a given financial time period. Directly related to revenues and expenses from the statement of operations, an organization is profitable if gross revenues are greater than gross expenses. However, these gross (total) accounts may be evaluated at a more intricate level to provide additional profitability information for the organizational leaders (see Table 12.3).

Ratio category	Ratio	Formula	Reason to assess?	Trend direction?
Profitability	Total margin	(revenue – expenses)/ revenue	"What is the relationship between our organization's profit margin and the total (gross) revenue for our organization?"	Upward
Profitability	Operating margin	(revenue – expenses)/ operating revenue	"What is the relationship between our organization's gross profit and the revenue earned (or received) from the provision of patient care services only?"	Upward

It should be stressed that a constant upward trend in organizational effectiveness (profitability) is required in today's healthcare industry. This statement applies to both for-profit and not-for-profit healthcare organizations. As the old adage states, "If you're not growing, you're dying." Healthcare leaders must constantly monitor the organization's financial effectiveness to ensure the facility will remain open and successful in providing healthcare services to the surrounding community. A closed hospital due to poor operational effectiveness and an inability to pay the bills does a community no good.

Note: Additional, important organizational profitability ratios exist in the discipline of healthcare financial management, such as return on assets and return on net assets, among many others. Because they are beyond the scope of this textbook, they are not addressed.

Financial Statement Analysis—Efficiency Ratios

When discussing how efficiently a healthcare organization is operating, the analysis of how well it is performing on an operational standpoint (formative analysis) comes into question. In other words, how efficient is the organization's processes in getting to the end goal (effective patient care and quality patient treatment outcomes)? This journey to the end point of care is evaluated using efficiency ratios. One can be quite efficient in their efforts to get a job or task completed or quite inefficient—yet still yield the same outcome in the end.

Helpful tip: There really is not a perfect answer to the question "What level of liquidity should our organization maintain on a regular basis?" that applies to all healthcare organizations. While ratios exist to assess liquidity at a specific point in time, the ongoing monitoring and adjustment of organizational liquidity is independent to each healthcare organization. This is because every healthcare organization exists within its own specific (and dynamic) economic environment. Healthcare administrators are trusted with the financial position and performance of the entire organization—to assess and respond to liquidity-specific requirements to enable the organization to meet ongoing strategic initiatives that require varying liquidity levels for any given financial period and related environmental/market conditions.

Helpful tip: It is assumed that while a thorough analysis of healthcare effectiveness (profitability) is important to organizational vitality for the long term, healthcare leaders' decisions regarding the ongoing attempt to increase revenues and decrease expenses should never result in a decrease in the quality of care provided to patients.

Two common healthcare efficiency ratios are shown in Table 12.4.

TABLE 12.4   Financial ratios to assist in evaluating organizational efficiency

Ratio category	Ratio	Formula	Reason to assess?	Trend direction?
Efficiency	Days in A/R	A/R, net/(net patient revenue/ 365)	"How long does it take us to collect on an invoice for services already provided?"	Downward with expectations for trend line to often remain close to electronic payer agreement time-line (if present).
Efficiency	Days in A/P	A/P/[(operating expenses – depreciation expense)/365]	"How long does it take us to pay on an invoice for goods or services our organiza-tion has already received?"	Trend line should be stable across all trade-credit agree-ment discount period timelines. Otherwise, if not trade-credit agree-ment, downward trend preferred.

Both the days in A/R and days in A/P ratio are unique in that their ratio cal-culation does not yield a monetary value but rather a number that represents a number of days (this is why there is a 365 value in these two efficiency ratio formulas). For days in A/R, an assessment of how many days (on average) it takes from the date of service until the organization receives reimbursement for the service provided is calculated. It is understood that in the healthcare industry the organization is not paid at the time of service, since a third-party payer is often involved. This third party must be billed after the service has been provided. However, as the claim for reimbursement continues to age well beyond 90, 120, and even 150+ days in A/R, the probability of collection from the responsible party continues to decline rapidly.

Days in A/P is quite similar to days in A/R, only in reverse. Instead of assess-ing how many days (on average) it takes to obtain reimbursement for service provided, an assessment regarding how many days it takes the healthcare organization to pay on obligations is made. Most often, such ratios should resemble average days in A/P similar to that of their trade credit agreements with external vendors for medical supplies and other services rendered on credit terms to the organization (Chapter 5).

Helpful tip: The health-care administrator should attempt to have all service/ supply contracts based on similar trade credit arrangements (percentage discounts, discount time period, and full invoice due date). This will assist in the interpretation of efficiency ratios, while also enabling the healthcare leader to maintain a more systematic approach to routine orga-nizational A/P processes and protocols.

Note: Additional, important organizational efficiency ratios exist in the discipline of healthcare financial management, such as total asset turnover, among many others. Because they are beyond the scope of this textbook, they are not addressed.

Financial Statement Analysis—Solvency

It is very common for healthcare organizations to have current and long-term economic obligations. Such liabilities may be in the form of bonds, loans, long-term construction contracts with accrued and future liabilities, and even deferred liabilities (tuition, rent payments received). At any one time, the healthcare organization will require a balance between its ability to access economic resources (assets) using either liability accounts or its net assets (specifically unrestricted NA/the operating fund account).

With any economic obligation comes risk. Banks are in the business of loaning money not only to organizations that need the quick access to capital funds for investment projects but also to those who are trustworthy and have a good potential to pay back the loan (creditworthiness), with interest. Solvency ratios are one way to assess an organization's financial statements to determine the overall risk involved with any single healthcare organization requesting a loan. Table 12.5 demonstrates two common solvency ratios that assess the organization's ability to simply pay the regular (e.g., monthly) fee for using the bank's money (interest expense), as well as an ability to pay both the interest and principal on the face value of the loan.

TABLE 12.5   Financial ratios to assist in evaluating organizational solvency

Ratio category	Ratio	Formula	Reason to assess?	Trend direction?
Solvency	Interest coverage	(excess of revenue over expenses + interest expense)/ interest expense	"Is our organization able to cover the interest charges on the loan?"	The higher the ratio calculated, the less risk is assessed by the creditor organization.
Solvency	Debt service coverage	(excess of revenue over expenses + interest expense + depreciation expense)/ (interest expense + principal payment amount)	"Is our organization able to cover the interest charges and principal amount on the loan?"	The higher the ratio calculated, the less risk is assessed by the creditor organization.

TRY ON YOUR OWN

If you are purchasing a
vehicle, which solvency
ratio would you use in evaluating your personal ability
to make monthly payments
on your new car? Why is
one solvency ratio in this
scenario better than the
other?
*Note: Additional, import-
ant organizational solvency
ratios exist in the discipline
of healthcare financial
management, such as long-
term debt to NA, among
many others. Because they
are beyond the scope of
this textbook, they are not
addressed.*

The better the organization's solvency ratios look, the more likely it is that the lending organization will be willing to offer the loan, and at a better interest rate (since low risk often results in a lower interest rate). However, as the solvency ratios trend in an unfavorable direction for the healthcare organization, the lending organization begins to be more restrictive with its lending options and availability, including higher interest rates and less access to principal loan funding. It is not a coincidence that banks favor lending to organizations that have current offsetting funds (assets) rather than assuming much higher risk with organizations that do not have sufficient solvency figures at the time of the loan request.

In Summary

Assessing a healthcare organization's financial position and performance falls within the discipline of healthcare financial management. Several financial management concepts are briefly reviewed to help bring the two disciplines together, while also demonstrating the necessity of generating valid and reliable financial statements. Future financial management ratios and follow-on decisions are made based the organization's financial statements. Therefore, it is imperative that the financial statements are correct and consistent with GAAP and ongoing FASB Accounting Standards Updates. Otherwise, if the statement values (and processes leading to the accumulation of these values) is incorrect, the resulting financial management ratio analyses will also be incorrect. This leads to poor management of the organization and decisions being made based on faulty data. A strong knowledge of healthcare financial accounting is imperative for the healthcare administrator to engage in effective healthcare financial management decisions.

The healthcare administrator is responsible for the financial position and performance of the organization. A solid foundation in financial accounting, related GAAP procedures, and specific healthcare policies is crucial. Data collection, recording and posting transactions, and presentation of valid and reliable financial statements are important preceding steps prior to any organizational decision making taking place. A strong competency in healthcare financial accounting will enable the healthcare leader to manage the organization into the future—to include furthering its strategic plan, adjusting for environmental changes, and—most importantly—ensuring the delivery of quality patient care.

Chapter Questions

1. Identify two asset and two liability subaccounts and discuss how an inaccurate financial accounting background may lead to incorrect figures. Next, review how the future financial management analysis(es) for a healthcare organization will be affected in this situation.

2. Review your personal finances and discuss what an optimal level of liquidity may be on any given week during a regular semester (fall and/or spring). Does this level stay the same, or does it vary throughout the semester? Why?

3. Using an Internet search engine, locate any organization's financial statements. Perform two financial ratio analyses using the ratio formulas in this chapter. Next, compare these values and interpret the directionality of both ratios from one statement to the next.

4. Identify and discuss several GAAP concepts specifically related to the healthcare industry that are important to understand prior to enrollment in a healthcare financial management course.

Appendix A: Basic Financial Statement Formats

T HESE BASIC FINANCIAL statement formats are provided to introduce the four financial statements in their simplest form as the journey toward generating them begins. These template formats will be expanded on throughout the textbook, to include ongoing FASB/GAAP format updates for specific healthcare organization types. Leaders are encouraged to learn these basic formats to assist in the interpretation and ongoing financial accounting updates that continue to evolve.

Formatting note: GAAP requires financial statements to be correctly labeled with the following items listed at the top of each statement:

    a)   Name of the healthcare organization
    b)   Date (or date range)
    c)   Type of financial statement

1.   Balance Sheet
    Healthcare Organization Name
    Single Date
    Balance Sheet

Assets	$50,000
Liabilities	$20,000
Net Assets	$30,000

2.   Statement of Operations
    Healthcare Organization Name
    Date Range

Statement of Operations

Revenue	$14,000
Expense	$9,500
Net Revenue	$4,500

3. Statement of Net Assets

Healthcare Organization Name

Single Date

Statement of Net Assets*

Unrestricted Net Assets	$56,000
Temporarily Restricted Net Assets	$24,000
Permanently Restricted Net Assets	$35,000
Total Net Assets	$115,000

*See Chapter 13 on the Cognella Active Learning website for additional updates to this financial statement format for healthcare organizations.

Healthcare Organization Name

Date Range

Statement of Changes in Net Assets

Beginning Net Assets, January 1, 20X1	$143,000
Change in Net Assets	+$52,500
Ending Net Assets, December 31, 20X1	$195,500

4. Statement of Cash Flows

Healthcare Organization Name

Date Range

Statement of Changes in Net Assets—Direct Method

Cash Flows from Operating Activities	
Net Cash Flows from Operating Activities (see Schedule A)	$35,000

Cash Flows from Investing Activities	
Net Cash Flows from Investing Activities	$15,000
Cash Flows from Financing Activities	
Net Cash Flows from Financing Activities	$6,500
Schedule A	
Net Cash Inflow from Operating Activities	*$35,000*

Healthcare Organization Name

Date Range

Statement of Changes in Net Assets—Indirect Method

Cash Flows from Operating Activities	
Net Cash Flows from Operating Activities	$35,000
Cash Flows from Investing Activities	
Net Cash Flows from Investing Activities	$15,000
Cash Flows from Financing Activities	
Net Cash Flows from Financing Activities	$6,500

Appendix B: Chart of Accounts

100	Assets		400	Revenue
101	Cash		401	Routine Services Revenue
102	Temporary Investments		402	Ancillary Services Revenue
103	Accrued Interest Receivable		403	Premium Revenue
104	Accounts Receivable (A/R)		404	Other Operating Revenue
105	Allowance for Uncollectible Accounts (AUCAs)		405	Rental Revenue
106	Inventory (Supply)		406	Tuition Revenue
107	Prepaid Insurance Expense		407	Interest Revenue
108	Prepaid Rent Expense		408	Non-Operating Revenue
109	Prepaid Interest Expense		500	Revenue Deductions
150	Land		501	Contractual Adjustments
160	Buildings(s)		502	Charity Care Adjustments
161	Accumulated Depreciation – Building(s)		600	Expenses
170	Equipment		601	Salary and Wages (S/W) Expense
171	Accumulated Depreciation – Equipment		602	Inventory (Supply) Expense
200	Liabilities		603	Utilities Expense
201	Accounts Payable (A/P)		604	Insurance Expense
202	Notes Payable (N/P)		605	Repairs Expense
203	Accrued Interest Payable		606	Rent Expense
204	Accrued Salaries and Wages (S/W) Payable		607	Depreciation Expense
205	Deferred Rental Revenue (Income)		608	Interest Expense
206	Deferred Tuition Revenue (Income)		609	Bad Debt Expense
220	Bonds Payable		610	Other (Miscellaneous) Expenses
300	Net Assets (Equity)			
301	Hospital Net Assets (NA)			
302	Revenue and Expense Summary			

Appendix C: Real/Nominal Subaccount Definitions

T HIS SECTION IS provided to encourage readers to begin learning the specific subaccount definitions and debit/credit effects for specific healthcare organizational transactions. All subaccounts below are located on the chart of accounts provided in Appendix B and will be frequently utilized in future accounting cycle process examples.

Asset Subaccounts

As previously discussed, organizational assets are composed of subaccounts that represent the *economic resources* that enable the healthcare organization to conduct operations (the delivery of patient care). Naturally, one would expect an organization's total assets to be a very high number, depending on the overall size of the organization.

Asset subaccounts are listed in order of *liquidity* on the balance sheet financial statement, with the most liquid assets listed first, and the least liquid assets to follow. Liquidity is an assessment of how long it will take to turn any specific organizational asset into cash. Asset subaccounts are also categorized into two groups: current and noncurrent assets. *Current assets* are those that can typically be liquidated within a 1-year period from the date of the balance sheet financial statement. *Noncurrent assets* are those accounts that will typically take longer than a 1-year period (on average) to liquidate.

Below is a description of each asset subaccount most utilized by any typical healthcare organization. It should be emphasized that while many of these account definitions may seem quite basic, a thorough understanding of each subaccount is important to correctly apply the principles of GAAP in everyday operations. While this list is not all inclusive, most healthcare operational examples in this textbook will involve the following asset subaccounts.

Cash

Cash is the most liquid organizational asset (being in its true form already) and represents dollar bills on hand, as well as monies being held by banking institutions that are readily available for spending (i.e., the organization's operational checking account or accounts). The healthcare organization can pay bills using the cash account and receives payments (from patients and third-party payers) to its cash account.

- Cash will be debited (increased) when monies are received by the organization.
- Cash will be credited (decreased) when monies are paid by the organization.

Temporary Investments

These are organizational short-term assets in third-party ventures that can typically be liquidated within a 1-year period from the date of the balance sheet. Examples include money market fund accounts and other liquid investment accounts that term (end) within a 1-year period.

- Temporary investments are debited (increased) when purchased by the organization.
- Temporary investments are credited (decreased) when sold by the organization.

Accrued Interest Receivable*

Related to any organizational investments with external firms, this account represents any interest earned by the healthcare organization in such investments but not yet received as of the date of the balance sheet financial statement.

- Accrued interest receivable is debited (increased) when the organization earns interest over a certain time period for an investment but has yet to be paid for this amount.
- Accrued interest receivable is credited (decreased) when the organization receives a payment for interest previously earned on an investment.

Accounts Receivable (A/R)*

Utilized to capture gross (volume × charges) revenue earned by the healthcare organization through the provision of healthcare services that are not yet paid (or received/reimbursed to the organization) by the patient or third-party payer. This gross (unadjusted) A/R value represents the organization's amounts billed for the delivery of care, including potential, future organizational write-offs such as contractual adjustments and/or charity care adjustments.

- A/R is debited (increased) when the organization provides a good or service but has yet to be paid.
- A/R is credited (decreased) when the organization receives a payment for a good or service previously provided.

Note: The A/R account and its presentation on a healthcare organization's statement of operations financial statement is addressed in Chapter 9. Additional A/R FASB updates are addressed in Chapter 13 (Cognella Active Learning website).

Allowance for Uncollectable Accounts (AUCA)

This account is classified as a contra-asset, working against the A/R account directly above it on the balance sheet. It captures the estimated, future potential write-offs from the gross A/R account directly above it. These estimated adjustments are related to both estimated, future contractual adjustments and estimated, future charity care adjustments for the healthcare organization.

- The AUCA is debited (decreased) only when estimated charity care and contractual adjustment accounts are objectively determined in value and adjusted or corrected to match the estimated amount to the actual amounts for these revenue deductions.
- The AUCA is credited (increased) when the organization has determined estimated, future charity care and contractual adjustment values to obtain a net realizable value for the gross A/R account.

Note: The AUCA account and its presentation on a healthcare organization's balance sheet financial statement are addressed in Chapter 8. Additional A/R FASB updates are addressed in Chapter 13 (Cognella Active Learning website).

Supply/Inventory

Supplies and inventory (synonymous terms in this textbook) represent one-time use (disposable) medical and nonmedical supplies utilized by the organization to assist in achieving its mission. These supplies are readily available on the inventory shelf, owned by the healthcare organization, and awaiting use in future patient care delivery.

- The supply/inventory account is debited (increased) when supplies are purchased by the organization in preparation for future use.
- The supply/inventory account is credited (decreased) when supplies are used by the organization in the delivery of patient care.

Prepaid Expenses (Insurance, Rent, and Interest)*

Prepaid insurance, prepaid rent, and prepaid interest expenses are not true expense accounts, even though they have the word "expense" in their account names. Rather, the "prepaid" qualifier at the beginning of these account names classifies them as organizational assets (which therefore appear on the balance sheet) and not expenses (which are presented on the statement of operations). These account values represent items/initiatives that the organization has paid for ahead of time (prepaid) that will benefit both current and future financial accounting periods.

- Prepaid tuition, prepaid rent, or prepaid interest expense accounts are debited (increased) when the organization purchases one of these assets that will benefit future accounting periods.
- Prepaid tuition, prepaid rent, or prepaid interest expense accounts are credited (decreased) as they are used and are to be adjusted to reflect current-day, remaining prepaid values.

Land

In its simplest form, land is the dirt the healthcare organization is built on. Land does not include land improvements (such as parking lot lighting, landscaping, and sprinkler systems). It is important to note that land does not depreciate.

- Land is debited (increased) when purchased by the organization.
- Land is credited (decreased) when sold by the organization.

Note: Depreciation and its presentation on a healthcare organization's balance sheet financial statement are addressed in Chapter 7.

Land Improvements

The value of all enhancements to the land that the organization is built on (not including land itself). Examples include sidewalks/pavement, parking lot striping, lighting, and even an outside therapeutic (walking) labyrinth. Land improvements can be depreciated.

- Land improvements are debited (increased) when purchased/added to the organization's property.
- Land improvements are credited (decreased) when sold, which is uncommon or only applicable when the organization's property is also sold.

Building(s)

The structure (four walls and roof) that constitute the healthcare organization's location(s) used for the provision of care. Buildings depreciate in book value over time.

- The building account is debited (increased) when a building is purchased.
- The building account is credited (decreased) when a building is sold.

Accumulated Depreciation—Building(s)

The to-date amount of depreciation that has accrued since the original purchase date of the structure(s).

- The accumulated depreciation—building account (a contra-asset account) is debited (decreased) when funds are removed for the upkeep and possible replacement of a building.
- The accumulated depreciation—building account is credited (increased) when a building's wear-and-tear value has been systematically calculated and captured as the building ages.

Equipment

Multiuse tools/machinery (both medical and nonmedical) used to achieve the healthcare organization's mission. Examples include desks, trash cans, elevators, gurneys, IV poles, MRI scanners, and ventilators.

- The equipment account is debited (increased) when equipment is purchased.
- The equipment account is credited (decreased) when equipment is sold.

Accumulated Depreciation—Equipment

The to-date amount of depreciation that has accrued since the original purchase date of the equipment.

- The accumulated depreciation—equipment account (a contra-asset account) is debited (decreased) when funds are removed for the upkeep and possible replacement of equipment.
- The accumulated depreciation—equipment account is credited (increased) when equipment's wear-and-tear value has been systematically calculated and captured as the equipment ages.

Liability Subaccounts

Healthcare organization liabilities are *economic obligations* that have yet to be paid. While the total value of liability accounts is initially subtracted from total assets to identify an organization's net worth (original, basic accounting equation: A − L = NA), the − L variable in the equation is moved to the right side of the equal sign in the equation, therefore making all liability values positive (the updated, basic accounting equation: A = L + NA). Therefore, while liabilities are presented as a positive value on the balance sheet financial statement, it is a number that should be kept lower in value, as opposed to asset accounts. The higher the value of organizational liabilities, the lower the organization's net worth (net assets).

Further discussed in Chapter 5, it is important to note that healthcare organizations often have ongoing liabilities to ensure they have the resources required to conduct their mission. A challenge for the healthcare leader is to ensure that all organizational needs are met to ensure the highest quality of care yet also contain the total amount of liabilities at any one time owed by the organization to external, third-party organizations.

Accounts Payable (A/P)*

This account represents the total value owed to external organizations for any goods or services provided to the healthcare organization already but not yet paid by the healthcare organization. Bills and other current liabilities with qualifying *trade credit terms* for medical supplies received and not yet paid for by the organization fall under this account until they are paid.

- A/P is debited (decreased) when the organization pays a bill for a good or service that was previously provided.
- A/P is credited (increased) when the organization receives a good or service and will pay for it later.

Note: Trade credit terms and related discounts will be addressed in Chapter 5.

Notes Payable (N/P)

A loan to the healthcare organization from a single entity—the bank. The value for this account represents the principal value of the loan remaining on the date the financial statement is generated.

- N/P is debited (decreased) as the organization pays down its loan obligation over time.
- N/P is credited (increased) when the organization is issued a loan by the bank.

Accrued Interest Payable*

The amount of interest for any organizational liability that continues to grow larger as every month (or other financial time period) passes but has yet to be paid by the healthcare organization (per the liability's terms). This account represents accrued interest over a time period only, not the principal balance of the liability itself.

- Accrued interest payable is debited (decreased) when the organization pays an interest bill for interest that has accrued in value to date.
- Accrued interest payable is credited (increased) as time passes and interest accrues against the organization's liability (e.g., a loan) but is not scheduled to be paid until sometime in the determined future.

Accrued Salary and Wages (S/W) Payable*

The value of payroll (human resources) that has been provided by organizational employees to the organization to assist in the delivery of care but has yet to be paid. This account will grow higher in value as the organization's scheduled pay date approaches and will then be reduced when the organization processes payroll and pays its employees.

- Accrued S/W payable is debited (decreased) when the organization pays its employees for services previously provided to the organization.
- Accrued S/W payable is credited (increased) as time passes and employees continue to work for the organization yet are awaiting a future pay date for their efforts already provided to the healthcare organization.

Deferred Rent Revenue*

This liability account represents the amount prepaid by an outside organization or individual to the healthcare organization in return for the healthcare organization providing space (e.g., a treatment room and/or office space) that is being leased/rented by the third party. Until the space has been fully provided over a specified time period, the prepayment by the third-party organization remains a liability (a deferred revenue) to the healthcare organization, and it will only be considered an experienced revenue (and not a liability) once it has been earned/completed over the established length of the lease.

- Deferred rent revenue is debited (decreased) when the organization has provided space (square footage) within the organization over a specified time period for which it was previously paid.

- Deferred rent revenue is credited (increased) when the organization receives a rent payment for space (square footage) that has been scheduled to be leased out but has yet to be provided to the lessee.

Deferred Tuition Revenue*

Like deferred rent revenue, this account represents the value of prepayments received from students registering for continuing education/classes to be provided by the healthcare organization. Therefore, these payments are received in advance, prior to the service (education) being delivered by the organization. Once the continuing education has been completed, this value is no longer prepaid by the students and has also been fully earned by the healthcare organization. This value (the original prepayment amount) is then moved from the liability (deferred tuition) account to a true revenue account once earned by the organization providing the education event.

- Deferred tuition revenue is debited (decreased) as the organization provides continuing education or other tuition-related services within the organization over a specified time period for which it was previously paid ahead of time.
- Deferred tuition revenue is credited (increased) when the organization receives a tuition payment for continuing education or other tuition-related services within the organization but has yet to provide the education.

Bond(s) Payable

A bond is a loan from the community, not the bank. Often extending over a very long time period (10-, 20-, even 30-year terms), a bond pays qualified investors a set percentage of interest every year during the life of the bond. When the bond terms (ends) on its final scheduled year, the last interest payment is paid to the investors, and their original investment amount is returned to the inventor at that time.

- Bond payable is debited (decreased) as the organization pays down its bond obligation over time.
- Bond payable is credited (increased) when the organization issues a bond.

Net Asset Subaccounts

Unrestricted Net Assets

This equity account houses the value of any profit experienced by the healthcare organization from previous accounting periods. Likewise, it will also lower in value of there is any loss experienced by the organization from a prior financial accounting period. In effect, it is either increased (a profit) or decreased (a loss) based on the net effect of total revenues and expenses of the organization over time.

Note: Philanthropic donations to the healthcare organization that are not restricted are also captured under the unrestricted net asset account.

Temporarily Restricted Net Assets
Philanthropic donations to the healthcare organization that increase its overall net worth (value) yet are not able to be utilized (spent) until a specified date in the future, per the donor's terms.

Permanently Restricted Net Assets
Philanthropic donations to the healthcare organization that increase its overall net worth (value) yet are only able to be utilized for a specific purpose or initiative, as stipulated by the donor.

- All NA account values are debited (decreased) when the organization's net worth is decreased.
- All NA accounts values are credited (increased) when the organization's net worth is increased.

Note: FASB changes to the presentation of the NA accounts and additional details are further reviewed in Chapter 13 (Cognella Active Learning website).

*The above notated asset and liability subaccounts are specifically utilized with the accrual method of account and related transaction.

Appendix D: Flash Cards for Common Healthcare Operations Accounting Transactions

WHILE CERTAINLY NOT all encompassing, the typical healthcare organization will conduct a handful of similar transactions repeatedly throughout any single day of regular operations. The following flash cards are offered to assist in memorizing the debit and credit subaccounts affected by any specific healthcare transaction.

Note: Many of the accounts used under the accrual accounting method are notated (*).

1.

A hospital purchased supplies for cash.	D) inventory/supply C) cash Explanation: Supplies increase in value because more were purchased. Cash lowers in value because it was used to acquire the supplies.

2.

A hospital purchased supplies on account (i.e., credit).	D) inventory/supply C) A/P* Explanation: Supplies increase in value because more were purchased. A/P is increased because the supplies were purchased now and will be paid for (in cash) later, increasing this liability account.

3.		
	A hospital mailed a check to pay its utility bill.	**D) utility expense** **C) cash** Explanation: The expense was paid, so the expense account increased in value to show it existing on the books. Cash was decreased because it was used to pay the expense.

4.		
	A hospital treated a patient and billed their insurance.	**D) A/R*** **C) operating revenue** Explanation: A/R was increased because the organization using the accrual accounting method earned revenue but will be paid later (not at the time of service). Revenue was increased because it was earned at the time of service (regardless of whether received).

5.		
	An outpatient medical clinic patient paid their copay at the time of service.	**D) cash** **C) operating revenue** Explanation: Cash increases in value because a positive cash flow is experienced. Revenue is increased because the organization using the cash method of accounting recognizes revenue only when received (paid).

6.		
	An organization made a payment on a loan which included $x of interest and $y of principal.	D) interest expense $x D) note payable $y C) cash Explanation: Expense is increased to show it now existing on the books, while the loan principle (N/P) is decreased due to payment on the loan. Cash is decreased because it was a cash outflow to pay these items.

7.		
	A hospital received a check from an insurance carrier for services previously provided to a patient.	D) cash C) A/R* Explanation: Cash is increased due to the positive cash flow (payment received). A/R is decreased because the organization is no longer expecting payment for a service previously provided (since the payment has now occurred and is no longer due).

8.		
	A hospital was provided a loan from the bank.	D) cash C) note payable Explanation: Cash is increased due to the positive cash inflow when a bank provides the loan principal value to the organization. N/P (a liability) is increased because this money is to be paid back to the bank over time.

9.

A hospital issued a bond to the local community.	**D) cash** **C) bond payable** Explanation: Similar to the organization receiving a loan from a bank, but the bond payable liability is increased to show the issuing authority to be the local community versus a bank.

10.

A hospital was billed for consultative services previously provided.	**D) other expenses** **C) A/P*** Explanation: Under the accrual method of accounting, the service (classified as "other expense") increased in value to show it recorded as an expense at the time it was incurred. A/P (liability) was increased to show a service was received but not yet paid.

11.

A hospital paid its employees.	**D) salary/wage expense** **C) cash** Explanation: The expense was increased to show it recorded on the books. It was paid with cash, so the negative cash flow is recorded as a credit to lower the cash account value.

A hospital paid its employees for a pay period that ended yesterday.	**D) salary/wages payable*** **C) cash** Explanation: The liability was decreased to show its value lowered since it is being paid and not owed to the employees anymore. It was paid with cash, so the cash account is lowered due to the negative cash flow.

12.

Glossary

Accelerated Depreciation Methods. An alternative to straight-line depreciation, these methods establish a systematic method to allocate depreciation expense in greater amounts earlier in the asset's useful life, and in lower amounts as the asset approaches the end of its useful life. Examples include 150%, 175%, and 200% accelerated depreciation methods, as well as the sum-of-years digits (SYD) depreciation method.

Accounts Payable (A/P). A liability account that represents the value of goods/services already received but yet to be paid for by the healthcare organization.

Accounts Receivable (A/R). An asset account that represents the value of goods/service already provided by the healthcare organization but not yet reimbursed.

Accrual Accounting Method. A method of financial accounting utilized primarily by hospitals and other large healthcare organizations that recognizes (records) revenues when earned and expenses when incurred, regardless of whether the organization has received payment and/or paid a bill.

Accrued Interest Payable. An accrual accounting liability account that records the value of interest expense that has accumulated since the last date the healthcare organization made an interest payment.

Accrued Interest Receivable. An accrual accounting asset account that records the value of interest revenue that has accumulated since the last date the healthcare organization received an interest payment.

Accrued Salary and Wages (S/W) Payable. An accrual accounting liability account that records the value of salary/wage expense that has accumulated since the last date the healthcare organization made a salary/wage payment (employee pay date).

Accumulated Depreciation. A contra-asset account that continuously retains all depreciation expense values for buildings and/or equipment assets being depreciated by the healthcare organization.

Accumulated Depreciation—Buildings. See Accumulated Depreciation.

Accumulated Depreciation—Equipment. See Accumulated Depreciation.

Adjustment (Adjusting Journal Entry). A journal entry that is utilized to increase or decrease the value of any account that has been changed over a specific time period. An adjustment may also be used to make a correction to any previously recorded transaction.

Allowance for Uncollectable Accounts (AUCA). A contra-asset account that is used to hold the value of any amounts of gross accounts receivable (A/R) that is estimated to possibly not be collected in the near future as a result of (a) charity care adjustments and/or (b) contractual adjustments. In effect, this action allows for the presentation of the net realizable A/R value, or what is actually expected to be collected for services provided and not yet reimbursed.

Alternative Payment Models (APMs). An alternative to the Merit-Based Incentive Payment System (MIPS) and part of the Medicare Quality Payment Program (QPP) that incorporates advanced pay-for-performance (P4P), provider risk-based reimbursement methods for specific healthcare organizations.

Ancillary (Operating) Service Revenue. Revenue that is earned/received for additional procedures or services ordered by a provider for specific patient care, in addition to routine service revenue.

A/P Voucher Process. A requirement maintained by the healthcare organization that requires a confirmation of delivered goods/services to be valued at the same amount as expected on the invoice received, as well as the amount the organization will pay in the transaction.

Asset Accrual Accounts. Asset subaccounts that are utilized under the accrual method of accounting to demonstrate accounts values growing systematically over time. Includes accrued interest receivable, accounts receivable, allowance for uncollectable accounts, and prepaid expenses.

Assets. Economic resources of the healthcare organization.

Balance Sheet. A financial statement that demonstrates the healthcare organization's financial position at any specific point in time.

Basic Accounting Equation. Assets – Liabilities = Net Assets.

Benchmark (External). Use of an outside financial accounting value (such as dollar amount, frequency of procedures, or financial ratio value) that is used as a comparison for the healthcare organization.

Benchmark (Internal). Use of an internal financial accounting value (such as a previous month's or year's value, or financial ratio value) that is used for the healthcare organization to compare its own values over time.

Bonds Payable. A liability account that shows the value of an outstanding bond at any specific point in time. Bonds are a loan from the community (multiple entities/stakeholders).

Book Value. The value of any account as demonstrated on the healthcare organization's financial records, independent of any market value influence.

Buildings. The structure in which healthcare operations are conducted by the healthcare organization.

Business Entity. An incorporated organization established to help with some (yet not exclusive) liability and debt protection.

Cash. The value of cash on hand by the healthcare organization, as well as any funds readily available in its operational (checking) accounts.

Cash Accounting Method. A method of financial accounting utilized by nonhospital entities that recognizes (records) revenues when payments are received and expenses when paid.

Cash (Sales) Receipt. Documentation (printed and/or electronic) that acknowledges the receipt of payment to the healthcare organization by a patient or other third party at the time of service.

Charge Master. An internal document that lists all frequently provided healthcare goods/services offered by the healthcare organization and their respective full-billed (gross) charge.

Charity Care Adjustment. The value of care provided to an indigent patient that is not expected to be collected due to the patient's inability to pay.

Chart of Accounts. A listing of all the healthcare organization's main and subaccounts in GAAP format with corresponding account numbers.

Coinsurance. An amount that the patient is expected to pay out of pocket to the healthcare organization after their insurance applies the contractual adjustment to discount the full-billed (gross) charge, after meeting their annual deductible, and after a percentage of coinsurance has been applied by the insurance company.

Conservativism. An accounting concept that involves the un-anticipation of revenues until actually received, and an anticipation of future expenses.

Consistency. An accounting concept that entails the healthcare organization keeping the same financial accounting processes and practices over time.

Contractual Adjustment. An agreed amount (via signed contract) to be discounted from the healthcare organization's full-billed (gross) charge for a good/service provided to a patient with third-party insurance coverage.

Copayment. A flat-fee (may increase for urgent/emergency care services) that is expected to be paid by the patient with third-party insurance coverage each time they access the healthcare system, regardless of whether they have met their annual deductible or not.

Corporations (C-corp). An incorporated business entity that is taxed separately from its ownership.

Cost-Shifting. The practice of private commercial health insurance organizations reimbursing a higher amount for services provided to their members (patients) in order to help offset lower allowable amounts paid by Medicare and/or Medicaid payers for that same service.

Credit. Used to document (record) the increase or decrease in an account value in the healthcare organization's journal and ledger.

Current (Short-Term) Assets. Asset accounts that are typically able to be liquidated within a 1-year time period.

Current (Short-Term) Liabilities. Liability accounts that are typically able to be paid off within a 1-year time period.

Days in A/R. A healthcare financial ratio that is used to monitor the age of pending A/R values, based on their initial date of service.

Debit. Used to document (record) the increase or decrease in an account value in the healthcare organization's journal and ledger.

Deductible. An amount established by the patient's third-party insurance plan that is required to be paid out of pocket by the patient each plan year (annually) before any insurance assistance (such as coinsurance) is available. The deductible is for all net values owed by the patient (the contractual adjustment is still applied to the full-billed (gross) charge).

Deferred Rent Revenue. A liability account that represents the amount of rent payments received (prepaid) from an outside entity, but the healthcare organization's rental space has yet to be provided.

Deferred Tuition Revenue. A liability account that represents the amount of tuition payments received (prepaid) from a continuing education student, but the healthcare organization has yet to provide the educational session.

Depreciation. The cost allocation of a calculated book value that represents the wear and tear (aging) of the healthcare organization's capital assets, such as buildings and equipment.

Depreciation Expense. An operating expense account that represents the wear and tear (aging) of the healthcare organization's capital assets, such as buildings and equipment.

Directionality. An assessment of healthcare data (e.g., healthcare financial statement ratios) that involves an identification and analysis of trending values over time (may trend up or down in value).

Dual-Entry System. The GAAP procedure that requires every financial accounting transaction to include at least one debit and one credit; the transaction's debit value must equal its credit value.

Effective Annualized Interest Rate. An analysis of an interest rate as applied to a 365-day period and based on the amount borrowed and the amount of trade discount percentage missed.

Efficiency Ratio Analysis. An analysis of specific healthcare financial statement data that provides information describing how well the organization is operating during the provision of patient care (formative evaluation process).

Electronic Fund Transfer (EFT). A transfer of money from one organization to another using a variety of electronic methods.

Equipment. A healthcare organizational asset that is reusable and helps support the organization's mission.

Equity. See *Net Assets*.

Expanded Accounting Equation. Assets + Expenses = Liabilities + Net Assets + Revenue.

Expense. The amount incurred (or paid) by the healthcare organization associated with the delivery of healthcare services and other mission-related initiatives.

Explicit Price Concession. (Chapter 13) The value of a known reduction from the full-billed (gross) charge for a healthcare service, such as a contractual adjustment with a third-party health insurance company.

Fair Market Value. The value of an asset as established between both the seller and a potential buyer in the marketplace.

Fee-for-Service (FFS). A healthcare reimbursement methodology that involves the healthcare organization providing and billing for each good/service delivered independently, and therefore reimbursed independently. Therefore, the more services the healthcare organization provides, the more it can bill and thereby be reimbursed. Also known as volume-based reimbursement.

Financial Accounting. A method of accounting that focuses on the accumulation and formation of valid and reliable financial statements for a healthcare organization.

Financial Accounting Cycle. The process of steps (initiatives) to support the accumulation of data and formulation of valid and reliable financial statements for a healthcare organization.

Financial Accounting Standards Board (FASB). An independent organization that establishes the standards and protocols to support Generally Accepted Accounting Principles (GAAP).

Financial Management. Decision-making processes and procedures that are based on the organization's financial statement (and the preceding financial accounting practices) to assist with ensuring the future viability and solvency of the healthcare organization.

Financial Period. An established time period (annual) that specifies when the healthcare organization finalizes and closes its books to determine operational effectiveness for the annual time period.

Financial Worksheet. A financial accounting tool (but not a financial statement) that assists the healthcare organization in establishing a balanced trial balance before and after adjusting entries are made, to ensure that the data supporting the three primary financial statements all balance accordingly.

Financing Activities. Utilized by the healthcare organization when it requires an additional resource (asset) and does not have the cash available to purchase the asset. Therefore, it acquires the asset using another organization's money to purchase the asset (e.g., a loan). The fee for this service is called interest.

First-in-First-Out (FIFO). An inventory costing (expensing) method that records the historical cost (purchase price) of the oldest asset in the inventory as the inventory (supply) expense value.

First-in-Still-Here (FISH). An inventory valuation method that records the historical cost (purchase price) of the oldest asset in the inventory as the inventory (supply) asset value.

Fund Account. A self-balancing subset of financial statements and/or financial resources that are earmarked for a specific use, often related to legal and/or ethical obligations or other organizational initiatives.

Future Profit Valuation. A healthcare asset valuation method that acknowledges an asset's future profits earned from its future workload, or otherwise assessed as an opportunity cost if the asset was sold instead.

Generally Accepted Accounting Principles (GAAP). An established set of processes and procedures that allows for consistency and conformity in the establishment and presentation of organizational financial statements.

General Partnership (GP). An agreement between two or more individuals (owners) of an organization in which they share equal responsibilities in ownership of assets, obligations of debt/liabilities, and experienced net assets of the organization.

Going Concern. An accounting concept that requires the healthcare leader to make decisions on behalf of the organization to ensure the longevity of the organization far into the future, versus simply focusing on short-term achievements/gains.

Goodwill. An asset account value presented on an organization's balance sheet financial statement to represent intangible organizational resources that help increase the value of the organization, truly represented (verified) in the actual sale of the organization. Examples include brand recognition, market and online perceived reputation, employee morale, and referring provider relationships.

Gross Patient Service Revenue (GPSR). Calculated in a fee-for-service (FFS) reimbursement environment by multiplying volumes by charges. The sum of all total billed charges for goods/services provided by the organization, without any adjustments.

Gross Revenue. The total amount of unadjusted, total revenue charged by an organization by multiplying the volume of procedures by the total billed charge for each respective procedure.

Historical Cost. The purchase price of an asset.

Implicit Price Concession. (Chapter 13) The amount adjusted from the patient's individual responsibility amount for healthcare goods/services previously delivered yet not expected to be collected in full due to patient financial constraints (e.g., indigent, charity care).

Income. See *Revenue*.

Indigent Patients. Patients who have received healthcare goods/services yet do not possess the financial resources to pay for the care received.

Investing Activities. Financial transactions related to third-party investments by a healthcare organization in order to outpace current inflation rates for unbudgeted cash on hand.

Inventory. An asset account that represents the value of expendable, one-time use supplies to assist the healthcare organization in achieving its mission. Also called supplies.

Inventory Expending/Usage. The value of all inventory items as pulled from the healthcare organization's supply shelf for use in the delivery of patient care.

Inventory Valuation. The value of all inventory items currently owned by the healthcare organization while remaining on the shelf and unused in anticipation of use in the provision of future patient care.

Invoice (Medical Invoice). A paper or electronic receipt to document healthcare services provided yet still not paid by the receiving patient and/or third-party payer.

Journal (Record). A book of all accounting transactions listed in chronological order, documenting the account names, debit/credit values, and date of the transaction.

Land. The dirt the healthcare organization is built on. Land is presented as an asset on the healthcare organization's balance sheet financial statement if it owns the land (does not lease, etc.).

Land Improvements. Additions to the dirt the healthcare organization is built on, including sprinkler systems, paved parking lots, parking lot striping, shrubbery/landscaping, and lighting.

Last-in-First-Out (LIFO). An inventory costing (expensing) method that records the historical cost (purchase price) of the newest asset in the inventory as the inventory (supply) expense value.

Last-in-Still-Here (LISH). An inventory valuation method that records the historical cost (purchase price) of the newest asset in the inventory as the inventory (supply) asset value.

Ledger (Post). A financial accounting tool that allows for the ongoing assessment of any healthcare organization's specific subaccount value at any point in time. Recognizable by the use of multiple T-accounts, one posts to a ledger after recording in a journal.

Liabilities. Economic obligations of the healthcare organization.

Liability Accrual Accounts. Liability subaccounts that are utilized under the accrual method of accounting to demonstrate account values growing systematically over time. Includes accrued interest payable, accrued salary and wages (S/W) payable, deferred rent revenue, and deferred tuition revenue.

Liquidity (Liquid) Ratio Analysis. An analysis of specific healthcare financial statement data that provides information describing how easily (quickly) the organization's noncash assets can be converted to cash.

Loss. A value as determined by the healthcare organization's statement of operations financial statement that demonstrates the financial period's total expenses being greater than the total revenue.

Market Value. Utilizing supply and demand economic theory, the value an asset can be sold for at any time in the dynamic market.

Matching Principle. An accounting concept that works to ensure that any expenses related to a specific good/service provided by the healthcare organization are able to be matched with the revenue earned (or received) from that same good/service within the same time period (e.g., month and/or year).

Materiality. An accounting concept that is used to describe data and/or a piece of financial accounting information that is of significance (big or important) to the healthcare organization.

Medicare Access and CHIP Reauthorization Act (MACRA) of 2015. Legislation following the PPACA that furthered pay-for-performance initiatives with the Medicare program by creating MIPS (Merit Based Incentive Payment Systems) and APMs (Alternative Payment Models). It also repealed the Sustainable Growth Rate (SGR) formula.

Merit-Based Incentive Payment System (MIPS). A Medicare Quality Payment Program (QPP) initiative that incorporates value-based reimbursement methods for healthcare organizations meeting specific, previously established quality standards.

Net. A financial accounting term used to denote "after." Example: net revenue = revenue – expenses. Therefore, revenue "after" subtracting expenses.

Net Assets. The value of the healthcare organization's net worth at any specific point in time as documented on the balance sheet financial statement by subtracting total liabilities from total assets. Also known as equity and/or net worth.

Net Operating Revenue. A value representing the profit or loss over a time period as related specifically to the prevision of healthcare services. Calculated by subtracting total expenses from total operating revenue.

Net Patient Service Revenue (NPSR). A value that represents gross patient service revenue (GPSR) minus the healthcare organization's revenue deduction accounts (contractual adjustments and charity care adjustments).

Net Realizable Value. An assessment of an asset's value (often at the time of sale) that represents additional charges (expenses) associated with the sale itself and/or additional nontangible asset values that increase the asset's market value.

Net Revenue. A value representing the profit or loss over a time period. Calculated by subtracting total expenses from total revenue.

Net Worth. See *Net Assets*.

Nominal Accounts. The category of accounts that close out and return to $0 value at the beginning of every new financial period. Includes all revenue and expense accounts.

Noncash Expenses. Healthcare organization operating expenses that do increase the organization's total expense value for any given financial period yet do not result in a negative cash flow. Examples include depreciation expenses and bad debt expenses.

Noncurrent (Long-Term) Assets. Asset accounts that are typically able to be liquidated beyond a 1-year time period.

Noncurrent (Long-Term) Liabilities. Liability accounts that are typically able to be paid off beyond a 1-year time period.

Non-Operating Revenue. Healthcare organization revenue earned (or received) from goods/services provided that are not related to the delivery of patient care; for example, interest revenue.

Nonprofit (Not-for-Profit) Corporations. Healthcare organizations that fall under section 501(c)(3) of the IRS tax code that utilize any profit experienced from a financial period to (a) reinvest in itself to assist with future healthcare operations and to (b) provide ongoing services to support community-based healthcare initiatives. As a result, the not-for-profit healthcare organization does not pay taxes.

Notes Payable (N/P). A liability subaccount that represents the value of an amount owed to a financial institution (i.e., the bank) for the balance of a loan.

Notes to the Financial Statements. A structured section of free-text written information at the end of the healthcare organization's financial statements that adds additional information and transparency to what is not obvious or otherwise provided in the financial statements themselves.

Operating Activities. Healthcare organization activities that are related to the provision of patient care services.

Opportunity Cost. The cost of making one decision that forgoes the alternate decision and all potential revenues and/or expenses that would have otherwise been experienced (obtained).

Other Operating Revenue Accounts. Revenue accounts related to regular operational activities for the healthcare organization yet unrelated to direct patient care services. Examples include rent revenue and tuition revenue.

Patient Protection and Affordable Care Act (PPACA) of 2010. The law that provides individual rights/protections for health care consumers. Subsidies and potential Medicaid expansion benefits are also included to assist those with low-income levels.

Pay-for-Performance (P4P). A healthcare reimbursement method that includes a multitude of techniques to reimburse healthcare providers and/or healthcare organizations for quality outcomes, versus the standard fee-for-service (FFS) reimbursement method.

Periodic Inventory Method. An inventory method that assesses all available inventory inflow and outflow from the previous financial period.

Permanently Restricted Net Assets. Philanthropic donations received by the healthcare organization that have legal and ethical obligation requirements to be enforced, as dictated by the donor.

Perpetual Inventory Method. An inventory method that assesses all available inventory inflow and outflow concurrently or during the current financial period.

Premium. A patient cost-sharing technique that involves a set monthly fee that is paid by the patient in order to maintain an active health insurance policy and related coverage.

Premium Revenue. Healthcare organization revenue earned (or received) by engaging in a contractual arrangement with an external entity that provides a set (fixed) payment for healthcare coverage and related services to a specific patient population, regardless of their utilization rates or acuity of illnesses and related expenses. Also known as capitated revenue and/or capitation.

Prepaid Expenses. An asset subaccount that represents payment for goods/services that will benefit the healthcare organization in a future financial period(s).

Profit (Margin). A value as determined by the healthcare organization's statement of operations financial statement that demonstrates the financial period's total revenue being greater than the total expenses.

Profitability Ratio Analysis. An analysis of specific healthcare financial statement data that provides information describing how well the organization has performed financially (summative evaluation process).

Provision for Bad Debts. A value that is deducted from net patient service revenue (NPSR) for unreimbursed care when healthcare services are provided to a patient and their ability to pay is not determined at the time of service.

Quality Payment Program (QPP). A value-based performance (VBP) reimbursement initiative established by the Medicare Access and CHIP Reauthorization Act (2015) policy requiring healthcare providers to participate in either the Merit-Based Incentive Payment System (MIPS) or an Alternate Payment Model (APM) initiative.

Real Accounts. The category of accounts that do not close out and therefore carry over their values at the end of a financial period to the beginning of the next financial period. Includes all asset, liability, and net asset accounts.

Restricted Net Assets. A category of net asset accounts and their respective values that have ethical and legal obligations as tied to them for predesignated, specific purposes.

Revenue. The amount earned (or received) by the healthcare organization associated with the delivery of healthcare services and other mission-related initiatives.

Revenue and Expense Summary Account. An account that follows the same debit/credit methodology as net assets and is utilized to help close out nominal (revenue and expense) accounts at the end of a financial accounting period.

Revenue Cycle Management. A healthcare organization's process that documents, identifies, accumulates, and works to collect all amounts owed for services provided and outstanding as accounts receivable (A/R).

Revenue Deductions. Healthcare industry–specific accounts that are subtracted from gross patient service revenue (GPSR) to result in net patient service revenue (NPSR). Includes contractual adjustments and charity care adjustments.

Routine (Operating) Service Revenue. Revenue that is earned (or received) as a result of routine care for patients within the healthcare organization related to room/board and regular nursing care.

Salvage Value. An estimated value often provided by the medical vendor and/or sales representative that represents what the asset could be sold for at the end of its prescribed useful life.

S Corporation. A business entity that utilizes a "pass-through" taxation option to allow for the healthcare organization's profits and/or losses to be assumed directly by the organization's shareholders (owners).

Sole Proprietorship. An individual who assumes personal responsibility for the organization, including any profits and/or losses and debts.

Specific Identification. A healthcare inventory valuation and expensing method that involves labeling individual pieces of supply (inventory) with their historical cost at the time of purchase.

Statement of Cash Flows. A healthcare financial statement that utilizes the cash method of accounting to identify cash inflows and outflows, as related to operating, financing, and investing activities.

Statement of Changes in Net Assets. A healthcare financial statement that demonstrates a beginning and ending net asset value based on experienced profit or loss.

Statement of Net Assets. A healthcare financial statement that describes the organization's net asset account by identifying values associated with restricted, temporarily restricted, and unrestricted net assets subaccounts.

Statement of Operations. A healthcare financial statement that demonstrates the organization's revenue earned (or received) and expenses incurred (or paid) and the resulting profit/loss value during a specific financial accounting period. Also called the statement of revenue over expenses, income statement, and the profit/loss statement.

Straight-Line Depreciation Method. A healthcare inventory valuation and expensing method that involves calculation of a fixed depreciation expense allocation amount to systematically lower the asset's book value throughout its prescribed useful life.

Solvency. The ability of a healthcare organization to meet not only its short-term obligations but also its long-term liabilities (long-term viability).

Solvency Ratio Analysis. An analysis of specific healthcare financial statement data that provides information describing how well the organization is able to meet its long-term debt obligations.

Sum-of-Years Digits (SYD) Depreciation Method. An alternative to straight-line depreciation, this method establishes a systematic method to allocate depreciation expense in greater amounts earlier in the asset's useful life and in lower amounts as the asset approaches the end of its useful life.

Sunk Cost. A cost (expense) during the financial management process that has already been incurred (or paid) by the healthcare organization and cannot be recovered, regardless of which decision is made moving forward.

Supply. See *Inventory*.

T-account. See *Ledger*.

Temporarily Restricted Net Assets. Philanthropic donations received by the healthcare organization that have legal and ethical time obligation requirements to be enforced, as dictated by the donor.

Temporary Investments. Short-term securities, often purchased with unbudgeted, excess cash on hand that allow the healthcare organization to earn interest revenue in the meantime.

Trade-Credit Discount. A contractual arrangement between a healthcare organization and an external business (e.g., a medical supply vendor) that offers a specific discount from the total billed charge for goods/services if payment by the healthcare organization is made early and within a prescribed time period from the date of the invoice.

Transaction (Accounting Transaction). The event that initiates the accounting cycle for the healthcare organization when at least one of the following occur between two entities: transfer of money, transfer of goods, or transfer of services.

Transfers to Parent Organization. Identified on the healthcare organization's statement of operations, this account represents an excess amount of profit experienced by the organization over a specific financial accounting period that is sent to a higher entity or governing body for redistribution to another healthcare location within the same organization.

Transparency. A financial accounting concept that requires the provision of any/all information needed to fully represent the healthcare organization and its financial status.

Trial Balance. A tool used in financial accounting that assesses the total sum of all debits and compares to the total sum of all credits for all accounts used by the healthcare organization to assist in confirming the use of a balanced, dual-entry process for all organizational transactions.

Unrestricted Net Assets. The value of healthcare organization profits experienced as documented on the statement of operation that can be utilized by the healthcare organization for any reason necessary (not restricted to donor requirements).

Useful Life. An estimated value often provided by the medical vendor and/or sales representative that represents how long the asset should remain productive if utilized under normal operating conditions.

Weighted Average (**WA**). A healthcare inventory valuation and expensing method that involves calculating a per-unit average cost during any specific financial accounting period to then determine the total inventory expense (based on usage) for that item, and therefore the remaining value of items left unused to date.

Recommended References for Additional Study

Finkler, S. A., Ward, D. M., & Calabrese, T. (2019). *Accounting fundamentals for health care management* (3rd ed.). Jones & Bartlett Learning.

Gapenski, L. C., & Reiter, K. L. (2016). *Healthcare finance: An introduction to accounting & financial management* (6th ed.). Health Administration Press.

Nowicki, M., & Berger, S. H. (2006). *HFMA's introduction to hospital accounting* (5th ed.). Health Administration Press.

Weygandt, J. J., Kieso, D. E., & Kimmel, P. D. (2014). *Financial accounting* (9th ed.). John Wiley & Sons.

About the Author

D R. CRISTIAN LIENECK has over 10 years of practical experience in the field of healthcare administration with a strong focus in medical group practice management (physician practice administration) and over a decade of preparing future healthcare leaders in higher education.

He began working in the healthcare field while in high school as a licensed emergency medical technician and later commissioned as a Medical Service Corps officer in the U.S. Army. As a lieutenant, Dr. Lieneck led a garrison medical clinic and a field medical evacuation platoon in the Third Armored Cavalry Regiment. Upon promotion to the rank of captain, he served as the executive officer and dental company commander for the Fort Carson Dental Activity, consisting of four outpatient dental practices and one hospital-based oral surgery clinic.

Dr. Lieneck's military leadership as a healthcare administrator has been recognized by all of his previous senior combat-arms (armor) and combat service-support (medical/dental) military officers, including having been awarded the Meritorious Service Medal upon completion of his ROTC scholarship service obligation.

Dr. Lieneck has since held healthcare leadership positions in organizations such as the Community Living Assistance Support Services program for the Texas Medicaid-Waiver Program (Texas Department of Aging and Disability Services), Austin Radiological Association, as well as serving as the medical group practice administrator of an Austin-based physiatry and pain medicine physician group practice, consisting of multiple locations and an outpatient procedure suite in central Texas.

Dr. Lieneck is a fellow and is board certified in medical group practice management by the American College of Medical Practice Executives, the credentialing body of the Medical Group Management Association (MGMA), the premier professional association for medical group/ambulatory care practice administrators. He is a fellow and is board certified in healthcare management by the American College of Healthcare Executives and a fellow in the Academy of Healthcare Management. He is also a Certified Professional in Health

Information and Management Systems, credentialed through the Health Information and Management Systems Society.

Dr. Lieneck continues to participate in professional leadership roles at national, state, and local levels. He is a faculty member with the American College of Healthcare Executives and teaches the Healthcare Finance module for the Board of Governors exam review course. He has been appointed and continues to serve as the MGMA Forum Representative for the state of Texas. He serves the profession by participating on various committees with other local, state, and national professional organizations. He is an active member of the Association of University Programs in Health Administration and serves as a program reviewer to ensure the quality of healthcare management education.

His research interests include healthcare value (directed toward finance and marketing perspectives), physician practice administration, and healthcare administration andragogy. He enjoys conducting research, teaching and developing future healthcare leaders, playing music (classic rock/guitar and bluegrass/mandolin), and most importantly, spending time with family.

Cristian and his wife, Lindsey, and their children, Emery and Eve, live in Austin, Texas.

Printed in the USA
CPSIA information can be obtained
at www.ICGtesting.com
LVHW080249281124
797814LV00001B/2